9/9   598 4634

C K
150 mb

Willard B. Anderson

Tacoma

Oct. 6, 1909   Wash.

THE ANCESTRY OF OUR
ENGLISH BIBLE

Hebrew Text on Papyrus from the Second Century (Cook).
Exodus 20 : 2-17

The Ancestry of Our English Bible

AN ACCOUNT OF MANUSCRIPTS, TEXTS,
AND VERSIONS OF THE BIBLE

BY

IRA MAURICE PRICE, PH.D.

Professor of the Semitic Languages and Literatures
in the University of Chicago

THIRD EDITION

Cincinnati : JENNINGS & GRAHAM
New York : EATON & MAINS

TO THE MEMORY OF

Jennie Rhoads Price

INSPIRING, DEVOTED WIFE AND MOTHER,
DURING WHOSE LAST YEAR OF PATIENT AND PATHETIC
SUFFERING THESE PAGES WERE PENNED,

THIS VOLUME IS
LOVINGLY DEDICATED

PREFACE

Our English Bible is the descendant of a long line of ancestors. It is the gathering up, the focalization, of the best that is found in all the manuscripts and versions extant. It is the result of the best efforts of about seventy-five of the leading scholars of the last quarter century.

How did these scholars produce our English Bible? What were the sources of their materials? Where were these materials found? What is their character? Where are they preserved? How were they used by scholars in the production, for example, of our Revised Version? These are a few of the questions that arise in the minds of every earnest, thoughtful student of the Bible. They can be answered only by a somewhat extended description and by references to many books and articles.

These questions were discussed in a popular vein in a series of eleven articles in The Sunday School Times during the first three-quarters of the year 1904. Their publication in book form was announced for the autumn of the same year. But long, distressing and fatal illness in the family of the writer, and the decision to expand the material to more than twice its original size, necessitated the postponement of its publication.

The purpose of this volume is to present in as concise and popular form as possible a description of the principal versions and texts of the Bible, from the earliest known translations and manuscripts down through the middle ages, even to modern times. Now and then a version or manuscript is prefaced by a statement of the historical background, where such is required to bring out more sharply the characteristics of such document. This has been done especially in the discussion of the early versions of the English Bible, for the Bible work is best understood if we appreciate the historical conditions of those days.

The division of the book into three parts is natural, though it may, at first, seem to need justification. The earliest versions and manuscripts do not all contain both the Old Testament and the New. In fact, the originals of the two being written in different languages, is sufficient ground for treating them in two parts. Then the existence of some versions, such as the Samaritan Pentateuch, in the Old Testament alone, calls for such a division of the theme. It soon becomes apparent, however, that the line between Parts I and II cannot always be sharply drawn; for, as in the case of the Vulgate, both Testaments are included. There is consequently some almost unavoidable overlapping, where the version is discussed both in Parts I and II. This disadvantage is partly overcome in the case of the Vulgate by devoting the chapter in Part I to early Latin Old Testament manuscripts, and the Vulgate down to the ninth century, and that in Part II to early Latin New Testament manuscripts and the Vulgate down to modern times. In Part III, "The English Bible," no division is made between the Old Testament and the New, both being treated under each chapter.

Some portion of each chapter descriptive of a version is given to an account of the principal manuscripts. Only such facts are mentioned as serve prominently to distinguish those documents in the history of the text. Of some of the great manuscripts, such as the Sinaitic, a few essential facts regarding its discovery are given, that we may the better know the cost of some of our most valued treasures.

The illustrations are designed to set vividly before the eyes of the reader facsimile specimens of some of the earliest and most important texts and versions now in possession of the great libraries of the world, and of some private collections. These have been gathered from a large variety of sources, as is indicated in the "List of Illustrations." Full acknowledgment is here made to the firms and individuals who have so generously granted permission to reproduce them for this volume. The names of such grantors appear in full in the "List of Illustrations."

The Bibliography gives merely a selection of the literature that will prove most helpful in further investigation of the theme of each chapter.

The Chronological Table is intended to present only such dates as are essential in the best scheme for fastening outline facts regarding Bible translations and texts.

The diagrams illustrative of the relations of the versions and transcripts present to the eye some patent facts that should be remembered.

The author acknowledges his indebtedness to many writers and authors from whom the material of this volume has been gathered and reconstructed. The Bibliography cites almost in full the sources employed in its production.

The thanks of the author are due his colleagues, Professor Ernest D. Burton, for his kindness in reading the manuscript of Part II, "The New Testament," and for making valuable suggestions; and to Professor C. W. Votaw for reading the proofs of the same, and for indicating points of improvement in the matter and forms of statements. The author, however, is alone responsible for the method of treatment.

To the Publishers, who have spared no pains in making the volume attractive in form and make-up, there is also due a debt of thanks.

IRA MAURICE PRICE.

The University of Chicago,
New-Year, 1907.

CONTENTS

(Parentheses enclose Illustrations.)

CHAPTER I.

THE ENGLISH BIBLE OF TO-DAY.

1. Versions in use to-day.—2. Reasons for these versions.—3. Variants in the Old Testament. (*American Standard Revised Version, specimen page, p. 4).—4. Variants in the New Testament.—5. Interpretative marginal readings.—6. Variant readings of Hebrew and Greek manuscripts.—7. Variant readings from ancient versions.—8. Classes of marginal readings.—9. Reasons for the variants . . **Pages 1–12**

CHAPTER II.

THE BASES OF OUR PRESENT VERSIONS.

10. Available sources.—11. The Hebrew and Greek texts used.—12. The use of the manuscripts. (*Codex Sinaiticus (S) from Mt. Sinai, p. 16).—13. The use of the ancient versions.—14. The Targums and quotations in ancient writers.—15. The revisers' *apparatus criticus* . . . . **Pages 13–19**

PART I. THE OLD TESTAMENT.

CHAPTER III.

HEBREW WRITING, TEXT, AND MANUSCRIPTS.

16. The Hebrew of the Old Testament.—17. Writing and writers in the Old Testament.—18. Other Hebrew documents in O. T. times.—19. Probable

destruction of Hebrew books.—20. Hebrew language.—21. Origin of changes in the Hebrew text.
—22. Divisions of the Hebrew text.—23. The vocal-
izing of the Hebrew text.—24. Hebrew manuscripts. (* St. Petersburg Hebrew manuscript, 916
A. D., p. 34)—25. Printed editions of the Hebrew Old
Testament.—26. Published list of Hebrew variants.
(*First Hebrew Bible published in America p. 38)
. . . . Pages 20–38

CHAPTER IV.

THE SAMARITAN BIBLE: THE PENTATEUCH.

27. Samaritan peculiarities.—28. Policy that originated
the Samaritans.—29. Composition of the Samaritans.—30. Manasseh's migration to Samaria.—31.
Mt. Gerizim a center of Jehovah worship.—32. Pentateuch the Samaritan Scriptures.—33. Samaritan
manuscripts. (*Jacob ben Aaron, high priest of
Samaritans at Nablous, p. 46).—34. Printed texts.—
35. Significance of differences between the Samaritan and Hebrew texts . . . . Pages 39–48

CHAPTER V.

THE GREEK BIBLE: THE SEPTUAGINT.

36. The spread of Greek civilization.—37. Jews in Alexandria.—38. Prevalence of the Septuagint.—39.
Time of translation of the law.—40. Character of
the translation.—41. Purpose of the translation.—
42. Contents of the Septuagint.—43 Septuagint
manuscripts in general. (*Septuagint papyrus from
Oxyrhynchus, Egypt, p. 56).—44. The great Septuagint manuscripts. (*Psalter fragment of papyrus,

p. 58).—45. The smaller Septuagint manuscripts.—
46. Printed editions of the Septuagint.—47. Value
of the Septuagint . . . . Pages 49–61

CHAPTER VI.

RIVAL GREEK BIBLES, AND REVISIONS OF THE SEPTUAGINT.

48. Reasons for rival Greek versions.—49. Aquila's
Greek version. (*Aquila's Version, p. 64).—50.
Theodotion's Greek version.—51. Symmachus'
Greek version.—52. Origen and his Hexapla.—53.
Origen's purpose and method.—54. Remains of
Origen's work.—55. Revisions of Eusebius, Lucian,
and Hesychius.—56. Some manuscripts of these re-
visions. (*Codex Marchalianus (q.) p. 72) Pages 62–73

CHAPTER VII.

THE LATIN BIBLES, THE VULGATE.

57. The Roman world Latin, and Christian Church
Greek.—58. Early Latin versions.—59. Origin of
Old Latin texts.—60. Classification of Old Latin
texts.—61. Jerome's early life and training. (*Jerome's Vulgate, p. 78).—62. Jerome's revision
work.—63. Jerome's translations.—64. Jerome's
personality.—65. Criticism and reception of Jerome's translation.—66. Adoption of Jerome's translation.—67. Latin Manuscripts. (*Ashburnham
Pentateuch, p. 84) . . . . Pages 74–84

CHAPTER VIII.

THE SYRIAC BIBLE, AND THE PESHITTA.

68. The demand for a Syriac Bible.—69. Theories of
the origin of the Syriac Old Testament.—70.
Earliest traces of the Syriac Old Testament.—71.

Contents of the Syriac Old Testament.—72. Manu-
scripts of the Syriac Bible.—73. Some critical value.
(*Syriac Peshitta, p. 90).—74. Printed editions
. . . . Pages 85–91

CHAPTER IX.

THE TARGUMS: JEWISH PARAPHRASES.

75. The Aramaic of Palestine.—76. Written Targums.—
77. The first Targums. (*Targum interlined with
Hebrew, p. 94).—78. Targums of the Pentateuch.—
79. Targums of the Prophets.—80. Targums of the
Hagiographa.—81. Some value of the Targums
. . . . Pages 92–98

CHAPTER X.

OTHER EASTERN VERSIONS OF THE OLD TESTAMENT.

82. Versions for far-away provinces.—83. Coptic versions.—84. The Ethiopic version. (*Ethiopic text,
p. 102).—85. The Gothic Version.—86. The Georgian version.—87. The Slavonic version.—88. The
Armenian version.—89. Arabic versions.   Pages 99–109

CHAPTER XI.

SUMMARY OF OLD TESTAMENT VERSIONS.

90. Direct and indirect translations.—91. Charts of
versions.—92. The relation of Hebrew to other versions.—93. The Samaritan Pentateuch.—94. The
Septuagint and Greek versions.—95. The Vulgate.
(*Complutensian Polyglot, p. 116).—96. The Syriac
version.—97. The Targums . . . . Pages 110–118

CHAPTER XII.

THE APOCRYPHA.

98. The existence of the Apocryphal Old Testament.—99. "Apocrypha" defined.—100. The apocryphal books.—101. Historical and legendary Apocryphal books.—102. Prophetic and didactic Apocryphal books. (*Ecclesiasticus, newly discovered Hebrew Manuscript, p. 124).—103. The Pseudepigraphical books.—104. The Apocrypha's existence and expulsion from the English Bible.—105. Reasons for rejecting the books of the Apocrypha . Pages 119–130

PART II. THE NEW TESTAMENT.

CHAPTER XIII.

WRITING AND MANUSCRIPTS IN GENERAL.

106. Comparative abundance of Old and New Testament material.—107. The character of the New Testament writings.—108. Original documents all lost.—109. Bases of the true text. (*Codex Vaticanus (B), p. 136).—110. Uncial manuscripts.—111. Fixing the date of uncial manuscripts.—112. Cursive manuscripts. (*University of Chicago, New Testament Manuscript, p. 140) . Pages 131–140

CHAPTER XIV.

SOME GREAT NEW TESTAMENT MANUSCRIPTS.

113. Uncials and cursives designated.—114. The perils through which manuscripts pass.—115. Tischendorf's discovery of Codex Sinaiticus. (*St. Catharine, Convent of, at Mt. Sinai, p. 144.)—116. Codex

Sinaiticus deposited in St. Petersburg.—117. Character of the contents.—118. Codex Alexandrinus (A)—history. (*Codex Alexandrinus (A), p. 148.)—119. Codex Alexandrinus (A)—contents.—120. Codex Vaticanus (B)—history.—121. Codex Vaticanus (B)—contents.—122. Codex Ephræm (C). (*Codex Ephræmi (C), p. 154)—123. Codex Bezæ (D).—124. Other New Testament manuscripts . . . . Pages 141-157

CHAPTER XV.

THE OLD LATIN AND THE VULGATE.

125. New Testament versions and their evidence.—126. Old Latin Texts.—127. Manuscripts of Old Latin Gospels. (*Old Latin Gospels, p. 162.)—128. Other Old Latin manuscripts. (*Codex Claromontanus, p. 164.)—129. Old Latin and Vulgate side by side.—130. Latin texts mixed. (*Codex Amiatinus, p. 166.)—131. Cassiodorus' revision and other peculiar texts.—132. Revisions of Alcuin and Theodulf. (*Alcuin's revision of Vulgate, p. 168.)—133. Decline in text purity.—134. Revisions in Paris.—135. The official Vulgate of the Council of Trent.—136. The Clementine text of 1592.—137. Vulgate's influence.—138. Preparations for a critical edition of the Vulgate . . . . Pages 158-175

CHAPTER XVI.

THE SYRIAC AND OTHER EASTERN VERSIONS.

139. The Diatessaron of Tatian.—140. "The Gospel of the Separated;" and The Peshitta.—141. Traces of Old Syriac epistles.—142. Revisions of the Syriac

Contents

Bible. (*Syriac Palimpsest from Mt. Sinai, p. 182.)
—143. The Palestinian version.—144. Egyptian
versions.—145. The Armenian version.—146. The
Ethiopic version.—147. The Gothic version. (The
Gothic Gospels, p. 187.)—148. Arabic, Georgian,
and Slavonic versions . . . . . . Pages 176-188

CHAPTER XVII.

THE GROUPING AND CLASSIFICATION OF MANUSCRIPTS, VERSIONS, AND OTHER WITNESSES.

149. The Textus Receptus. (*Codex Bezæ (D), p. 190.)
—150. Classification of manuscripts. (*Bishop B.
F. Westcott, p. 192.)—151. The Syrian group.—152.
The Western group.—153. The Alexandrian group.
(*Hort, F. J. A., p. 194.)—154. The Neutral group.
—155. Westcott and Hort's Greek New Testament . . . . Pages 189-196

CHAPTER XVIII.

HOW MANUSCRIPTS AND VERSIONS ARE USED.

156. The material at hand.—157. Textual and higher
criticism.—158. Necessity of textual criticism.—
159. Significance of variations.—160. Some rules
for textual critics.—161. Rules for textual critics
continued.—162. Rules for textual critics, concluded.—163. Our Greek New Testament result of
application of these rules . . . . . Pages 197-206

PART III. ENGLISH VERSIONS OF THE BIBLE.

CHAPTER XIX.

EARLY ENGLISH MANUSCRIPTS.

164. Christianity in early England.—165. Cædmon.—
166. Aldhelm and Egbert.—167. Bede.—168. King
Alfred.—169. The Lindisfarne Gospels. (*Cotton

Manuscript, or Lindisfarne Gospels, p. 212.)—170. Tenth century Gospels and the Old Testament.—171. The Ormulum.—172. English Psalters of the fourteenth century.—173. Intellectual awakening of England in the fourteenth century . Pages 207–217

CHAPTER XX.

WYCLIFFE'S VERSION OF THE BIBLE.

174. John Wycliffe. (*John Wycliffe, p. 218.)—175. The fourteenth century.—176. Wycliffe's place in the controversies of the day.—177. Wycliffe's resolution.—178. Wycliffe's translation of the Latin Bible. (*Wycliffe's Bible, specimen page, p. 222.)—179. Wycliffe's plan for religious extension.—180. Revision of Wycliffe's Bible.—181. Adoption of the revision of Wycliffe's version.—182. Some characteristics of Wycliffe's version.—183. The Lord's Prayer in three tongues . . . . . Pages 218–229

CHAPTER XXI.

TYNDALE'S VERSION OF THE BIBLE.

184. Wycliffe's version in the fourteenth century. (*William Tyndale, p. 230)—185. Fifteenth century regeneration.—186. Progressive events of the fifteenth century.—187. Tyndale's birth and education.—188. Tyndale in London.—189. Tyndale at Hamburg, Wittenberg, and Cologne.—190. Tyndale at Worms. (*Tyndale's New Testament, p. 238.)—191. Reception of Tyndale's New Testament in England.—192. Success of Tyndale's opponents in England.—193. Reasons for opposition to Tyndale's work.—194. Tyndale's last published translations.—195. Tyndale's arrest at Antwerp, im-

prisonment and martyrdom.—196. Crowning work
of Tyndale.—197. Tyndale's influence on the version
of 1611, and on English style . . . . Pages 230-246

CHAPTER XXII.

VERSIONS CLOSE TO TYNDALE'S.

198. Myles Coverdale. (*Myles Coverdale, p. 248.)—
199. Appearance of Coverdale's Bible. (*Coverdale's Bible, p. 250).—200. Character of Coverdale's
Bible.—201. Tyndale and Coverdale compared.—
202. John Rogers' "Thomas Matthew" Bible.—203.
Royal favor for the Matthew Bible.—204. Coverdale
engaged to edit another version.—205. "The Great
Bible" printed. (*The Great Bible, p. 254.)—206.
Contents of the Great Bible.—207. Public use of
the Great Bible.—208. Influence of the Great Bible.
—209. Taverner's Bible . . . . . Pages 247-259

CHAPTER XXIII.

THE GENEVAN, BISHOPS', AND DOUAI VERSIONS.

210. The anti-reformation movement.—211. Edward
VI.—212. Mary's persecutions and death.—213.
The Geneva New Testament.—214. The Geneva
Bible. (*The Geneva Bible, p. 264.)—215. Its popu-
larity and use.—216. Appearance of the Bishops'
Bible. (*The Bishops' Bible, p. 266.)—217. Char-
acter of the Bishops' Bible.—218. The Rheims
and Douai version. (*The Rheims New Testament,
p. 270.)—219. Character of the Douai Bible.
. . . . Pages 260-271

CHAPTER XXIV.

THE AUTHORIZED VERSION OF 1611.

220 Queen Elizabeth's reign.—221. James I and Hampton Court Conference.—222. Steps toward a revision.—223. Organization of the revisers.—224. Work doing and done. (The Authorized Version of 1611, p. 278.)—225. Sources of the version of 1611. —226. Popularity of the Authorized Version.—227. Abortive attempt at revision by Long Parliament.— 228. Private revisions and additions to the Authorized Version.—229. The sway of the Authorized Version . . . . Pages 272–282

CHAPTER XXV.

THE REVISED VERSION.

230 Eighteenth century conditions.—231. Private translations and texts.—232. Formation of a Revision Committee.—233. Organization and beginning of work.—234. Organization of the American Revision Committee.—235. Completion of the New Testament.—236. Reception given the Revised New Testament.—237. Completion of the Old Testament.—238. Texts at the basis of the Revised Version.—239. Improvements in the translations. —240. Improvement in language.—241. Improvements in make-up or form.—242. Reasons for adoption of the Revised Version. (*American Standard Revised Version, Title-page, p. 298.)— 243. The American Committee and its restrictions. —244. The American Appendix to the Revised Version.—245. Anglicisms and Archaisms in the 1885 edition.—246. Marginal references.—247. The American Committee's task.—248. Contract with

Contents

Nelson & Sons.—249. The issuance of the American Standard Edition of the Revised Version.—250. The reception of the American Edition . Pages 283–305

BIBLIOGRAPHY 307–314
CHRONOLOGICAL TABLE 315–319
TOPICAL INDEX 321–328
SCRIPTURE INDEX 329, 330

ILLUSTRATIONS AND DIAGRAMS

[Numbers refer to pages ; arranged in alphabetical order.]

FACING
PAGE

Alcuin's Revision of the Vulgate 168
From Anderson and Rule, "Biblical Monuments"

Alexandrinus (A), Codex 148
From "The Palæographical Society's" Facsimiles, by
permission of Sir E. Maunde Thompson, Editor

American Standard Revised Version, specimen page . 4
By permission Thos. Nelson and Sons, publishers

American Standard Revised Version, Title-page . . . 298
By permission Thos. Nelson and Sons, publishers

Amiatinus (A), Codex, best Vulgate Manuscript . . . 166
From "The Palæographical Society" Facsimiles, by permission of Sir E. Maunde Thompson, Editor

Aquila's Version, Palimpsest 64
By permission of Cambridge University Press

Ashburnham Pentateuch 84
From "The Palæographical Society's" Facsimiles, by
permission of Sir E. Maunde Thompson, Editor

Authorized Version of 1611, specimen page 278
From "Bible Illustrations," by permission of Oxford
University Press

Bezæ (D), Codex 190
From "The Palæographical Society's" Facsimiles, by
permission of Sir E. Maunde Thompson, Editor

Bishops' Bible, specimen page 266
From "Bible Illustrations," by permission of Oxford
University Press

Catharine, St., Convent of, at Mt. Sinai 144
From "Bible Treasury," by permission of Thos. Nelson
and Sons, publishers

Claromontanus (d), Codex 164
From "The Palæographical Society's" Facsimiles, by
permission of Sir E. Maunde Thompson, Editor

FACING
PAGE

Complutensian Polyglot, specimen page 116
From "The Jewish Encyclopedia," Vol. III, Funk and
Wagnalls, publishers; by permission

Cottonianus (D), Codex 212
From Anderson and Rule, "Biblical Monuments"

Coverdale, Myles, portrait 248
From Hoare's "Evolution of the English Bible." By
permission of E. P. Dutton & Co., publishers

Coverdale Bible, specimen page 250
From "Bible Illustrations," by permission of Oxford
University press

Ecclesiasticus, new Hebrew Manuscript of 124
From "Facsimiles of the Book of Ecclesiasticus," by
permission of Clarendon Press

Ephræmi (C), Codex, Palimpsest 154
From "Bible Illustrations," by permission of Oxford
University Press

Ethiopic Text, specimen page 102
From Anderson and Rule, "Biblical Monuments"

Geneva Bible, specimen page 264
From "Bible Illustrations," by permission of Oxford
University Press

Gothic Gospels 187
From "The Palæographical Society's" Facsimiles, by
permission of Sir E. Maunde Thompson, Editor

Great Bible, specimen page 254
From "Bible Illustrations," by permission of Oxford
University Press

Hebrew Bible, first published in America 38
From Report of U. S. National Museum of 1896; by
permission

Hebrew Papyrus, Pre-Massoretic. . . . . Frontispiece
From "Proceedings of Society of Biblical Archæology,"
Vol. XXV

Hort, F. J. A., portrait 194
From "Life and Letters of Fenton John Anthony Hort,"
The Macmillan Company; by permission

Jacob ben Aaron, High Priest of Samaritans at Nablus 46
From collection of the Rev. W. E. Barton

FACING
PAGE

Latin Bible of Jerome 78
From "Bible Treasury," by permission of Thos. Nelson
and Sons, publishers

Marchalianus (Q), Codex 72
From Kenyon "Our Bible and the Ancient Manuscripts,"
by permission of the author

Old Latin Gospels, Codex Vercellensis, specimen page . 162
From "Bible Illustrations," by permission of Oxford
University Press

Psalter Fragment of Papyrus 58
From "Bible Treasury," by permission of Thos. Nelson
and Sons, publishers

Rheims New Testament, specimen page 270
From "Bible Illustrations," by permission of Oxford
University Press

St. Petersburg Hebrew Codex, 916 A.D. 34
From Weir, "History of the Hebrew Text of the Old
Testament," by permission of the author

Septuagint Papyrus of Third Century 56
From "Biblical World," by permission University of
Chicago

Sinaiticus (S), Codex 16
From "The Palæographical Society's" Facsimiles by
permission of Sir E. Maunde Thompson, Editor

Syriac Peshitta 90
From Anderson and Rule, "Biblical Monuments,"

Syriac Codex, Palimpsest 182
From "Studia Sinaitica," X, by permission of Mrs. A. S.
Lewis, the author

Targum in alternate verses 94
From "Jewish Encyclopedia," Vol. Il1, Funk & Wagnalls, publishers; by permission.

Tyndale, William, portrait 230

Tyndale's New Testament, specimen page 238
From "Bible Illustrations," by permission Oxford
University Press

University of Chicago, N. T. Manuscript 140

FACING
PAGE

Vaticanus (B), Codex............................... 136
    From Kenyon's "Handbook to Textual Criticism of the
    New Testament," by permission of the author

Westcott, Brooke Foss, portrait..................... 192
    From a photograph in possession of author

Wycliffe, John, portrait............................. 218

Wycliffe Bible, specimen pages...................... 222
    From " The Palæographical Society's " Facsimiles by
    permission of Sir E. Maunde Thompson, Editor

DIAGRAMS

Form of Origen's Hexapla..........................on   67

The Relation of the Rival Greek Bibles and Revisions
    to the Septuagint...............................   72

The Sources in General of the Minor Eastern Versions   105

The General Relations of the Ancient Versions to the
    Hebrew   111

The Beginnings of Modern Versions, Early in the Six-
    teenth Century.................................   245

Principal Sources Employed by the Translators of
    King James Version of 1611.....................   276

Main Sources of Old Testament of the Revised Ver-
    sion ....op.   286

CHAPTER I

THE ENGLISH BIBLE AND ITS MARGINAL READINGS

1. The English Bible holds a pre-eminent position in the worlds of religion and literature. For three centuries it has easily and gracefully occupied such a place among English-speaking peoples. Its power and influence to-day permeate every avenue of religious and literary life. Its increasing importance has required that it represent the best scholarship and the best statements of its truths for the popular mind of this day. Endeavors to answer these requirements have provided us with more than one version of the English Bible. In fact, students and readers of the Holy Scriptures are confronted to-day with several editions or versions of the Bible, each claiming superior qualities of its own. The presence of these several versions is not an unmitigated evil for most Bible readers. They rather confuse than illuminate the questions that touch the origin of The Book. Some of the versions that lie all about us, and are found in every community, are The Authorized or King James Version, The Revised Version of 1885, and The American Standard Revised Version of 1901. In addition to these we find several translations and editions, which are the products either of private enterprise or of Bible translation societies.

1

Some of these are Spurrell's "A Translation of the Old Testament Scriptures from the Original Hebrew;" Fenton's "The Bible in Modern English;" and the translations of the American Bible Union. Then there are some editions which have for their purpose the presentation of the Authorized or Revised Versions in an improved literary form, with introductions and notes. Notable specimens of this kind of work are found in The Temple Bible, an arrangement of the Authorized Version; and Moulton's "The Modern Reader's Bible," a literary distribution of the matter of the Revised Version of 1885.

2. An examination and comparison of these several versions point distinctly to the reasons for their production. The translators of the Hebrew and Greek of the Old and New Testaments respectively into English had no small task. They were obliged to translate texts that had been copied over and over again by the hand of man for hundreds, and, in the case of the Old Testament, for thousands, of years. There must inevitably have been mistakes by scribes and copyists that have never been corrected. No one of us could copy by hand ten pages of manuscript without making some errors. We would at least forget to dot some "i's" or cross some "t's"; but the most of us would leave out words, write some words twice, leave out some lines, repeat some lines, and make many other blunders that would cause our copy to vary from the original. Just these things have happened with the manuscripts of the Bible.

Fortunately, at different periods in the history of Bible manuscripts, translations were made into other languages. Many of these translations, such as the Greek and Latin and Syriac, are now available for scholars. By their help we can often detect and locate an error in the Hebrew or Greek text, and thus give a better rendering into English of what we estimate was the original text. Such variations and helps are noted in the margins of our Revised Version, and constitute a valuable source of aid in comprehending the real meaning of the original text.

3. The quantity of these variations is sometimes alarming until one begins to understand the close relation they sustain to a true conception of the text. As a rule the more the marginal notes, the better a text is understood. They are a most welcome light to those of us who wish better to understand the meaning of some obscure passage in the text; and also an index to the industry of scholars in ascertaining the readings of the text when corrected by the various ancient translations. So that we should always regard with careful discrimination every marginal note if we are endeavoring to find out just what scholars have concluded as to the meaning of the text which we are reading or studying.

These variant readings are not confined either to the Old or to the New Testament, but are found in every part of the Bible. A few examples may best illustrate this point: In Genesis 6: 3 we find, "My spirit shall not strive with man for ever;" the margin reads for " strive," " Or, rule in ;" " for that he also is flesh," has as its alternative in the margin, " Or, in their going astray they are flesh." The margin then reads the verse in this way: " My spirit shall not rule in man[kind] for ever, for in their going astray they are [have become] flesh "—quite a different conception from that in the text, either of the Authorized or the Revised Version. Genesis 49: 10, " Until Shiloh come; And unto him shall the obedience of the peoples be," has a margin as follows: " Or, till he come to Shiloh; having the obedience of the peoples." Again, in that passage that describes Samuel's first anointing of Saul, 1 Samuel 9: 20, we find in the text, " And for whom is all that is desirable in Israel? Is it not for thee, and for all thy father's house?" the margin reads, " Or, on whom is all the desire of Israel? Is it not on thee, and on all, etc.?" That difficult passage in 2 Samuel 5: 8 presents some interesting variations, " And David said on that day, Whosoever smiteth the Jebusites, let him get up to the water-course, and smite the lame and the blind, that are hated of David's soul;" the margin reads, " Or, and as for the lame and the blind, that are hated of David's soul—;" " Another reading is, that hate David's soul." The text goes on to say: " Wherefore they say, There are the blind and the lame; he cannot come into the house;" the margin says, " Or, The blind and the lame shall not come into the house." These margins show the variant translations of the revisers of the original Hebrew describing this event. In Isaiah

1 22   I. SAMUEL   2 15

Samuel given to Jehovah   Hannah's Song of Thanksgiving.   The Sin of Eli's Sons

and his vow 22 But Hannah went not up ; for she said unto her husband, *I will not go up* until the child be weaned ; and then I will *a* bring him, that he may appear before Jehovah, and *b* there abide for ever. 23 And *c* Elkanah her husband said unto her, Do what seemeth thee good; tarry until thou have weaned him; only *d* Jehovah establish his word So the woman tarried and gave her son suck, until she weaned him. 24 And when she had weaned him, *e* she took him up with her, [1] three bullocks, and one ephah of meal, and a [2] bottle of wine, and brought him unto *f* the house of Jehovah in Shiloh : and the child was young. 25 And *g* they slew the bullock, and *h* brought the child to Eli. 26 And she said, Oh, my lord, [3] as thy soul liveth, my lord, I am the woman that stood by thee here, praying unto Jehovah. 27 *k* For this child I prayed; and Jehovah hath given me my petition which I asked of him: 28 therefore also I have [3] granted him to Jehovah; as long as he liveth he is granted to Jehovah. And he worshipped Jehovah there.

2 And Hannah *m* prayed, and said:

My heart exulteth in Jehovah;
n My horn is exalted in Jehovah;
My mouth is enlarged over mine enemies,
Because *o* I rejoice in thy salvation.
2 *p* There is none holy as Jehovah;
For *q* there is none besides thee,
Neither is there any rock like our God.
3 Talk no more so exceeding proudly,
r Let not arrogancy come out of your mouth;
s For Jehovah is a God of knowledge,
[4] *t* And by him actions are weighed
4 *u* The bows of the mighty men are broken ;
x And they that stumbled are girded with strength.
5 They that were full have hired out themselves for bread;

And they that were hungry
b have ceased *to hunger* :
y Yea, the barren hath borne seven;
And *z* she that hath many children languisheth
6 *a* Jehovah killeth, and maketh alive
b He bringeth down to Sheol and bringeth up.
7 *c* Jehovah maketh poor, and maketh rich .
d He bringeth low he also lifteth up.
8 *e* He raiseth up the poor out of the dust,
f He lifteth up the needy from the dunghill,
g To make them sit with princes,
And inherit the throne of glory
h For the pillars of the earth are Jehovah's,
And he hath set the world upon them.
9 *i* He will keep the feet of his holy ones ;
k But the wicked shall be put to silence in darkness ;
l For by strength shall no man prevail.
10 *m* They that strive with Jehovah shall be broken to pieces;
n Against them will he thunder in heaven :
o Jehovah will judge the ends of the earth ;
p And he will give strength unto his king,
q And exalt the horn of his anointed.
11 And Elkanah went to *r* Ramah to his house. *s* And the child did minister unto Jehovah before Eli the priest.
12 Now the sons of Eli were base men ; *t* they knew not Jehovah. 13 *u* And the custom of the priests with the people was, that, when any man offered sacrifice, the priest's servant came, while the flesh was boiling, with a flesh-hook of three teeth in his hand ; 14 and he struck it into the pan, or kettle, or caldron, or pot; all that the flesh-hook brought up the priest took therewith. So they did in Shiloh unto all the Israelites that came thither. 15 Yea, before *x* they burnt the fat, the priest's servant

Marginal notes (left):
[1] The Sept and Syriac have, *a bullock three years old*
[2] Or *skin*
[3] Or, *lent*
[4] According to another reading, *Though actions be not weighed*

Marginal notes (right):
[5] Or *have rest*
[6] Or *godly ones* Another reading is *holy one*
[7] Or, *they knew not Jehovah, nor the due of the priests from the people. When any man &c.*

Page of the American Standard Revised Version, showing Marginal References and Variant Readings

there are many and striking variant readings. In chapter 8: 20, we read: "if they speak not according to this word, surely there is no morning for them;" the margin says, "Or, surely according to this word shall they speak for whom there is no morning." Isaiah 23: 13 reads: "this people was not; the Assyrian founded it for them that dwell in the wilderness;" the margin reads: "This people is no more; the Assyrian hath appointed it for the beasts of the wilderness." Isaiah 40: 9, "O thou that tellest good tidings to Jerusalem;" margin, "Or, O Jerusalem, that bringest good tidings." Isaiah 53: 1, "Who hath believed our message?" margin for "our message," "Or, that which we have heard."

4. The New Testament carries on its margins scores of important variations in translation from that in the text. Matthew 2: 2 reads: "Where is he that is born King of the Jews?" the margin says, "Or, where is the King of the Jews that is born?" In Matthew 25: 41, we find, "Depart from me, ye cursed;" but in the margin, "Or, Depart from me under a curse." Luke 1: 4, "that thou mightest know the certainty concerning the things wherein thou wast instructed;" the last phrase reads in the margin, "Or, which thou wast taught by word of mouth." Luke 1: 35, last half: "The holy thing which is begotten shall be called the Son of God;" margin, "Or, that which is to be born shall be called holy, the Son of God." John 1: 9, "There was the true light, even the light which lighteth every man,

coming into the world;" margin, "Or, the true light, which lighteth every man, was coming;" another marginal rendering is, "Or, every man as he cometh." Paul's epistles have striking variant renderings of the original Greek: I Corinthians 2: 13, "combining spiritual things with spiritual words;" the margin reads, "Or, interpreting spiritual things to spiritual men." 2 Corinthians 2: 17, "corrupting the word of God;" but in the margin, "Or, making merchandise of the word of God." Colossians 1: 2 reads, "to the saints and faithful brethren in Christ that are at Colossæ;" but in the margin we find, "Or, to those that are at Colossæ, holy and faithful brethren in Christ."

These variant marginal renderings in the Old and New Testaments are sufficient evidence to the thoughtful reader that there may be more than one correct translation of the original text as we have it to-day. These variant renderings furnish us with one important class of alternative readings in our present day versions of the English Bible.

5. A second class of marginal notes consists of those that are interpretations or explanations of the original Hebrew or Greek; some give a literal translation of the Hebrew, the meaning of proper names, an explanation of some obscure linguistic idiom, or of some custom. Such readings contribute valuable aid to the understanding of the text, and bring the reader closer to the warmth of the original. The margins of the Revised Versions are replete with

such help.   In Genesis 1 : 20, we find : " in the open
firmament of heaven," where the margin gives, "Heb.
on the face of the expanse of the heavens."   In Genesis 3 : 20, " Eve " is explained in the margin, " Heb.
Havvah, that is, Living, or Life."   The word
" South," in Genesis 12 : 9, is commented on in the
margin, " Heb. Negeb, the southern tract of Judah."
" Mesopotamia " in Genesis 24 : 10, is treated in the
margin as follows : " Heb. Aram-naharaim, that is,
Aram of the two rivers."   Genesis 43 : 9 gives the
conclusion of Judah's vow to Jacob in these words,
" then let me bear the blame for ever," whereas the
margin reads, " Heb. I shall have sinned against thee
for ever."   Job 40 : 15, for " behemoth " has in the
margin, " That is, the hippopotamus ; " and Job 41 : 1
for " leviathan " has as its marginal note, " That is,
the crocodile."   Jeremiah 51 : 1 contains that strange
name, " Leb-kamai," explained in the margin, " That
is, The heart of them that rise up against me."   In
Matthew 5 : 46, " publicans " is explained in the margin, " That is, collectors or renters of Roman taxes."
That passage in the Lord's prayer, Matthew 6 : 11,
" Give us this day our daily bread," has this marginal note, " Gr. our bread for the coming day.   Or,
our needful bread."   In Jesus' prayer, John 17 : 2,
" to all whom thou hast given him he should give
eternal life," the margin reads, " Gr. whatsoever thou
hast given him, to them he, &c."   Such marginal
notes are a kind of commentary, adding material that
is often essential to the understanding of the text.

6. A third class of marginal readings is made up of those notes which are quotations from Hebrew or Greek manuscripts, other than those upon which the translated text is based. These variant manuscript readings often throw welcome light on the true meaning of a difficult verse, by furnishing some reading that could be substituted for that in the commonly accepted Hebrew or Greek text. That difficult passage in which Elisha sends word to Benhadad, King of Syria, through Hazael (2 Kings 8: 10), saying, " Go, say unto him, Thou shalt surely recover, howbeit Jehovah," etc., has a marginal note that says, " Another reading is, Thou shalt not recover, for Jehovah, &c." In Isaiah 9: 3, "thou hast increased their joy," has a marginal note, " Another reading is, thou didst not increase the joy." Isaiah 52: 2, " loose thyself from the bonds of thy neck," has in the margin, " Another reading is, the bonds of thy neck are loosed." In the Lord's prayer, in Matthew 6: 13, there is a marginal note which says, " Many authorities, some ancient, but with variations, add, For thine is the kingdom, and the power, and the glory, for ever. Amen." To Mark 16: 9f., there is this marginal remark, " The two oldest Greek manuscripts, and some other authorities, omit from ver. 9 to the end. Some other authorities have a different ending to the Gospel." In John 3: 31b, 32a, . . . " he that cometh from heaven is above all. What he hath seen and heard, of that he beareth witness," is noted in the margin by, " Some ancient authorities read, he

that cometh from heaven beareth witness of what he hath seen and heard." Examples of this class of readings might be multiplied indefinitely to show that there are variant readings of the Hebrew and Greek manuscripts which are worth careful study on the part of every diligent student of the Bible.

7. A fourth class of marginal readings reaches out still farther into the field of contributory literature. These notes are made up of variations from the original texts, as we have them, of the Old and New Testaments, which are found in the best ancient versions, such as those of the Greek Bible or Septuagint, the Latin Bible or Vulgate, and the Syriac Bible or Peshitta. The American Revised Version of the Old Testament usually names specifically the ancient version whose reading is quoted in the margin, but the New Testament conceals its sources under some such phrases as " Some ancient authorities," " Many ancient authorities," etc. Such sources are quoted rather sparingly in the Old Testament, and only where the contribution is of some genuine worth. In Genesis 6: 3, " My spirit shall not strive with man for ever," the margin says, " Acc[ording] to Sept [uagint], Vulg[ate], and Syr[iac], abide in." Genesis 49: 10, " until Shiloh come " has a variant in the margin, " Or, acc. to Syr., Till he come whose it is, &c." 1 Samuel 14: 18, where Saul says, " Bring hither the ark of God. For the ark of God was there at that time with the children of Israel," carries in the margin, " Some editions of the Sept. have.

Bring hither the ephod. For he wore the ephod at
that time before Israel." In 2 Chronicles 1 : 13 the
translators adopted the reading of three ancient versions as against that of the Heb., as seen in the marginal note, " So Sept., Vulg., and Syr. The Heb. has,
to." This same policy was adopted in Psalm 22: 16,
" They pierced my hands and my feet," since the
margin says, " So the Sept., Vulg., and Syr. The
Hebrew text as pointed reads, Like a lion, my, &c."
The fact that the New Testament does not name
the ancient sources of its variants, allows us to pass
by this class in that division of the Bible. We learn
at least from this class of marginal notes that there is
considerable matter, valuable both for the translation and interpretation, found outside of the commonly accepted original texts of the Old and New
Testaments.

8. The marginal readings classified in the preceding sections bristle with questions concerning the
" whence " of our English Bible. They point to
scores of manuscripts which do not agree in all respects, to ancient versions that preserve in many
places a different reading from that found in the commonly accepted original text of the Old and New
Testaments. At first thought these facts disturb the
mind of the student of the English Bible. He finds
at least four classes of marginal readings in the
American Standard Revised Version. They are (1)
a variant translation of the same Hebrew or Greek
text; (2) an explanation, interpretation or literal

interpretation of some Hebrew or Greek word or proper name; (3) quotations from, or variants of, some other than the regular Hebrew or Greek text upon which the translation of the English Bible is based; (4) readings found in the ancient translations or versions of the Bible.

9. If the original texts of the Old and New Testaments were in each Testament one text, how could all these variations arise? How could there be such a vast collection of variants as that found, for example, in the Variorum Teachers' Bible? This question is easily answered. Before the invention of printing from movable types, books were multiplied solely by the hand of fallible man. A slip of the pen, an error of sight, an error of hearing, or an error of memory, on the part of a scribe or copyist, would be preserved and perpetuated with the same care as that exercised in preserving the best text. Subsequent copyists and translators would not only perpetuate earlier errors, but would probably add the same kind of evidences of their own fallibility. This kind of multiplication of manuscripts, extending down through the centuries, opened the door to untold possibilities of many kinds of errors in the text that was thus treated. From the one original text of each of the two Testaments, copyists and translators multiplied copies and translations for more than two thousand years. The efforts of biblical scholars to-day are aimed at discovering, if possible, what the errors are, and what the original text may have been.

Subsequent chapters of this book will aim to look into the origin, character, and value of the principal ancient versions, and the early English Bibles, and to indicate approximately only the contribution that each has made to the up-to-date American Standard Revised Version of 1901.

CHAPTER II

THE BASES OF OUR PRESENT VERSIONS

10. The variety of the available marginal readings of our current versions of the English Bible point to several sources. We find references (1) to variant readings of manuscripts, and (2) to several ancient versions, such as the Septuagint, the Syriac, and the Vulgate. These versions were translated at an early date, and hence were made from texts that were in existence from fifteen hundred to twenty-two hundred years ago. They thus form an important evidence to the original texts as they existed in that far-off day. Our English Bible, with all its variants and readings, bases its best renderings and best thought, as we discover in its pages, upon at least four sources of supply: (1) the reconstructed original texts found in our best printed editions of the Hebrew Old Testament and the Greek New Testament; (2) the manuscripts of these Testaments as either collated and published, or as preserved in various great libraries of the world; (3) the most important ancient versions, whose translations were made more than a thousand years before the invention of printing; (4) paraphrases and quotations from ancient authors which may be valuable in the determination of some points in the text.

13

11. The first source of our English translation is the commonly received original Hebrew text of the Old Testament and the revisers' Greek text of the New Testament. The Hebrew text of the Old Testament as a whole has remained practically unchanged for centuries. There are published lists of variations of manuscripts which are used in making a critical study or translation of the received text. Except where stated differently in the margin, the Revised Version is practically a translation of this common text. On the other hand, the best printed text of the New Testament has been constructed within the last half-century on the basis of the readings of the best manuscripts. The Greek text from which the revisers made the translation of the Revised Version was constructed by the use of all the best documentary sources which have been discovered within the last three hundred years. It was then a resultant of the work of the best scholarship engaged on the Revision Committee. It was not the text of Westcott and Hort or of any other recognized authority, but that which was worked out by the best talent of the Committee. The difference between the "textus receptus" used as the basis for the Authorized and other versions, and that prepared by the revisers, is slight in substance, but very much in form. The latter is "shorter, but it is also older, purer and stronger." But since these texts from which the translations were made, particularly the New Testament, were prepared or reconstructed by the use of

manuscripts, let us pass on to inquire concerning this basis.

12. The manuscripts of the New Testament date, at the latest, from the invention of printing from movable types in 1455, back to the fourth century A. D. They were written on paper and vellum of various kinds, generally by persons who were skilled in such writing. They were copied directly from some other manuscript, or were written at the dictation of some reader. The oldest manuscript of the Hebrew Old Testament whose date is positively known, touches 916 A. D., much more than one thousand years after the writing of the latest book of the Old Testament. The oldest New Testament Greek manuscript reaches back into the fourth century, or is about five hundred years older than the oldest Hebrew manuscript.

In order to profit by these documents, scholars have started with some standard printed edition of the Old Testament as a basis, and then by a careful comparison of the various manuscripts with that printed text have collected all the variations in the readings supplied by these manuscripts. These documents are found in scores of libraries, and their examination and comparison involved long and patient work of a very taxing kind. In the Old Testament, particularly, there are two large collections of these variants which have not yet been embodied in any printed versions of the Hebrew. The revisers made use of these separate collections in preparing their Hebrew text from which they made their translation.

The best New Testament manuscripts have been thoroughly collated, and their valuable readings embodied in the text or margins of the latest and best printed texts of the Greek New Testament. Scholars who make use of these recently issued texts have at their disposal, in the margins, all the best variations of the New Testament manuscripts. In our Revised Version the marginal references to such variant readings are very numerous. They show the value which must be attached to the existence of a large number of manuscripts, and also to the nicety of discrimination which must be exercised by scholars in dealing with these variants. Taken together, they must yield, by careful critical judgment, a text that deserves the confidence of every earnest student of the New Testament.

13. Another and a very important basis of our present versions is made up of the contributions of the various ancient versions. As these will be treated in detail further on, the merest skeleton as to their value will be given here. (1) The Septuagint was translated out of the original Hebrew probably between 280 and 130 B. C. It was made at Alexandria under Hebrew-Greek influences, hence carries a distinctive Hebrew flavor. It sprang from an original Hebrew source more than a thousand years before the age of the oldest Hebrew manuscript. But this Bible, like the Hebrew, was multiplied by copyists, down to the fifteenth century, hence was subject to copyists' errors. To secure

Codex Sinaiticus (S).   Fourth Century (⅔ 12, 115·117)
Esther 1 : 15 to 2 : 14

a good text of the Septuagint scholars must use the same methods as those employed in fixing a Greek text of the New Testament. (2) The Syriac Version was made from the original Hebrew of the Old Testament and the Greek of the New Testament in the second century A. D. It seems to have suffered somewhat from the doctrinal beliefs of its translators. But it represents the original of the Old Testament about three centuries later than the Septuagint, and that of the New Testament within about one hundred years after it was completed. Its true text, however, must be determined by the same processes as those employed to fix the New Testament Greek text. (3) The Vulgate, so-called, was for the most part the translation into Latin by Jerome of the original texts of the Bible at the close of the fourth century A. D. This version, then, represents the condition of the original texts of the Bible about two centuries later than the Syrian, and about five to six centuries later than the Septuagint. The true text of the Vulgate, as of the Syrian and Septuagint, must be determined by the processes already mentioned.

These three ancient versions are our most valuable aids, among the translations of the Bible, in ascertaining just what the original text of the two Testaments must have been. The margins of our Revised Version of the Old Testament show that the translators carefully followed the texts of each of these ancient versions, and in a few cases adopted their readings in preference to the Hebrew original, and in a much more numerous list of cases regarded their readings of sufficient importance to quote them as valuable alternate readings or side-lights.

14. Before the careful translator has completed his preparation, he will consult for the Old Testament those notable Jewish paraphrases called the Targums. Though they are not always nor prevailingly accurate translations of the original, they still represent, often in fine form, the thought of the Hebrew. They sometimes aid, too, in giving a correct shade of meaning to a word whose form or meaning in the original Hebrew has become either obscure or altogether lost.

Both of the Testaments are frequently quoted in ancient literature, especially by the church fathers. These quotations were made in some cases merely from memory, and sometimes poor memory at that. In other cases they aim to give only the sense of the original. In still others, the words seem to be a faithful quotation, either from the Septuagint or Vulgate. Occasionally only they were translated from the original Hebrew. Such quotations, either fragmentary, or exact, furnish valuable material to the translator of the Bible, and have contributed no insignificant part to the proper understanding of some otherwise obscure passages of that Book.

15. It must be evident now that the translators of our present versions have had at their disposal an embarrassing amount of textual riches. It must be plain also that the abundance of this material has

imposed upon them heavy burdens. They have had to determine their texts of the Old and New Testaments on the basis of the manuscripts, ancient versions, and quotations. And in doing this they were practically obliged to use the best printed texts of the ancient versions, which are by no means the result of a collation of all the known manuscripts of those individual versions. This of itself, of course, deprived them of what may yet be valuable aids to future translators.

Our translators have used as the basis of their revision, then, all the available material that could be treated by a small body of scholars, limited as to time and strength. Their work is seen in the text itself, in the marginal notes, and in the appendices.

A treatment of each individual version, and its part in the work which culminated in our Revised English Bible, will be treated in succeeding chapters.

Part I.　The Old Testament

CHAPTER III

HEBREW WRITING, TEXT, AND MANUSCRIPTS

16. The Old Testament books were written in Hebrew,—the language used by Israel during all the years of its existence as a nation, in Egypt, the wilderness and in Palestine, stretching down into the centuries between the Old and the New Testament. Within these books, however, we find another language, a kind of modified Hebrew, employed in part by the Jews in the centuries immediately preceding, and during the Christian era. This is called Biblical Aramaic, and is found as the language of Daniel 2: 4 to 7: 28; Ezra 4: 8 to 6: 18; 7: 12-26, and Jeremiah 10: 11. A few words of this same tongue are found scattered here and there throughout the Hebrew Bible.

The oldest specimen of biblical Hebrew writing of any considerable size that we possess to-day is either that of the St. Petersburg codex of the prophets, dated 916 A. D., or a British Museum manuscript copy of the Pentateuch, which Ginsburg locates "at least half a century earlier." According to S. A. Cook the scrap which is figured in the frontispiece of this volume bears the palm for age. Both of these larger manuscripts are written in the so-called square character, similar to those found in our printed Hebrew Bibles. Prepared at that point in time, viz., 916 A. D., or even fifty years earlier, they represent the Hebrew script of at least a thousand years after the youngest book of the Old Testament was put into writing. One thousand years of multiplying books by the process of copying with the pen may introduce great changes in the character of the script. How many of us can read with ease English written documents of the fourteenth century? Again, the Hebrew found in the rabbinical writings of the last five centuries differs quite materially from that in the Hebrew Bible and manuscripts.

17. Every trace of the original manuscripts, or rolls upon which the Old Testament was written has totally disappeared. That Israel wrote down descriptions of events, bodies of laws, lyrical poems, etc., is certain from hints and direct references in the body of the Old Testament. The origin of their alphabet is as yet a conjecture, but its use from the time of David down to Judas Maccabæus is pretty definitely known to-day.

There is no mention in all the book of Genesis of writing. Abraham (Gen. 23) bought the cave of Machpelah from Ephron the Hittite, but nothing is said of any written contract. The first mention of writing in the Old Testament is in Exodus 17: 14, where Moses is commanded to write down in a book an account of Israel's victory over Amalek. In Ex-

odus 24: 7, Moses reads in the audience of the people
"the book of the covenant;" that is, the laws contained in Exodus 20-23. Very soon thereafter he
goes into the mount to receive the two stone tablets
upon which the law had been inscribed. Thereafter we
find frequent references to writing as a means of preserving records of events. In Jeremiah (32: 9-15) we
find that a deed for property was drawn up in two
forms, one sealed and one open. Both of these documents, which may have been made of clay, as they
were in Babylonia, were deposited in a jar for future
reference.

There is frequent mention, however, of certain
classes who were skilled in writing. In that exquisite
Song of Deborah (Judges 5: 14) there is doubtless
reference to " the staff of the scribe " (marg.). During the beginnings and ascendancy of the monarchy,
prophets, court officials and kings were able to record
the events, decrees and wisdom of their day. Samuel
(1 Sam. 10: 25), David (2 Sam. 11: 14), Nathan
the prophet, Gad the seer (1 Chron. 29: 29), and
a host of others, both inside and outside of court
circles, were able to make records in writing. Thus
before the close of the Old Testament, there is a su-
perabundance of evidence to show that among the
Hebrews there were not simply scribes, but men of
distinguished literary ability.

18. With all these Old Testament references to
writing and writers we do not possess a single Old
Testament document in its original form. There was

writing, too, long centuries prior to Moses, among
the Egyptians, the Babylonians, the Susians, the Assyrians, the Hittites, and other contemporaneous
peoples. And we possess great quantities of their
literary products, stretching back almost, if not quite,
to 5000 B. C. It is entirely reasonable to expect that
among the remnants of ancient oriental writing we
should find some scraps of old Hebrew. In this we
are not disappointed. In 1868 there was found east
of the Jordan, at the site of ancient Dibon, the now
famous Moabite Stone. Its fragments are now put
together, and it stands in the Louvre in Paris. It
carried on its surface thirty-four lines, written in the
Phœnician or archaic Hebrew of about 860 B. C.,
when this work was probably executed. It is the
oldest dated Hebrew document known to-day, for its
issuer was Mesha, King of Moab, mentioned in
2 Kings 1: 1 and 3: 4. It was rudely cut on a hard
stone. Several lion-weights found at Nineveh, and
dating from the latter part of the eighth century B. C.
also carry Phœnician and Assyrian characters.

To bring the case closer home, an inscription in
similar character was found in Jerusalem in 1880, cut
in the wall of the tunnel connecting the Pool of
Siloam with St. Mary's well. This short six-line inscription is written in elegant Hebrew—a little more
artistic in form than the Moabite Stone. It is
thought to date from Hezekiah's reign, where a con-
duit, probably this same one, was constructed (2 Kings
20: 20; 2 Chron. 32: 30; Ecclesiasticus 48: 17).

These two inscriptions are the best known examples of the written language of the children of Israel and their neighbors in Moab, during the regal period— that period when writing was prevalent among the prophets and court officials. Samples of the Hebrew and Phœnician of the fourth century B. C. (for example, the Carpentras stele found in Egypt), of the first three Christian centuries (in the Palmyrenian form) show the tendency of the letters of the alphabet to change as the centuries slide by. The oldest Hebrew inscription in the square character, such as we have seen in the oldest Hebrew manuscript, is found in a short inscription in a cave at Araq al Ameer near Heshbon, which was used as a place of retreat in 176 B. C. A few other fragments and coins distributed over a couple of later centuries show us how the letters gradually moved towards the later square character.

19. It is probable that the books of the Old Testament were written in the same kind of script that we find on the Moabite Stone. As the centuries swept by, the value of these books to succeeding generations became more and more apparent. They were not only carefully preserved, but were copied time and time again to perpetuate their usefulness, and to avoid the possibility of their being lost or destroyed. The ravages of war and persecution very greatly endangered these Hebrew rolls. There were at least three events which threatened the very life of the cherished records of the Hebrews. The first and

most critical of all was the destruction of Jerusalem
by Nebuchadrezzar, in 586 B. C., though at this time
it is probable that Ezekiel had carried some portions
of the Old Testament with him when he was taken
to Babylonia in 597 B. C., eleven years before the fall
of the capital. Again, when Antiochus Epiphanes (in
167 B. C.) ordered all the copies of the law to be destroyed (1 Macc. 1: 56, 57), his decree did not
reach to Babylonia, where Ezekiel and Ezra had been
busy in earlier centuries instructing their people, and
where doubtless copies of the Old Testament books
were extant. Nor did it reach to Egypt, where, at
least one hundred years before that day, translators
had busied themselves to put into Greek some at least
of the sacred books of the Hebrews.

The destruction of Jerusalem by Titus in 70 A. D.
was a third disaster at that place, that threatened the
life of the Old Testament. On the authority of the
Babylonian Talmud, Titus destroyed copies of the law.
Josephus (Wars 5: 5, 7) states that one single copy
of the law occupied a prominent place in the victory
of Vespasian. This is the earliest mentioned manuscript of the Old Testament, and was said to have
just thirty-two variations from the received text.
This document was later deposited in the royal library
at Rome, and later, in 220 A. D., was handed over to
the synagogue of Severus, probably by the emperor,
who was a good friend to the Jews.

These perils to the manuscript of the Old Testament did probably extinguish many of the sources of

some of the books. For we find to-day, mentioned
in the books of the Old Testament now extant, the
names and titles of twenty-four books that have perished. By far the largest number of these is found
in Kings and Chronicles. It is not impossible that
some of those works, if existent, would be found in
our Bible, but they were probably blotted out by the
dire disasters that befel Jerusalem and the Jews between 600 B. C. and A. D. 100.

20. The alphabet of the Hebrew language is made
up of twenty-two letters—all consonants. Four of
these are called vowel letters, for their presence indicated the use of certain vowel sounds in the pronunciation of a word. On the Moabite Stone and the
Siloam Inscription, the individual words are separated
by a small point. This is found also between the
words of the Samaritan Pentateuch. It is probable
that as soon as the writing became modified into the
square characters, as seen in the St. Petersburg codex,
that this dot was omitted. For there are many instances in the Old Testament where two Hebrew
words have been written as one. The continuous
multiplication of the biblical Hebrew rolls by the pen
of a scribe opened the door for numerous errors. If
any one is not convinced of this, let him try to make
an exact copy, through one solid week, or one entire
day, of any written or printed document. There were
not in these manuscripts any verse, paragraph, or
chapter divisions beyond small spaces. Even the
Psalms were not separated, so that the Septuagint

and the Hebrew do not everywhere agree in their arrangement. Such facts only make it the more apparent that copyists had no sinecure in the very arduous and careful work which they were obliged to do.

21. The changes charged to the scribes who did the copying are of two kinds, intentional and unintentional. Their intentional changes were made (1) to correct what they conceived to be an error in statement, or an error of a preceding copyist, as Job 7: 20, "I am become a burden to myself," for "I am become a burden upon thee," as the Septuagint reads: 1 Samuel 3: 13, "because his sons made themselves vile," is not a possible reading of the Hebrew; the Septuagint reads, "did revile God,"—without doubt a rendering of the proper original text; (2) to insert some euphemistic word or phrase in place of an indelicate one found in the text, the latter usually being dropped into the margin.

The unintentional changes are the more numerous. Scholars have practically agreed on this classification: (1) Failure to see the sense of a passage, as where words were incorrectly divided. A good example is found in Amos 6: 12, "Shall horses run upon the rock? Will one plow there with oxen?" The word for "oxen" should doubtless be divided into two words, and then it will read, "Do men plough the sea with oxen?" Another good illustration is Psalm 73: 4, "For there are no pangs in their death; but their strength is firm." Simply by separating the word translated "in their death" we can translate, "For they have no pangs, sound and firm is their strength"—a meaning that better fits both the thought in the context and the parallelism.

(2) Errors due to the eye: (a) Repetitions: in Leviticus 20: 10, omit the five words repeated; 1 Chronicles 9: 35-44 has been repeated, doubtless through an error, from 1 Chronicles 8: 29-38. (b) Omissions: as where, in Proverbs 10: 10b, the omission is made up from verse 8b; but the Septuagint and the Syriac read for 10b, "He that rebuketh boldly is a peacemaker." (c) Transposition of letters or words: 2 Chronicles 3: 4, represents the porch of the temple as one hundred and twenty cubits high. The Septuagint reads twenty cubits, and the Hebrew, by a transposition of two letters and the two words reads twenty cubits, which is certainly correct. Psalm 35: 7 reads, "For without cause have they hid for me their net in a pit, without cause have they digged a pit for my soul." By simply transposing the words pit and net, we read: "For without cause have they hidden their net for me, without cause have they digged a pit for my life." There are also numerous cases where one letter has been taken for another by the copyist. One of the familiar cases is that where "Nebuchadrezzar," the only correct reading, has been, by mistaking two Hebrew letters n (נ), r (ר), read "Nebuchadnezzar." Another error of the same kind, where "Hadadezer," has been erroneously read "Hadarezer," a mistaking of the Hebrew d (ד) for

r (ר). In Isaiah 39: 1, we find " Merodach-baladan,"
where the parallel in 2 Kings 20: 12, reads, " Bero-
dach-baladan "—a confusing of two Hebrew letters
m (מ) and b (ב).

(3) Errors due to the ear, where one read to a
number of copyists; these are seen mainly in the use
of one Hebrew word for another of almost or just
the same sound. A good example is found in Psalm
100: 3, where " and not we ourselves " should be
" and we are his." In 2 Chronicles 10: 18, " Hado-
ram " is " Adoram " in 1 Kings 12: 18.

(4) Errors of memory; these may be occasioned
by the fact that the copyist sometimes carried in his
mind the thought rather than the exact words of
what he was copying. In such a case he would be
apt to use synonyms, or nearly such, in place of the
word contained in the original. As an example of
this " Jehoiakim," in Jeremiah 27: 1, should be " Zede-
kiah," as in verse 3.

(5) Errors due to carelessness or ignorance. Of
this type there are many examples. In 1 Samuel 13: 1
we find " Saul was — years old;" some copyist care-
lessly neglected to put down the number. In 2 Samuel 3: 7, " Ish-bosheth " is missing, but is found here
in the Septuagint, Syriac and Vulgate. 2 Samuel 11:
21 has " Jerubbesheth," a careless writing for " Je-
rubbaal " (Judges 6: 32). In 1 Samuel 27: 8, " Gir-
zites " is read in some manuscripts " Gizrites." 1 Samuel 12: 11 has " Bedan," where the word should be
read according to the Septuagint, the Syriac, and the

original narrative as the story is told in the book of Judges 4, " Barak."

Such errors as these crept into the text gradually, and were transmitted by copyists from one manuscript to another continuously down through the centuries.

As a prevention against further errors the scribes counted the number of verses (though they were not yet formally numbered) and even letters in the various books, and then made note of the middle verse, the middle word, and the middle letter of each book. These are found at the end of each book in our Hebrew Bibles to-day. The middle verse of the Pentateuch is Leviticus 8: 7; the middle verse of Joshua is chapter 13: 26; of Judges, chapter 10: 8. The middle verse of the Hebrew Bible is Jeremiah 6: 7. If a scribe, after he had finished his work, could not make his count tally with these notations, there was some error in his copy of the manuscript, which must either be corrected or his copy discarded.

22. The Hebrews classified the books of the Old Testament under three heads: (1) The Law, consisting of the first five books, or the Pentateuch; (2) The Prophets, subdivided into (a) the Earlier Prophets, consisting of four books, Joshua, Judges, Samuel and Kings; (b) the Latter Prophets, containing four books, Jeremiah, Ezekiel, Isaiah and The Twelve (one book) ; (3) the Hagiographa, containing eleven books, Ruth, Psalms, Job, Proverbs, Ecclesiastes, Song of Songs, Lamentations, Daniel, Esther, Ezra (including Nehemiah) and Chronicles. Of these the

Five Rolls, so often mentioned, are Song of Songs, Ruth, Lamentations, Ecclesiastes and Esther. The whole number according to the Jewish reckoning was therefore twenty-four books. Josephus and some others, by combining Ruth with Judges, and Lamentations with Jeremiah, made them twenty-two—the same in number as the letters of the Hebrew alphabet.

Then the Law, after the exile at least, was arranged to be read in regular course. In Acts 15: 21, we read that, " Moses from generations of old hath in every city them that preach him, being read in the synagogues every sabbath." This custom has continued to the present day. In Palestine it was read through in three and one-half years. To facilitate this plan the law was early divided into sections, called parâshahs. There are now fifty-four of these sections or paragraphs found in Hebrew manuscripts and printed texts, and since the fourteenth century an annual reading of the whole law has become universal among the Jews.

After the Law was read in the synagogue a corresponding, or appropriate, passage was read from the prophets. An example of this is seen in the synagogue at Nazareth (Luke 4: 17f.) when Jesus read from the prophet Isaiah (61: 1f.). But the sections into which the prophets were divided are not definitely known.

Some of the poetical portions of the Old Testament (such as the Song of Moses, Exodus 15, the Song of Deborah, Judges 5, the Psalm of David in

2 Samuel 22 (Psalm 18), are written in a peculiar
form, to represent some phantasy of the scribes. In
the Septuagint the Psalms are arranged in a form to
represent the fact of Hebrew parallelism.

There was no early division into chapters, nor into
formal or numbered verses, though the latter became,
in fact, a necessity for reasons of interpretation.
When a reader in the synagogue in the time of Christ
and for centuries thereafter, had read two or three
verses, an interpreter would translate it into the
spoken Aramaic, or language of the times (compare Nehemiah 8: 8)—an indication that there were
regularly recognized divisions in the text.

23. The early Hebrew writing, as has already been
stated, consisted of consonants only. Four of these
possessed vowel values, and wherever any one or
more of them happened to stand in a word, they gave
some key to its pronunciation. But all the known
Hebrew Old Testament manuscripts and printed
texts are supplied with a complicated and scientific
system of points, which give us exact sounds and
pronunciations for words, and some individual consonants. These are placed below, within, or above the
consonants, as the varying sounds require.

When were these vowel points first used? We
know through hints in Jerome (who died 420), the
Targums and the Talmud, that there was no pointed
or voweled Hebrew at the end of the sixth century.
On the other hand, we know that two of the greatest
authorities on the use of the vowel points lived about

the beginning of the tenth century. Ben Asher, one of these men, was descended from a notable family of Massoretes, or students of the text, who had devoted at least one hundred and twenty years to that study. None of their records tell of the origin of these points. But popular tradition has so far connected that family with the origin of the Hebrew vowel points that the Hebrew text supplied with them is called the Massoretic text. Since we know that at 600 A. D. there were no points, and at about 900 A. D. there was a full developed system, it is evident that its growth fell within those limits. Scholars are now practically agreed that it arose about the end of the seventh or the beginning of the eighth century.

The reason for the invention of these vowel points lies in the fact that Hebrew, as a spoken tongue, was passing away. Its teachers, fearful lest its proper pronunciation should be lost, saw that some helps to preserve it were becoming necessary. Syriac had only recently adopted the use of vowel points, and the Greek language had just begun to make use of accents. It was then in accord with the tendency of the age that some system be devised to preserve the traditional pronunciation of the Hebrew language of the Old Testament. The Massorah means, " what is handed down," and as applied to the Old Testament, its traditional text.

When the Hebrew was supplied with those points, those voweled words bore the marks of the interpretation that the " pointers " gave them. The conso-

nants of many words in Hebrew can be pointed with
vowels in more than one way, thus conveying different ideas. This may be illustrated by noting the use
of the same consonants in English to mean different
things, according to the vowels used. Take such consonants as f r; with different vowels we have f(a)r,
f(i)r, f(u)r; c(a)p, c(o)p, c(u)p; b(a)d, b(e)d,
b(i)d, b(u)d. Now and then in the Old Testament
a slightly different pointing changes entirely the mean-
ng of a word. In Psalm 50: 18, the word translated
" thou consentedst " by different vowel points reads,
    thou didst run." Psalm 59: 10 reads as it stands
" God with his lovingkindness; " by the simple change
oᶠ one vowel point we read, " My God, by his lovingkindness."

The vowel points at best are simply the interpretation of the text as fixed by the Massoretes at the end
of the seventh or beginning of the eighth century A. D.

24. Manuscripts of the Hebrew Old Testament
are comparatively young. The oldest dated document belonging, as we have seen, to 916 A. D., is
called the St. Petersburg codex of the prophets. Dr.
Ginsburg puts a British Museum manuscript (of the
Pentateuch) (Orient. No. 4445), " at least half a century earlier." This consists of 186 folios, fifty-five
of which were added in 1540 A. D. Each page carries three columns of about twenty-one lines each.
the Massorah magna has been put above and below
the columns, while the Massorah parva has place in the
side margins. The St. Petersburg codex consists of

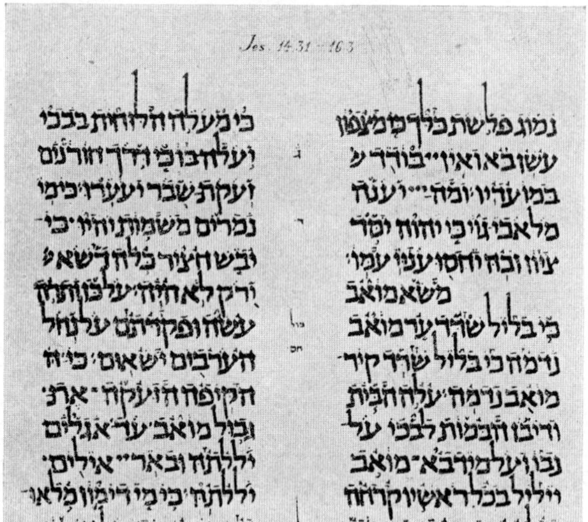

St. Petersburg Hebrew Codex. A.D. 916
Isaiah 14 : 31 to 16 : 3

225 folios, each of two columns of twenty-one lines. Its system of punctuation is that called the super-linear, or sometimes Babylonian. It contains Isaiah, Jeremiah, Ezekiel and The Twelve.

The oldest manuscript of the whole Old Testament is another of the famous Firkowitzsch collection brought from the Crimea. This one dates from 1010 A. D., though its correctness is disputed. The number of manuscripts of the entire Hebrew Old Testament is very small, though partial or fragment documents run up into the neighborhood of 1700.

The most of the variant readings of these manuscripts may be charged to scribal errors of some kind. For example, one manuscript omits nine words of Genesis 19: 20, and in Exodus 8 omits verses 10 and 11. In 1 Chronicles 2, one manuscript has twenty-two variations from the common Massoretic text. Errors from mistaking one Hebrew letter for another as seen in Section 21, occur more frequently in Hebrew than in Greek and Latin manuscripts.

The close resemblance of all existing Hebrew manuscripts has led scholars to conjecture that at some period before the invention of the Hebrew vowel points, all known Hebrew manuscripts were either reduced to one or all other existing documents besides the one model were destroyed. Every subsequent copy was then made from this model; and the variations after the letters received their vowels, were reduced to a minimum.

25. The first part of the Old Testament to be put

into print was the Psalter, in 1477. It was printed
in Hebrew with the rabbinical commentary of Kim-
chi, text and commentary alternating at every verse.
The typographical difficulties were so great that only
the first few psalms were printed with vowel points.
The work was full of errors of many kinds. During
the next ten years (1477-87), at least four editions,
covering all the Old Testament were printed in as
many different cities. The first complete edition of
the whole Hebrew Old Testament with vowel points
and accents was finished at Soncino, February 14,
1488. It was issued next at Naples, 1491-93; and a
third time in the Brescia Bible in 1494—the text used
by Luther. A fourth edition appeared at Pesaro in
1511-17. All these editions were issued under the direction of Jewish authors.

The first edition of the Hebrew text to be published under the direction and authority of Christian
influences was that found in the so-called Complutensian Polyglot. This great work carried in parallel
columns the Hebrew text, the Septuagint, the Vulgate, and the Hebrew paraphrase, or Targum, of Onkelos, for the Pentateuch. It was edited by Cardinal
Ximenes and printed at the University founded by
him at Alcala, Spain, 1514-1517. The magnitude of
this undertaking may be partially understood when it
is said that the Cardinal had to cast all his own type
before he began the printing. The critical value of
this first polyglot was slight, because of its defects
and frequent errors.

The first Hebrew Bible with full vowel points and
all the Rabbinic material for interpretation of the text,
was printed by Daniel Bomberg at Venice, 1516-17.
This is the first Hebrew text to divide Samuel, Kings
and Chronicles, each into two books; and the book
of Ezra into Ezra and Nehemiah. The so-called
" editio princeps " of the Hebrew Bible, with all Rabbinic helps, was Bomberg's second edition, edited by
Jacob ben Chayim, a Jew of Tunis, 1524-25. This
formed the standard edition of the Massoretic text
of the Hebrew Bible.

The great Paris Polyglot, found to-day in a few
of our large libraries, was edited by le Jay, and
printed 1629-45 in ten folio volumes. A rival of this
stupendous work was the London Polyglot, edited by
Walton in London, in 1657, in six folio volumes.

The Hebrew Bible of to-day is divided into chapters and verses. This chapter division had its origin
in the Vulgate, and is accredited to Lanfranc, Archbishop of Canterbury, who died 1089; to Stephen
Langton, who died 1228; and to Hugo de Sancto
Caro in the thirteenth century. The numbers of the
chapters were first inserted in the margin, even in
the Complutensian Polyglot. The first edition to
insert the chapter numbers in the text was that of
Arias Montanus, who edited an interlinear Latin
translation at Antwerp in 1571. The first clear Hebrew text to insert chapter numbers in the text appeared in 1573-4.

26. Naturally the printing of so large a number

of Hebrew Bibles at so many places, and based on
the readings of so many different manuscripts, led to
confusion in interpretation, and anxiety regarding the
true text of the Old Testament.   This led to the
doing of just what appears in the margins of our
English Bibles, viz: the collecting of the variants or
differences in the readings of the known manuscripts.
Without giving the history of this kind of work, it is
sufficient to say that the first great collector and publisher of variants was Kennicott, an Englishman.   He
employed a number of scholars, and spent £9000
sterling in carrying on his work.   At the conclusion he had succeeded in collecting and having
collected the various readings of 694 manuscripts and
almost numberless editions.   These pertain to consonants only.   His collection was published at Oxford, 1776-80, in two folio volumes.

A professor in Parma, Italy, by name of de Rossi,
collected the readings of 732 manuscripts and 310
editions.   Of all this number Kennicott had seen only
eighty, so that de Rossi compared 652 new ones.   In
1784-88, he published in Parma four volumes quarto,
and in 1798 a supplemental volume.

Kennicott and de Rossi together compared 1,346
different Hebrew manuscripts of the Old Testament,
and 342 reported editions, or 1,686 different manuscripts.   The value of their work is seen in that it
showed that the underlying Hebrew of all the manuscripts examined by these two scholars and their
assistants was practically one and the same text.

First American Edition of the Hebrew Bible. Philadelphia, 1814

CHAPTER IV

27. The Samaritans were and are a peculiar people. Their idiosyncrasies are found on every page of Palestinian history since 400 B. C. Their friendship for, or antipathy against, the Jews rests upon definite historical facts. Their religious proclivities appear in some periods of history in strangely opposing relations. When it was to their advantage to be Jews, they were Jews, when derogatory to such a claim, they were not Jews. They seemed to stand alone for long centuries, and not to mingle freely with any people. In New Testament times they looked with disdain upon the Jews, and this spirit was heartily reciprocated. The few New Testament references to their beliefs and spirit classify them among the enemies of the Jews. It also locates their seat of worship at Shechem in opposition to that carried on in Jerusalem. The clannish, provincial character of these people is doubtless due in large part to their composite origin. The same spirit that made them clannish also stimulated them in their opposition to the Jews, and whatever they believed and held sacred.

28. These strange peoples owe their origin to the governmental policy of the new Assyrian empire, established by Tiglath-pileser III (745-727 B. C.).

From a purely military control of his provinces, he established a civil government, imposing definite local responsibility. In order to compensate for the deported peoples of any province, and also to lessen the liability to revolt among new subjects, he imported peoples from distant provinces and compelled the two to reside side by side. This mingling and commingling of foreign peoples resulted, within a few years, in a confusion of customs, religions and nationalities. Such conglomeration only served to make the province thus constituted less liable to stir up trouble for Assyria, and better able to take part in some local government.

29. The specific instances that brought about the beginnings of the Samaritans occurred in 722 B. C., when Sargon II captured Samaria, the capital of the northern kingdom of Israel. His own records tell us that he carried away 27,290 of its inhabitants. The Old Testament (2 Kings 17 : 24) records read in these words: " And the king of Assyria brought men from Babylon and from Cuthah, and from Avva, and from Hamath and Sepharvaim, and placed them in the cities of [the province of] Samaria instead of the children of Israel, and they possessed Samaria, and dwelt in the cities thereof." Sargon himself in his own inscriptions which were found in the ruins of his old palace at Khorsabad, just north of Nineveh (Annals, 95-97), says: " The tribes of the Tamud, Ibadid, Marsiman, Chayapa, the distant Arabians who inhabit the desert, whom no scholar or writer knew, who had

paid tribute to no king, I smote in the service of Asshur my lord; the remaining inhabitants I carried away and settled in Samaria." In other words, Sargon and 2 Kings agree on the general policy that was carried out regarding the re-populating of the northern kingdom from which captives had been carried to the East.

Both records together give the names of ten different nationalities, including the Jews already there, who were settled down in the same territory together. Within a few generations they intermarried, they combined heathen and Jehovah worship, and formed a distinct and unique population (compare 2 Kings 17: 24-41). To this conglomerate, other peoples were added at a later time, as seen in Ezra (4: 2), where the Samaritans say to the Jews: "Let us build with you; for we seek your God, as ye do; and we sacrifice unto him since the days of Esarhaddon, king of Assyria [681-668 B. C.], who brought us up hither." In the formal protest against the building activities of the Jews, sent to Artaxerxes, king of Persia, the Samaritans give this astounding list of foreign peoples who made up their populace, imported at a still later date (Ezra 4: 9, 10): "Then wrote Rehum the chancellor, and Shimshai the scribe, and the rest of their companions, the Dinaites, and the Apharsathchites, the Tarpelites, the Apharsites, the Archevites, the Babylonians, the Shushanchites, the Dehaites, the Elamites, and the rest of the nations whom the great and noble Osnappar [Assurbanipal, king of Assyria, 668-626 B. C.] brought over, and set in the city of Samaria, and in the rest of the country beyond the River, and so forth."

30. What a background for the Samaritans! Out of this composite sprung the peoples who developed such rivalry with the Jews as appears immediately after the exile. The Samaritan antagonism to Israel on the latter's return to Jerusalem, and their attempt to rebuild their temple and city, must have gradually cooled off. For Ezra and Nehemiah find the Jews had not only formed friendly relations with all the surrounding peoples, but had freely intermarried with them. This infraction of Jewish law grieved Ezra and angered Nehemiah. They adopted drastic and cruel measures to break off all domestic relations with these foreigners (Neh. 13: 23-27). In his investigations Nehemiah (13: 28) found that " one of the sons of Joiada, the son of Eliashib the high priest, was son-in-law to Sanballat the Horonite," therefore he drove him out. Josephus (Antiquities 11, 8, 2) tells us that this grandson of the high priest was Manasseh; that he preferred rather to lose his wife than his prospects of the high priesthood in Jerusalem. His father-in-law promised him, however, if he would go with his wife and forsake Jerusalem that he (Sanballat) would build a temple for him on Mount Gerizim like that in Jerusalem, and furthermore would see that the Persian king should bestow on him the high priesthood. Elated by such promises, Manasseh forsook Jerusalem, his prospects of promotion, and

the temple, and followed his wife and his father-in-law to Samaria.

31. This expulsion of Manasseh from Jerusalem (in 433 B. C.) engendered only bitterness and enmity between the Samaritans and the Jews. It meant, too, for the former a new fixed religious trend. The temple is said to have been built on Mount Gerizim as a rival of that at Jerusalem. Its first high priest, Manasseh, had sufficient regard for the law of Jehovah to make it a basis for worship on Gerizim. It is generally believed that this was the time that the Pentateuch was adopted as the authoritative scriptures of the Samaritans. With Gerizim as a place for the worship of Jehovah, and influential officials and friends to support him, Manasseh could gradually crowd out and eradicate the various species of idolatry that had been dominant among these nations since the time of Sargon II. In fact, the worship of Jehovah and heathen divinities had existed side by side, and had even commingled for centuries. Manasseh's great missionary endeavor had now given the worship of Israel's God first place in the hearts and life of the Samaritans, and established the Pentateuch as their sacred book. It is thought that this was the only portion of the Old Testament at that time that had been recognized by the Jews as holy scriptures. When the Prophets and Hagiographa were adopted at a later time, the Samaritans refused to adopt them.

32. The Samaritan Pentateuch is not a transla-

tion of the original Hebrew, and so properly not a version. It is a Hebrew text, which has been maintained independently since the fifth century B. C., but written in the old Hebrew characters that were extant before the beginning of the use of the square characters. Hence it reaches back farther for its origin than any other except the Hebrew text itself. Its adoption by the Samaritans may have been attended by certain changes in the text conformable to their place of worship and their peculiar beliefs. One of the most striking deliberate changes in the text is the substitution, in Deuteronomy 27: 4, of " Gerizim " for " Ebal " in the Hebrew text, thus pointing to the pre-eminence of Gerizim, the seat of their temple, over Ebal.

The chief value of the Samaritan Pentateuch is that it is an independent text that has had its own transmission by copyists from the time of Manasseh without any known contact with the numerous Hebrew texts. It is thus a check on the errors and corruptions that may have crept into the Hebrew text in its numerous copyings from the fifth century B. C. down to the time of the printing of the Hebrew Old Testament.

33. The existence of the Pentateuch as the Bible of the Samaritans was known to European scholars in the sixteenth century. Joseph Scaliger, the famous linguist, complained that Christians traveling in the East took no pains to secure a copy of it. The first specimen of it to be seen in Europe was brought

by the Italian traveler, Pietro de la Valle, in 1616. He spent twelve years in visiting the East, and published the best information then extant about Turkey, Persia, Egypt and India. The Samaritans, though now confined to modern Nablus, the ancient Shechem, consisted in his day of several small communities, located at Gaza, Cairo and Damascus. Pietro de la Valle, at the urgent request of the French ambassador at Constantinople, M. de Sarcey, attempted to secure a copy of the Samaritan Bible. After failure at three of the places, he finally succeeded in buying two copies from the Samaritan colony at Damascus. The first was the Hebrew text of the Pentateuch in Samaritan characters on parchment. This he presented to the ambassador, who in turn deposited it in the library of the Oratoire in Paris. The second, a Samaritan version of the same, written on paper, he kept for himself. Since that day scholars and travelers have secured a goodly number of these sacred documents, and they are now found either as private possessions or in various libraries of Europe and America.

The most sacred copy of the Samaritan law is securely kept and guarded in the synagogue at Nablus. It has this subscription: "I, Abishua, the son of Phinehas, the son of Eleazar, the son of Aaron the priest, wrote this copy in the court of the tabernacle, on Mount Gerizim in the thirteenth year of the settlement of the children of Israel in the land of Canaan." Scholars put no confidence in this subscription.

Kennicott, the textual critic (see §26), collated sixteen Samaritan manuscripts. None of these documents stretches back into an extreme antiquity. The oldest manuscript is in Rome and is dated 1227 A. D., though there is another whose oldest portions claim as its date 656 A. D. Of modern prepared manuscripts there are several in this country: Drew Theological Seminary has one; the New York Public Library, one; the Rev. W. Scott Watson, one; and the Rev. W. E. Barton, of Oak Park, Ill., two.

34. The first edition of the Samaritan Pentateuch was printed under the supervision of John Morinus in 1632, and then in the Paris Polyglot in 1645. It was also included in the London Polyglot in 1657. It was later published in the square character by Blayney of Oxford, in 1790. Kennicott, who collated the known manuscripts, published the variants in his great work already referred to. In 1868, Petermann published a grammar of the language, including in it the whole book of Genesis, as it was read by the at-that-time high priest to the little Samaritan body at Nablus, consisting of about 165 persons at the present time (1906).

35. Now what is the value of this Samaritan Pentateuch? It differs from the text of the Hebrew in about 6,000 items. A large part of these consists of insertions of vowel letters, insertion or omission of conjunctions, and such other variations as have no real effect on the sense. There are more than a thousand characteristic variations that have some real

Jacob ben Aaron, present High-Priest of the Samaritans at Nablous,
with Pentateuch Roll

significance. These variants from the Hebrew text
are of several kinds : (1) explanatory additions to the
text, as in Genesis 4: 8, to the Hebrew, " And Cain
said to Abel his brother," the Samaritan, as well as
the Septuagint, adds, " Let us go into the field."
Genesis 7: 3, to " of the fowls of the air," the Samaritan adds, " which are clean." Genesis 44: 31, to
" the lad is not," the Samaritan adds " with us."
(2) Conjectural emendations by changing a letter or
two, either to improve the sense or avoid some difficulty as in Genesis 49: 10, " The sceptre shall not depart from Judah, nor the ruler's staff from between
his feet," by the change of a single letter (r to d) the
Samaritan reads, " from amidst his standards."   (3)
Corrections to agree with some parallel passage,
Genesis 11: 10f., " and he died " is added to what is
said of each patriarch, as in Genesis 5. In Exodus
4: 18, for the Hebrew " Jether," the Samaritan reads
" Jethro," as in Exodus 18: 1.   (4) Corrections to
relieve some supposed historical difficulty; thus in
Exodus 12: 40, the four hundred and thirty years are
said to cover the whole period of wanderings by the
additions for " in Egypt," " in the land of Egypt and
in the land of Canaan." The most notable variation
of this kind is found in the genealogical tables of
Genesis 5 and 11. The Samaritans seem to have
assumed that no one would have been more than one
hundred and fifty years old at the birth of his first
son ; when this number is exceeded, as in the case of
Methuselah and Lamech, one hundred years or more

are taken from it. If the remaining years were unchanged they would survive the flood. But such changes are made as to allow them all to die in the year of the flood. (5) Variations made to present Samaritan ideas, and to remove anthropomorphisms. The chief passage is Deuteronomy 27: 4, where "Ebal" is displaced by "Gerizim;" and this is incorporated in Exodus 20: 17, and Deuteronomy 5: 21. In Genesis 49: 7, Jacob's rebuke of Simeon and Levi, "cursed be their anger," is changed to read, "noble was their anger."

These are the most important classes of variations for our study. They are so important that the editors of the Teachers' Variorum Bible mention more than thirty of them in their footnotes, and every commentator of the Pentateuch must reckon with them before he concludes his investigations.

CHAPTER V

36. The military campaigns carried into Western Asia and Egypt by Alexander the Great opened the door for a literary conquest. Alexander's troops were the forerunners of Greek civilization. Wherever his invincible battalions beat down the enemy, there the Greek language secured a foothold. Its conquests, however, were most marked and permanent on the shores of the Mediterranean Sea. Here the Greek language displaced in some countries the native tongues, and became the language not only of culture, but of commerce and religion. Greek literature secured a firm footing, and prepared in a most remarkable manner for the advent and expansion of Christianity several centuries later.

Alexander's conquest of Egypt meant an open door into that country for Greek settlers, commerce, culture and religion. His magnificent foresight led to the founding of Alexandria, that soon became the most important of all ports on the shore lines of the eastern section of the Mediterranean Sea. Its attractive features soon filled it with the strength of Greek civilization and learning. But it also became more or less a cosmopolitan city. Its commercial advantages drew to it tradesmen from all Oriental lands.

49

With their products and articles of trade they also took with them their customs and religion; and in turn themselves fell under the spell of Greek learning.

37. Egypt had been the home of some Jews at least since early in the life of Jeremiah the prophet (comp. Jeremiah, chapters 43 and 44). At various periods in their history they had gone down for one reason or another to sojourn in the land of sunshine. Famines, wars, trading facilities and governmental reasons had all conspired to bring about such migrations. Alexander's liberal governmental policy encouraged the settlement of Jews in Egypt, and they were industrious, thrifty, temperate, intelligent, and comparatively loyal to any ruler whose policy did not hamper their religious liberty.

It is reported that in the times of the Ptolemies one-third of the population of Alexandria was Jewish. This large Jewish element was, of course, imbued with Greek culture and civilization. It spoke the Greek language, and adopted some Greek methods of thought and systems of belief. Its sympathies even were falling away to things Greek and to persons Greek.

But among this multitude of Greek-speaking Jews there were some who tenaciously held to the beliefs of their fathers. While they believed in the God of Abraham, Isaac, and Jacob, they were steeped in the language and culture of a foreign people. The requirements of these very Jews brought about an event most important to Bible students—the translation of the Hebrew Old Testament into the Greek language, the adopted language of these Egyptian Jews.

38. This is the first foreign tongue into which the Old Testament was translated. Therefore its why? how? wherefore? are of intense interest to every Bible student. This translation became not simply the Bible of the Greek-speaking Jews of Alexandria and Egypt, but of all the Jews in the countries about the Mediterranean Sea, in the times of Christ and in the early Christian centuries. It was the Old Testament of Paul and the apostles, and was in constant use by the church fathers in the first few centuries of the Christian church. It was the mother-text, too, for several translations which will be examined farther on in our discussion, and it has been the Bible of the Greek church from its organization to the present day.

39. There are several stories of the origin of this remarkable book. One based on the now famous letter of Aristeas, about seventy-two translators completing the work in seventy-two days, has been shown to be a forgery. When all the stories have been sifted there still remain some kernels of truth. It seems to be a fact that the translation of the Law, at least, was made in the reign of Ptolemy Philadelphus (285-247 B. C.). This bare fact, preserved by tradition, has been gorgeously arrayed in the spurious letter of Aristeas, and imbedded as credible statements in the writings of many of the early church fathers. The authority of the king doubtless made for this new trans-

lation a ready and willing acceptance among the Jews of that and succeeding centuries. The name " Septuagint," meaning " seventy " (often written " LXX ") was probably given it on the basis of a tradition of seventy translators, though some have thought it was derived from the sanction of the translation by an Egyptian Jewish Sanhedrin of seventy members.

40. It is now certain that the books were not all translated in the time of Ptolemy Philadelphus, nor were they all translated by the same person. The work was done by different men, extending over a period approximating 150 years, or from 285-130 B. C. The former fact is certain from the varying degrees of accuracy observable in the whole volume. The Pentateuch is a creditable translation, especially of Leviticus and Deuteronomy. Ecclesiastes is so slavishly literal that it is little more than a Græcized Hebrew. Daniel is so poor a translation that the church ruled it out and substituted for it the Greek translation of Theodotion. The book of Esther has a note attached to it stating that it was translated by Lysimachus of Jerusalem, and taken to Egypt in the fourth year of Ptolemy Philometer, 185 B. C. The prologue to the book of Ecclestiasticus speaks of the whole Old Testament as completed before 132 B. C. In some of the books, notably Proverbs and Jeremiah, verses and chapters, and even a body of chapters are transposed. For example, immediately after Jeremiah 25: 13, chapters 46-51 are introduced in the following order: 49: 34-39; 46; 50; 51; 47: 1-7, 7-22;

49: 1-5, 28-33, 23-27; 48; then the Hebrew order is followed up from chapter 25: 15. In 1 Samuel the Septuagint either so cut the Hebrew text as to relieve it of difficulties, or had a different original as the basis of its translation.

41. These liberties taken with the Hebrew text may be due in large part to the purpose for which the translation was made. The aim of these translators was to cast the Hebrew thought of the Old Testament into Greek moulds, so that it might be plain to ordinary Hebrew-Greek readers. Therefore fidelity to sense was more essential than fidelity to form. They seemed to be perfectly ready to make such slight changes or additions as were necessary to clear up the sense of any passage. They now and then substituted literal for figurative expressions. They inserted or omitted words and clauses, and added or changed clauses as they saw fit, as in Genesis 4: 8, " and Cain said unto Abel, let us go into the field " (agreeing with the Samaritan reading). In 2 Samuel 6: 5, they read, for " on all manner of instruments made of fir wood," " with all [their] might and with singing." In Jeremiah 15: 19, the clause, " bring thee again," is read in the Septuagint, " give thee a habitation." Ezekiel 23: 42, " and the voice of a multitude being at ease was with her," is read in the Septuagint, " And with a loud noise did they sing therein." The Septuagint omits in Ezekiel 32: 31, " even Pharaoh and all his army, slain by the sword." In Ezekiel 34: 16, " but I will destroy the fat and the strong," is

made to read, " and I will keep the fat and the
strong." Then in Exodus 12: 40, the same addition
is made as already noted under the " Samaritan Pentateuch." These examples indicate a few of the
multitude of variations that this, our oldest translation
of the Hebrew Old Testament presents. Doubtless in
many cases they were the translation of a Hebrew
text differing from the one we possess to-day. This
fact is made use of in many passages of the Revised
Version as seen in the marginal notes and readings.

42. The Septuagint, as it has come down to us,
embodies not simply a translation of our Hebrew
Bible, but also of many of the so-called apocryphal
books. This may be due to the fact that the Jews
of Alexandria took a more liberal view of what constituted their sacred books than had the Jews at
Jerusalem. It shows either that there was not yet a
sharp distinction made between the sacred and secu-
lar in Jewish literature, or that the Greek-Jews wished
to include with their sacred books other portions
of their writings. These apocryphal books are distributed among the other books. In order properly
to locate them, we present below the order of the
books in the Septuagint. The so-called historical
books, while differing from the order in the Hebrew
Bible, follow in the same succession as they do in the
English Bible, until 2 Chronicles is concluded. From
this point the apocryphal books will appear among
the regular books in the order found in the best manuscripts, and will be numbered successively. Immedi-

ately following 2 Chronicles we find (1) Esdras,
followed by Ezra (called 2 Esdras). Then follow
in order, Psalms, Proverbs, Ecclesiastes, Song of Solomon, Job, (2) Wisdom of Solomon, (3) Wisdom of
Sirach (or Ecclesiasticus), Esther, with (4) The Rest
of Esther, (5) Judith, (6) Tobit, Hosea, Amos,
Micah, Joel, Obadiah, Jonah, Nahum, Habakkuk,
Zephaniah, Haggai, Zechariah, Malachi, Isaiah, Jeremiah, (7) Baruch, Lamentations, (8) Epistle of Jeremiah, Ezekiel, Daniel, opened by (9) Susanna; after
Daniel 3: 23, (10) The Song of the Three Children,
after the close of Daniel, (11) Bel and the Dragon,
(12) 1 Maccabees, (13) 2 Maccabees, (14) 3 Maccabees, and in some manuscripts (15) 4 Maccabees. Several of the apocryphal books are not known to have
existed in Hebrew. These are The Rest of Esther, a
part of Baruch, The Song of the Three Children, and
2 Maccabees. On the completion of the canon
of the Old Testament, even those written in Hebrew
were left out. This fact left them outside the regard
given the canonical books, and they practically ceased
to be copied by the biblical scribes. Thus we know
them almost exclusively in translations. Jerome's
fidelity to what he knew to be the canonical books
led him to disregard them in his great work. Their
appearance in the Vulgate was in spite of Jerome's
opinion of their real value.

43. We have already noted the fact that our oldest Hebrew manuscript dates from the tenth century
—more than a thousand years after the last word of

the Old Testament was written. Though the original Septuagint translation was made after the close of the Hebrew canon, there are manuscripts of this version that antedate the oldest known Hebrew manuscripts by five or six hundred years. This fact makes them of superior importance in determining the early text of the Hebrew Old Testament.

Manuscripts of the Septuagint are fortunately quite plentiful in the great libraries of Europe. They are written in two kinds of script. Those dating from the fourth to the ninth centuries were written in uncials, that is, in large, separate letters, practically capitals; those from the ninth century to the close of pen transcriptions in cursives, that is, small, running-hand script. The uncial manuscripts are designated by capital letters, and the cursives by numbers. There are about thirty known uncials, more or less fragmentary, stretching over five centuries of time. The great importance of these documents requires some further notice.

44. The oldest scrap of a Septuagint manuscript is a piece of papyrus found at Oxyrhynchus, in Egypt, in 1903, shown in the illustration (opposite page). There are also two others in the British Museum of the third century, containing Genesis 14: 17, and a fragment of a Psalter containing Psalms 12: 7 to 15: 4 respectively. There are four invaluable large, ancient manuscripts of the Septuagint now available for the use of Bible students: (1) The oldest and most complete known manuscript of the Greek Bible, cov-

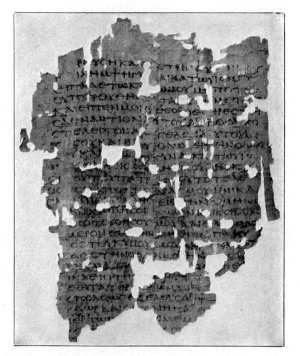

Septuagint Papyrus of the Third Century, from Oxyrhynchus, Egypt
Genesis 24 : 38-43

ering the Old and New Testaments, is Codex Vaticanus (marked " B " in catalogues), in the Vatican library at Rome. It was written in the fourth century. It lacks only Genesis 1: 1 to 46: 28; 2 Kings 2: 5-7, 10-13; Psalms 106: 27 to 138: 6 in the Old Testament; the books of Maccabees are not in it. This manuscript formed the basis of our current critical edition of the Septuagint.

The next most valuable manuscript text is the Codex Alexandrinus (marked " A " in catalogues), in the British Museum. It is estimated to have been written in the first half of the fifth century. This, too, covers the entire Bible. But the following passages of the Old Testament are lacking: Genesis 14: 14-17; 15: 1-5, 16-19; 16: 6-9; 1 Kings 12: 20 to 14: 9; Psalms 1: 20 to 80: 11. It contains all four books of the Maccabees, and "the Epistle of Athanasius to Marcellinus on the Psalter;" a summary of the contents of the Psalms by Eusebius stands before the Psalms. At the close of the 150 Psalms stands the apocryphal 151st Psalm, also some canticles or chants from other parts of the Old Testament, such as Deuteronomy 32 and 1 Samuel 2: 1-10.

The third prize manuscript of the Septuagint is the Codex Sinaiticus (marked "S"). Though this document ranks in age with the Vatican manuscript, its fragmentary character would rather give it third place in value. It was discovered in 1844 by Tischendorf in the monastery of St. Catharine, at Mt. Sinai (§115). In a later visit he secured one hundred and fifty-six leaves of the Old Testament and the entire New Testament, all of which ultimately found their home in the Imperial Library at St. Petersburg. The parts of the manuscript intact for scholars are fragments of Genesis 23 and 24, of Numbers 5, 6 and 7; 1 Chronicles 9: 27 to 19: 17; Ezra 9: 9 to 10: 44; Nehemiah, Esther, Tobit, Judith, 1 Maccabees, 4 Maccabees, Isaiah, Jeremiah, Lamentations 1: 1 to 2: 20; Joel, Obadiah, Jonah, Nahum to Malachi, Psalms, Proverbs, Ecclesiastes, Song of Solomon, Wisdom of Solomon, Wisdom of Sirach, and Job.

The fourth important manuscript of the Septuagint is the Codex Ephraemi (marked " C "), written in the fifth century, now in the Bibliotheque Nationale in Paris. This is a palimpsest; that is, the biblical manuscript has been partly erased, and over it is written a treatise in Syriac composed by St. Ephraem, of Syria, somewhere about the twelfth century. It is with great difficulty that some parts of the underlying biblical text can be made out. There are sixty-four leaves containing parts of the Old Testament. These are parts of Job, Proverbs, Ecclesiastes, Wisdom of Solomon, Wisdom of Sirach, and the Song of Solomon.

45. The following are some of the most valuable smaller or fragmentary manuscripts of the Septuagint. The letter or number in parentheses following the name is the catalogue designation of the document: Codex Cottonianus (D) is a charred manuscript of the fifth century, now in the British Museum. It

Fragment of Septuagint written in Greek Uncials on Papyrus, about Third
Century. Found in Egypt in 1892. Now in the British Museum
Papyrus contains Psalms 11 : 7 to 15 : 4

was partially destroyed by a fire in the library of Sir R. Cotton in 1731. It was written in a beautiful uncial character, and furnished with 250 illustrations that carry the evidence of close relation to the mosaics of San Marco in Venice. Had not the text been carefully collated before the fire, its real value would have been greatly diminished.

The Bodleian Genesis (E) at Oxford, was written in the eighth century. It contains in a good state of preservation Genesis 1: 1 to 14: 5; 18: 25 to 20: 13; 24: 55 to 42: 17. Codex Ambrosianus (F) at Milan, written in the fifth century. It carries three columns to the page, and is fully punctuated, accented and supplied with breathings. Its contents are Genesis 31: 15 to Joshua 12: 12, with a few lacunæ here and there; also fragments of Isaiah and Malachi. The Vienna Genesis (L), written in silver letters on purple vellum, belongs to the fifth or sixth century. It contains the whole of Genesis. Codex Basiliano-Vaticanus (N) at Rome and Venice, belongs to the eighth or ninth century. It consists of two volumes, somewhat mutilated, and is written in sloping uncials. Its special importance is due to its having been used with the Codex Vaticanus (B) as the basis of the Roman edition of the Septuagint issued in 1587.

These are a few of the more than thirty uncial manuscripts of the Septuagint now known to be in existence. Of cursives, there are more than 300 (Holmes and Parsons name 313, though it is known that their collators failed properly to describe the writing of some of the texts). Many of these have not been carefully studied in connection with the issuance of Septuagint texts.

46. The first printed copy of the Septuagint was embodied in the Complutensian Polyglot, issued under the supervision of Cardinal Ximenes in 1514-1517. The Aldus edition, based on manuscripts in Venice, appeared in 1518. But the great edition of the Septuagint in those centuries was that published under the patronage of Pope Sixtus in 1587. The Codex Alexandrinus, supplemented by other manuscripts, was published in 1707-1728 by Grabe. The greatest work of all was that issued at Oxford by Holmes and Parsons, 1798-1827. This gives us the Roman edition of 1587, with variant readings of about 325 manuscripts. Tischendorf published a revision of the Roman texts with variants from S, A and C. Swete published a three-volume edition of the Septuagint (1887-1894), according to the best extant manuscript of each part of the Old Testament, with all the variants in three or four of the next best manuscripts. A new Cambridge edition is now being edited by Brooke and McLean that will give a much larger amount of variant material for critical work, collated from the different types of text.

47. What can be the inherent value of such a mass of manuscripts, dating from the third to the sixteenth centuries? They were inscribed in uncial and cursive writing, by various writers, and are preserved with the most scrupulous care. The whole purpose of

scholars is (1) to determine as near as may be, by a study of all the best manuscripts, the text of the Septuagint as it was originally translated from the Hebrew; (2) to determine by the use of that best text of the Septuagint the text of the Hebrew Old Testament from which the Septuagint translation was made; (3) to determine, by a comparison of this text with the Massoretic text, as nearly as may be, the original form of the Hebrew books of the Old Testament. Such determinations, even approximately, clear up many serious difficulties, and aid us greatly in translating the original text into good idiomatic English. Even a glance at the footnotes of the Variorum Teachers' Bible shows how useful the Septuagint variations are in the fixing of the meaning of the original text. The value of the Septuagint expands as one studies it, and indicates that that will be one of the fruitful fields of research in the near future, for finding as near as possible the Hebrew text that was in use in the centuries preceding the Christian era, when from it the Septuagint was translated.

CHAPTER VI

48. The Septuagint was the Old Testament of
the times of Christ and the Apostles. From its pages,
in its language, the New Testament writers usually
quoted. The early Christian church all about the
shores of the Mediterranean Sea adopted generally
that version of the Old Testament. It was by the
use of it that they proved that Jesus was the promised Messiah, that all the law and the prophets were
fulfilled in him. Such general adoption and use of
its form and thought by the leaders of the Christian
church, naturally aroused the antagonism of the Jews,
who could not agree with the new sect. This
estrangement of the Jews from their formerly cherished Old Testament led them to consider very cau-
tiously how they could avoid the adoption of the same
thought and creed that inspired the followers of Jesus
of Nazareth. Often when the Septuagint was quoted
against them the Jews affirmed something wrong in
the translation. Such opposition could not long remain fruitless. The Jews finally repudiated the time-
old translation as the Christians' Old Testament, and
resorted to other means to better their doctrinal rivals
and secure for themselves an authoritative transla-

tion of their own Hebrew Scriptures. In fact, it was not long before there were several rival translations, each bidding for favor as being the most faithful rendering of the Hebrew original.

49. The first scholar to respond to the call for a new translation of the Hebrew into Greek was Aquila. From the scanty information that we can find he was a proselyte to Judaism from Sinope in Pontus, Asia Minor, who flourished, on the authority of Epiphanius, about 128 A. D. He is reported by Jerome to have been a pupil of Rabbi Akiba between 95 and 135 A. D. Such training would have made him a reverer of the very letter of the text, as he, in his subsequent work, proved to be. Aquila's translation of the Hebrew is slavishly literal, trying to translate every word and particle, regardless of literary form, the requirements of the Greek language, or the conveyance of clear thought. He often "follows Hebrew idioms in violation of Greek usage," casts new words to suit his convenience, carries Hebrew words bodily over into Greek spelling, and generally violates principles of grammar and syntax to put the Hebrew into a cold, literal Greek. Such renderings have some value for the study of etymology, lexicography and the text, but are far from being helpful in an exegetical line. Aquila's translation soon came to the front among the anti-Christian Jews, and became their official Greek version of the Old Testament. His translation is known to have been in use by 177 A. D., as Irenæus makes mention of it. Some writers identify

Aquila with Onkelos, the author to whom the principal Targum of the Pentateuch is ascribed. But the
evidence is not such as to convince the most careful
or thoughtful of students of the literature of that
early period of Semitic culture.

50. This rival Jewish translation aroused the Christians of the second century, and a new translator
appeared in the person of Theodotion, who is thought
by every reference to him to have been an Ebionite
Christian of Pontus, or of Ephesus. His translation
is located between 180 and 192 A. D., in the reign
of Commodus. It was based on the Hebrew, and in
style and character, in some parts, closely followed
the Septuagint. In fact, it is called by some scholars
rather a revision of that venerable version than a new
translation. It is clear that its purpose often seems
to have been to make a correction of that work.
Theodotion, in contrast with Aquila, gave a free rendering of the Hebrew, and had due regard to correct
and idiomatic Greek. He is the only one of the three
translators (Aquila, Theodotion and Symmachus)
that paid any attention to the Apocrypha. He inserted the postscript to Job, and the additions to Daniel, viz.: Susanna, Song of the Three Children, and
Bel and the Dragon. His translation soon won its
way in the Christian church for its fidelity to the
Hebrew and its improvement on the translations of
some of the books of the Septuagint. Indeed, this
translation became so much in favor that it exercised
a large influence upon the further revisions of the

Aquila's Version of Greek Bible (§ 49). A Palimpsest with Hebrew written over the Greek. 2 Kings 23 : 15-19

Septuagint. Theodotion's own version of Daniel was so much superior to that of the Septuagint that it soon displaced that version in the Septuagint manuscripts. The old Septuagint original of Daniel was so completely discarded that only a single copy, written in the ninth century, has come down to us. The book of Job in the Septuagint lacked about one-sixth of the matter found in the Hebrew text. These gaps have been filled out from Theodotion's translation.

51. The third great translator of the Hebrew into Greek in this period was Symmachus, who, on the authority of Eusebius and Jerome, was an Ebionite. His activity as a translator fell within the reign of Severus 193-211 A. D. His translation is remarkable for its fidelity to the original Hebrew, for its pure and even elegant Greek, and for its display of literary skill as a piece of good literature. Like Jerome, he had a high conception of a translator's duty. Symmachus' translation is referred to in Jerome in a second edition. Jerome had high regard for Symmachus, and made use of him in his great work. In fact, Jerome characterized these three versions by saying " Aquila translates word for word, Symmachus follows the sense, and Theodotion differs slightly from the Septuagint." Symmachus' influence on our English Bible came by way of Jerome's Vulgate, upon which the translators of the Authorized Version leaned so heavily.

52. The greatest biblical scholar of the early Christian centuries was Origen. He was born at

Alexandria, 186 A. D., and was surnamed Adaman-
tios because of his untiring energy. His early life
and training, his skill as a schoolmaster, and the
broad scope of his scholarship, were famed and lauded
all down the Christian centuries, and are an inspiration
to us of later days. His tremendous energy and skill
in biblical lines of research laid the foundation for
critical biblical study. Indeed, the first half of the
third century marked an epoch in the history of biblical textual study. Origen found in existence and in
use in his day, besides the Old Testament in Hebrew,
the Septuagint and the three Greek versions noted
above. He complained that every manuscript contained a different text from its next. He conceived
the idea of carefully studying by comparison all these
different versions and manuscripts, and of producing
therefrom the best possible manuscript or version. In
order to accomplish this, not only for himself but for
all who should study the Scriptures, he planned a stupendous work, called "The Hexapla," upon which he,
with helpers, occupied twenty-eight years of his life.
It was the arrangement in six parallel columns of (1)
the Hebrew text then current, (2) this same Hebrew
text put into Greek letters, (3) the Greek translation
of Aquila, (4) the Greek translation of Symmachus,
(5) the Septuagint, revised by himself, and (6) the
Greek translation of Theodotion. These versions
were arranged so carefully and adjusted so nicely
that the ordinary Bible student who could read Greek
could make use of this Hexapla.

ORIGEN'S HEXAPLA (SIX-FOLD)

HEBREW.	HEBREW IN GREEK LETTERS.	AQUILA.	SYMMACHUS.	ORIGEN'S SEPTUAGINT.	THEODOTION.
This was practically the Massoretic Hebrew text current to-day.	For those who could not read the Hebrew, that they might get as near as possible to the original, and to its correct pronunciation.	The first anti-Christian version intended to displace the Septuagint among the Jews.	The most artistic literary translation of the Hebrew into Greek.	By the use of other manuscripts and the Hebrew, Origen tried to get the best possible Septuagint version.	The second rival version of the Septuagint, so valuable that its Daniel is found in the Septuagint proper.

For some of the Old Testament books, chiefly the poetical, Origen added a fifth (Quinta), a sixth (Sexta), and even a seventh (Septima) Greek text. This made a seventh, eighth and ninth parallel column. Then there seems to have been extant an edition which consisted of the four Greek versions, the four columns to the right, as seen above, called the Tetrapla, or four-fold version. Such a version would give the reader a comparative view of the work of all previous translators into the Greek, and of Origen's text.

53. The real purpose of Origen's Hexapla was not a restoration of the original text of the Septuagint, but to make it correctly and adequately represent the Hebrew original. The fifth column of the Hexapla is the most important, touching Origen's work, for it was his revision of the Septuagint. He revised

the regular Septuagint text on this wise : If the manuscripts of the Septuagint differed he chose that one
that was the best translation of the Hebrew original.
In case there were words in the Hebrew that had no
adequate representation in the Septuagint, he inserted in the Septuagint text such translation of these
words as was found in one of the other three Greek
versions, preferably from Theodotion. Such insertion
was marked by an asterisk (* or *) at the beginning,
and a metobelus (ⲩ) at the close of the passage. A
passage which was found in the Septuagint, but had
no equivalent in the Hebrew was marked in Origen's
Septuagint by an obelus (—), or a horizontal line,
but it was not expunged.

These are a few of the critical marks introduced
by Origen to specify the sources and variations of
his version of the Septuagint. He did a large service
for the biblical scholarship of his own and succeeding centuries. The magnitude of this Hexapla can
scarcely be conceived until we realize that the whole
Hebrew Bible carried out on that plan would have
filled, according to Professor Nestle's calculation,
more than 6,000 leaves, or 12,000 pages of carefully
copied and critically worked over Hebrew and Greek
manuscripts.

54. Our only descriptions of Origen's Hexapla,
until recently, have been those of Eusebius, the historian, of Epiphanius, and of Jerome, and scattered
specimens in biblical manuscripts. In 1896, however,
Giovanni Mercati discovered in a palimpsest manu-

script of the tenth century, in the Ambrosian library, in Milan, the first continuous fragments of a copy of the Psalter of the Hexapla. It gives us a good idea of the tremendous amount of close critical work necessary to finish one page of that Hexapla. Again, in 1898, there was found in the so-called Genizah collection of palimpsests brought to Cambridge from Cairo, Egypt, a Hexaplar fragment of Psalm 22, dating probably from the eighth century. Though this double leaf, containing 105 lines of Hebrew, is badly worn, enough remains to make it plain that Origen's method was to put one Hebrew word, and at most two in a line, in the first column, and its exact equivalent in the Greek column. This plan was followed in both the Milan and the Cairo palimpsests. The entire Psalter written as were these lines would cover about 450 leaves, and include 19,000 words.

Origen's great Hexapla has survived only in fragments scattered here and there in the works of such ancient writers as Eusebius, or noted in the margins of manuscripts. The original manuscript seems to have been preserved in the library at Cæsarea, and was seen there at the beginning of the seventh century. At this place Jerome consulted it; and here Bishop Paul of Tella in Mesopotamia translated Origen's fifth column, or his Septuagint revision, into Syriac, 617-618 A. D. In his translation he copied with care Origen's critical symbols. A part of Bishop Paul's work, written in the eighth century, is now found in the Ambrosian library at Milan. This contains the

prophets and the most of the Hagiographa. The
Codex Sarravianus (G) at Leyden, containing the
Pentateuch, with portions of Joshua and Judges, is a
manuscript of Origen's fifth column, partially provided
with his critical symbols. It probably dates from the
fifth century—less than 300 years after Origen laid
down his work. Twenty-two leaves of this manuscript are in Paris (Codex Colbertinus), and one in
St. Petersburg. The Codex Coislinianus (M) in
Paris, from the seventh century, covering Genesis to
1 Kings 8: 40, with some breaks, contains a Hexaplar
text. Field carefully collated and published in two
large volumes the various known material of Origen's
Hexapla in 1875.

55. Origen's work did not unify existing Greek
texts of the Old Testament, but rather opened the
door for revisions. Three great scholars arose in
the third century who gave themselves to this work:
(1) Eusebius of Cæsarea (260-340), the first church
historian, assisted by Pamphilus or vice versa, issued
with all its critical marks the fifth column of the Hexapla, with alternative readings from the other columns,
for use in Palestine. The Emperor Constantine gave
orders that fifty copies of this edition should be prepared for use in the churches.

(2) Lucian of Samosata prepared a revision of the
Septuagint that far outstripped that of Eusebius in
original methods. He supplied its omissions from
other Greek versions, and sometimes modified its expressions; where the translation, in his opinion, did

not correctly represent the Hebrew, he added a correct translation of the passage in question. He did not hesitate to add explanatory clauses, and even to substitute synonymous words where it would make the meaning clearer. His revision was adopted throughout Asia Minor from Antioch to Constantinople. Lucian fell a martyr to the persecution of Maximus in 311.

(3) The person and work of Hesychius are quite unknown. He is thought to have been the martyr-bishop mentioned in Eusebius, who fell under the persecution that destroyed Lucian. His revision was adopted as the Septuagint in Alexandria and Egypt, for he was one of the Alexandrian school of learned men.

These three revisers furnished Greek revisions for all the eastern coasts of the Mediterranean Sea. Eusebius for Palestine, Lucian for Asia Minor, and Hesychius for Egypt.

56. The manuscripts that preserve the above revisions of the Septuagint are not numerous. There is in Trinity College, Dublin, a palimpsest, Codex Dublinensis Rescriptus, similar to the Codex Ephræm, consisting of only eight leaves of Isaiah. It was written in Egypt in the sixth century, and is credited with relations with the revision of Hesychius. The finest manuscript relative to this group of revisions is the Codex Marchalianus in the Vatican library at Rome. It was written in Egypt in the sixth century, and contains the books of the prophets. The editor

of this manuscript, Dr. Ceriani, shows that it was originally the text of Hesychius. Its value is greatly enhanced by marginal readings taken from a text of Origen's Hexapla, with initial letters indicating the source of the readings.

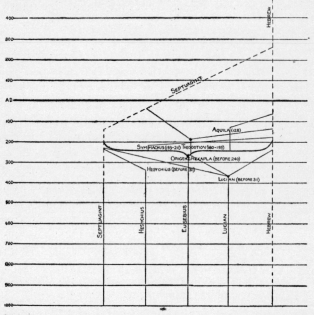

DIAGRAM SHOWING THE RELATION OF THE RIVAL GREEK BIBLES AND REVISIONS TO THE SEPTUAGINT (CHAP. VI)

Notes in the Syro-Hexaplar version of Paul of Tella and a statement of Theodoret led Field and Lagarde to identify the manuscripts of the Lucian text. This Lucian revision is of great value in the

Codex Marchalianus (Q). Sixth Century
Ezekiel 5 : 12-17

criticism of the Hebrew Old Testament; for Lucian used Hebrew manuscripts at Antioch that were different from those employed by Origen. He also differs from the Septuagint, and probably was well acquainted with the Syriac version.

These three revisions of the Septuagint, while not superseding that venerable text, added valuable elements to the matter for textual biblical criticism, for better determining the original text of the Septuagint, and of estimating with a good degree of probability the true readings of some difficult texts in the Hebrew Old Testament.

CHAPTER VII

THE LATIN BIBLES, THE VULGATE

57. The official language of the Roman empire was Latin. But this tongue was not at first, nor even at last, the language generally in use throughout all the provinces of the empire. In all those countries most contiguous to Rome it gradually became the language not simply of officialdom, but of all important public institutions. The Christian church in the first century, and well along into the second, seems to have made Greek its everyday tongue. The books of the New Testament were all first written in Greek, unless Matthew be an exception; and Paul's preaching and writing were done in the same tongue. Even the early bishops of Rome were Greek. One of the oldest manuscripts of the New Testament—the Codex Alexandrinus—contains an epistle of Bishop Clement of Rome, written in Greek to the Corinthians. In fact, the early Christian church was Greek through and through, using the Septuagint as its Old Testament scriptures, and the Greek documents, the Gospels and Epistles, as its New Testament; that is, its Scriptures were all Greek.

58. But the constantly increasing influence of Rome gradually overcame the predominance of the Greek tongue. The Christian church, like all other

institutions, finally adopted Latin as the language of its ritual and services. This soon led to the requirement either of an interpretation into the Latin tongue by the leader of the church services, or of a translation into that tongue.

The current Latin Bible of to-day is the Vulgate, translated by Jerome at the close of the fourth century. But there is abundant evidence in the church fathers, in manuscripts, and in some other sources that there were Old Latin versions current before Jerome's day, as in Germany there were German translations of the Bible before Luther's day. Augustine (353-430 A. D.) says that "those who have translated the Scriptures from Hebrew into Greek can be numbered, but the Latin translators cannot, for every one into whose hands a Greek manuscript came in the first periods of the Christian faith, and who fancied that he had some skill in both languages, ventured to translate." It is now generally conceded that at the latest a Latin translation of the entire Bible was in circulation at Carthage 250 A. D. It is entirely probable that portions of the Bible, particularly the New Testament, for its immediate value to the Christian church, were extant in Latin as early as 200 A. D. Of course, the New Testament was translated immediately from the original Greek, but the Old Testament of the Old Latin versions was translated from the Septuagint—a translation of a translation of the Hebrew Bible.

59. From the fragments of manuscripts and other

remains of the Old Latin versions it is evident that there were different versions current in different parts of Christendom. Then the question might well be asked, Where was the Bible first translated into Latin,—in Rome, North Africa or Syria? For these were all important centers of Christianity. The late Dr. Hort and a company of modern scholars, have independently come to the conclusion that the Old Latin version had its origin in Syria or Asia Minor, probably at Antioch, that powerful literary and religious center in the early Christian centuries. Its faithfulness in some places to the Hebrew text, and its resemblances to Lucian's readings, and the certain knowledge of its translator of the administrative arrangements of Palestine in this period, are some of the many evidences for Dr. Hort's position. This Old Latin version made in Syria was carried to Rome, to the countries of Europe, and to North Africa, in the region of Carthage. Cyprian (about (200-258 A. D.) quotes freely from it, and apparently always from the same text. Tertullian, Cyprian's teacher, likewise quotes Scripture in his writings, but in a manner that strips his quotations of value in seeking the true readings of a text. He apparently paraphrases, quotes from memory, and so uses the matter as to lead one to suspect that he discounted the authoritative value of the text he quoted.

60. The Old Latin material such as manuscripts of which there is not a complete one of the whole Bible, quotations from the fathers, and other frag-

ments, are classified by Dr. Hort under three groups. The first is the "African," whose manuscripts and texts agree with the quotations of Cyprian. The second group is the "European," a text used in Western Europe and North Italy, and differing in many respects from the African. The third group was named "Italian," after a reference in Augustine (de Doct. Christ., vol. ii. 15) to a Latin translation which he called "Itala." This is smoother and more polished than the European, and is often supposed to be a revision of that text.

The three groups are constituted of texts that were translations of the Greek Bible, made at different times between 200 and 400 A. D. Their original was probably the Septuagint in different manuscripts before the preparation of the editions of Origen or the later revisionists already described. There are found to-day in various libraries of Europe about thirty manuscripts, and long authoritative quotations from the Old Latin canonical books of the Old Testament, and several complete texts of the apocryphal books. The manuscripts date as far back as the fifth century, at the very beginning of which Jerome laid down his pen.

We have to-day in complete form the Old Latin texts of Esdras, Wisdom of Solomon, Ecclesiasticus, Baruch, the Maccabees, the Rest of Esther and the Additions to Daniel. All these books, unrevised by Jerome, are retained to-day in their Old Latin form in the Vulgate.

61. The existence of several Latin versions, differing greatly in their texts, occasioned either by careless copying or translating, or both, soon aroused complaints and distrust in the authoritative value of the manuscripts. Jerome, a most accomplished scholar, who was born at Stridon, on the borders of Dalmatia and Pannonia about 340-342, came "to the kingdom for such a time as this." His parents were wealthy and he had the best school advantages of his day. His early training, his four years of travel in the East, his five years (374-379) spent in the desert of Chalcis in self-discipline, and a thorough study of the Hebrew language under a rabbi who had been converted to Christianity, prepared him for one of the great tasks of the ages. In this period, through correspondence and explanation of Scripture terms, he formed a close friendship with Pope Damasus. In 379 he moved to Antioch, where he was ordained presbyter. Later, at Constantinople, he became thoroughly imbued with the expositions of Gregory Nazianzen. In 382 he went to Rome, where he spent more than two years in close association with Pope Damasus.

62. At the request of the Pope, who had displayed large interest in the Scriptures, Jerome undertook a revision of the Old Latin version on the basis of the Greek text. He began by revising the Gospels which appeared in 383. This was followed very soon by the Acts and the rest of the New Testament. He seems to have confined his changes to as few pas-

EXPLICIT PRAEFATIO IN LIBRO IOB

INC LIB IOB

IR ERAT
IN TERRA
HUS
Nomine Iob et erat
uir ille simplex et recta
ac timens dm et recedens
a malo. Natiq; sunt ei septe
filii et tres filiae. Et fuit
possessio eius septe milia ouiu
et tria milia camelorum quinqua
ginta quoq; iugaboum et quingente
asinae ac familia multa nimis. Eratq; uir ille
magnus inter omnes orientales. et ibant filii eius
et faciebant conuiuiu per domos unusquisq; in die
suo. Et mittentes uocabant tres sorores suas ut come
derent & biberent cu eis. Cuq; in urbem transissent
dies conuiuii mittebat ad eos iob et sctificabat illos.
Consurgensq; diluculo offerebat holocausta p singu
los. Dicebat enim. ne forte peccauerint filii mei
et benedixerint deo in cordib; suis. sic faciebat iob
cunctis dieb;

Jerome's Version, Latin. About A.D. 840.
Job 1 : 1-8a

sages as consistent with faithfulness to the original text.

Jerome's first work on the Old Testament was a revision of the Old Latin Psalter, probably of the "Italian" version. He did his work on the basis of the Septuagint and made only such changes as the sense required. This very mild revision (of 384) was called "the Roman Psalter," in distinction from the Old Latin Psalter. By a decree of Pope Damasus, this became the official version of the Psalter in the churches of Rome and Italy until Pius V (1566-1572). It is still the official Psalter in St. Peter's at Rome, and at Milan, and partially in the Roman Missal, and in one place in the Breviary in the Invitatory psalm 94 (95)."

About the end of 384 A. D. Pope Damasus died, and in 385 Jerome left Rome for Palestine. After a prolonged study of its topography and cities, and a tour of Egypt, he, with his associates, settled in Bethlehem. Here in 389 he founded two monasteries over one of which he presided for at least fifteen years. Over the other, founded for nuns, Paula, the devout widow, was governess.

Somewhere during these years, probably about 387 A. D., in answer to requests, Jerome again revised the Psalter. In this work he used, in addition to the Septuagint, the Greek text of Origen's Hexapla, together with some of his critical symbols. This revision became known later as "the Gallican Psalter," for it was first adopted in Gaul. It was finally adopted

and decreed to be the official version of the
Psalter in the Latin Church, where it remains to-day
as the version of the Psalms embodied in the Vulgate.
Jerome also translated or revised other books of the
Old Testament on the basis of the Septuagint, but
only the Psalter and Job of this revision have been
preserved to this day.

63.   More and more Jerome came to see that the
work that he had been doing could be a better representation of the original Hebrew if it were not a
revision, but a new translation.   In his controversies
with Jews, he saw the disadvantage of appealing to
the Septuagint, for they denied that it truly represented the original Hebrew.   Jerome's friends, too,
were urgent that he undertake a new translation of
the Old Testament from the Hebrew.   In answer to
these requests, as he says in his prefaces, he began
little by little to translate the separate books, and to
send copies of them to his friends.   Thus the great
biblical scholar was led gradually and almost casually
into doing by piecemeal what later became his great
life-work.

His first translation (390 A. D.) dealt with the
easier historical narrative Hebrew of the Old Testament, the books of Samuel and Kings.   These books
were prefaced by the " helmeted prologue " (prologus
galeatus), which is practically an introduction to the
whole Old Testament, and one armed to meet his
antagonists on the issue of a new translation.

The next task that he set before himself was a new

translation of the Psalter, he having already twice revised it. The prophets and Job followed in order; then Ezra and Chronicles—all the translations thus far falling within the years 390-396 A. D. For two years he was laid aside by severe illness. He was able to take up his task again in 398 and translate Proverbs, Ecclesiastes and Song of Songs. The Pentateuch followed in order, and (in 404) Joshua, Judges, Ruth and Esther. The death of Paula, head over the convent, occurred in 404 A. D.; soon thereafter appeared the apocryphal parts of Daniel and Esther. Later followed the books of Tobit and Judith, translated from the Aramaic. These completed Jerome's translation of the Old Testament from the Hebrew text. He neither revised nor translated Wisdom of Solomon, Ecclesiasticus, the Maccabees, and Baruch.

64. Jerome's personality as reflected in the prefaces to his translations is extremely interesting. His profound scholarship did not deaden his sensitiveness to criticism and opposition. For fourteen years (390-404) he labored almost incessantly to produce a faithful rendering of the Hebrew, only to meet the sharpest, keenest antagonism of the churchmen all about him. These prefaces are defenses of his positions, and fairly ring with his denunciations of his ignorant, superstitious critics. He wielded a sharp pen, possessed a hot temper, and did not fail to combine them into cutting and caustic retorts and criticisms. He gives us, besides, in these prefaces, an idea of how

he worked, what difficulties he encountered, and how he finally succeeded in a task that gave to the church such a careful translation of the Hebrew text.

65. After the final work of translation was completed, Jerome had to endure a storm of criticism and invective. His own tempestuous replies to his critics only added strength to the irritation. The Septuagint's authority and accuracy being laid aside by Jerome's translation, the friends and devotees of the former version fiercely assailed him. Jerome asserted his reverence for the Septuagint, but at the same time said that his effort was only to render clearly the Hebrew passages that were obscure in the Septuagint and the Old Latin. The conservatives at that day, as in this, clung to the older versions because long use and familiarity had cast a halo of sanctity about them. But the wisest of the churchmen soon began to recognize the superiority of Jerome's work. As soon as the leaders expressed a preference for the best translation, the rank and file of the church fell into line. St. Augustine, who had expressed fear of the consequences of such work, now wisely set to praising it. But poor old Jerome saw only contention and strife to the end of his life (in 420) at Bethlehem. He had no satisfaction of seeing his all-important service to the cause of biblical learning publicly recognized for anything like its true worth. But its superior merit was enough to grant it a fair hearing, and win for it the place that it was destined soon to hold in the progress of Christianity.

66. Jerome died almost broken-hearted because of the denunciations of his fellow churchmen for his new translation of the Bible. But that century, the fifth, did not pass by without public recognition on the part of church leaders of his real service to biblical learning. Pope Gregory's commentary on Job (about 580 A. D.) recognized Jerome's translation as on a par with the Old Latin. In the next two centuries the church fathers quoted both the Old Latin and Jerome's versions, the latter gradually gaining favor over the former. The use of the two versions side by side led to the correction of one by the other, and finally to the mixing of the texts. In the sixth century, even, this corruption had gone so far that Cassiodorus took steps to correct the current versions by the old and best manuscripts. The work of Alcuin, under commission from Charlemagne and of Theodulf of Orleans, will be noted in §132.

Further consideration of the Vulgate's history will be found under Chapter XV. A few words concerning the earliest Old Latin and Vulgate manuscripts will conclude our present discussion of this theme.

67. There are thousands of Old Latin and Vulgate manuscripts in the public and private libraries of Europe. Professor Samuel Berger, of Paris, examined more than 800 in the libraries of Paris alone. It is thought that the total number will not be less than 8,000. The most of them are late thirteenth or fourteenth century documents that possess slight value.

Mention can be made here of only a few of the oldest and most valuable of these documents of the Old Testament: (1) One of the oldest of the Spanish texts is the "Ashburnham Pentateuch," now in the National Library at Paris (Nouv. acq. Lat. 2334), a beautiful Vulgate document with pictorial illustrations, from the seventh or eight century. (2) Codex Complutensis, in the library of the University of Madrid, Spain, belonging to the ninth or tenth century, an entire Vulgate Bible text, but Ruth, Esther, Tobit, Judith, and 1 and 2 Maccabees are from an Old Latin version. (3) Codex Amiatinus of the whole Bible at Florence, dating from the beginning of the eighth century. It was copied in England, either at Wearmouth or Jarrow, and carried by Abbot Ceolfrid in 715 A. D. as a present to the Pope. The large list of known manuscripts, by far the greater number being of the Gospels, is arranged in ten classes: (1) Early Italian texts; (2) early Spanish texts; (3) Italian texts transcribed in Britain; (4) Continental manuscripts written by Irish or Saxon scribes, showing a mixture of two types of text; (5) texts current in Languedoc; (6) other French texts; (7) Swiss manuscripts; (8) Alcuinian Revision; (9) Theodulfian Revision; and (10) medieval texts.

A discussion of the New Testament texts of the Old Latin and Vulgate, their confusion during the middle ages, and some attempts to reconstruct a pure text, and the Vulgate since the Council of Trent will be found in Chapter XV.

quos erus esi masculini auce
simoahnoeisupraprocedentii
adbellum quinquaginta nouem
liatrecenti deplus gad perge
nerationeseifamilias acdomos
cognationum suarum recensi
tisuntpernominasingulorum
auigintiannisetsupraomnes
quiadbellaprocederent xlum
hadd deplisiuda pergenera
tionessuas eifamilias acdomos
cognationumsuarumpernomi
nasingulorum auicesimoahno
eisupra omnesquipoterantad
bellaprocedererecensunt
lxxun miliasescenti deplisisachar
pergenerationessuas eifami
as acdomoscognationumsua
rum pernominasingulorum
auicesimo ahnoeisupraomnes
quipoterantadbellaprocedere
recensiisunt lun milia qua
dringenti deplis zulon per
generationeseifamilias acdo
moscognationumsuaruarie
censiisuntpernominasingulo
rumauicesimoahnoeisupra
omnesquipoterant adbellapro

cedere lun milia quadringerxi
deplisioseph filiorumephrai
pergenerationes acfami
lias eidomoscognationum
suorum recensiisunper
homina singulorumauice
simoahno eisupraomnes
quipoterant adbellaproce
dere xl milia quingenti
porrofiliorum manas sepen
generationes eifamilias
acdomosetcognationumsu
nuumrecensiisuntperno
minasingulorumauicesimo
ahnoeisupraomnesquipo
terantadbellaprocedere
xxii miliaducenti deplus
beniamin pergeneratio
neseifamilias acdomoscog
nationumsuarum recensii
suntpernominasingulorum
auicesimoahno eisupra
omnesquipoterantadbel
laprocedere xxv milia qua
dringenti deplisdan per
generationeseifamiliasac
domoscognationumsuaru
recensiisuntnominatibus
singuloro

Vulgate Manuscript formerly in Earl of Ashburnham's Library.
Seventh Century.   Numbers 1 : 22b-38a

CHAPTER VIII

THE SYRIAC BIBLES

68. The Syrians were the population of Syria, the country northeast of Palestine, and northwestern Mesopotamia. Their language was the Syriac, a Semitic tongue very closely allied with the Hebrew of the Old Testament. So far as known, there was no call for the Old Testament in the tongue of these peoples until after the introduction into their country of Christianity. The establishment of Christian churches within the bounds of Syria very soon must have been followed by a demand on the part of the communities in which these churches were located, for the sacred books of Christianity in their own tongue. The fact that the Old Testament original was written in Hebrew would greatly facilitate its translation into Syriac, a sister Semitic tongue. Similar idioms could thus be readily translated, even by one who was not well versed in other languages.

69. The existence to-day of one complete Syriac Bible, and of several versions of the Syriac New Testament, leads us to inquire as to their origin. The Syriac Old Testament will claim our attention here, while the New Testament versions will be reserved for Chapter XVII. The one complete Syriac Old Testament had an obscure beginning. Some scholars

of prominence claim that it had a Jewish origin, because of its faithfulness to the Hebrew, and the embodiment in the text of thoughts characteristically Jewish. On the other hand, it is thought that it must have had a Christian origin because of its faithful rendering of Messianic passages, that better agree with Christian than with Jewish ideas. In Leviticus 11 and Deuteronomy 14, there is a carelessness in translation, or ignorance of the details of ritualistic observance, that would oppose any thought of a Jewish origin. The absence of the apocryphal books from the earliest copies bespeak Jewish origin. The absence of Chronicles points to a current discussion of the canonical status of that book. The two groups of reasons given above regarding translators could be admirably harmonized on the supposition that it was the work of Jews who had been converted to Christianity. It is well known that this country was a favorite land for the abode of many Jews in the first Christian centuries, and that they, as at all times, were energetic promoters of learning.

70. If the Syriac Old Testament is of Christian origin, we must look for it at about 150 A. D. In the fourth century it was not simply extant, but was the basis of an elaborate commentary by Ephræm Syrus (who died in 373). He mentions the Syriac Old Testament as widely circulated in the churches of Syria in his time. It had been translated at so distant a day that some of the words had already become obscure to him, and required extensive com-

ments. Aphraates, a churchman at Mosul, about the
middle of the fourth century, quotes passages out of
all the canonical books of the Syriac Old Testament,
with the exception of Song of Songs; though he gives
none from the Apocrypha. Then still farther back,
just after the middle of the second century, Melito of
Sardis cites "the Syrian" in discussing the sacred
books. It is not certain, however, that he refers to
the Syriac Bible. Jacob of Edessa and Ephræm
affirm, however, that the early Syriac Bible was the
result of the labors of several translators. After some
centuries a part of the Syrians threw aside their old
Syriac Bible, translated from the Hebrew, for one
of the several translated from the beloved old Septuagint. Jacob of Edessa (about 704 A. D.) attempted to harmonize the old Syriac, or Peshitta
(the "simple," "literal"), and the Septuagint versions. Another translation was that made by Polycarp (in 508) at the instance of Bishop Philoxenus.
Of more importance was the Syriac translation from
the Hexaplar text of Eusebius and Pamphilus. This
was executed by Bishop Paul of Tella in Mesopotamia, at Alexandria, 617-618 A. D. It contains not
simply the critical symbols of Origen, but fragments
of other Greek translations as marginal notes. Other
comparatively unimportant Syriac editions and revisions were doubtless current during succeeding centuries, as seen among the various religious sects and
orders of Syria.

71. The contents of the Syriac Old Testament

cover about the same ground as the Hebrew or Massoretic text. Its number of books is twenty-two, and the arrangement of these books varies considerably in different manuscripts. The version current among the Nestorians lacked Chronicles, as did that among the Jacobites at Edessa. This book is found, however, in the manuscripts of the sixth century, though with a division in most of them at 2 Chronicles 6: 1. Esther is not found in the Nestorian version, nor is Ezra-Nehemiah in that of the Jacobites. In the latter version Esther, Judith, Ruth and Susanna form " the Book of the Women."

The arrangement of the books has several points in common with the Septuagint. Indeed, the resemblance is often so much nearer that of the Septuagint than of the Hebrew that one is led to suspect that the Septuagint was either freely used in making up the original order, or the Syriac at a later time was made to conform to that order. There is very slight probability that such revision was made after the time of Aphraates, the middle of the fourth century. In addition to the regular books of the Septuagint and Hebrew, complete Syriac manuscripts, like Codex Ambrosianus, contain the Apocalypse of Baruch, 4 Esdras and 4 and 5 Maccabees.

72. The extant manuscripts of this version are not numerous. One of the finest collections is found in the British Museum, secured mainly in 1842 from the monastery of St. Mary Deipara, which is situated in the Nitrian desert in Egypt. In this collection is

found one manuscript which bears the oldest date of any known manuscript of the Bible. This date is 464. It carries in it Genesis, Exodus, Numbers and Deuteronomy. This very text has been copiously copied by Ephræm and Aphraates in the fourth century. Another notable manuscript is the Codex Ambrosianus at Milan, out of the sixth or seventh century. The preface to the Psalter in this manuscript says the Psalms were translated from the Palestinian language into Hebrew, from Hebrew into Greek, from Greek into Syriac. In Codex Rich (No. 7154 Brit. Mus.) this claim covers the whole Syriac Old Testament, while it states that the (Syriac) Psalter was translated from the Palestinian language into Hebrew, according to the translation of Symmachus, the Samaritan. One of the notable things in the Syriac Psalter is the freedom with which the superscriptions are omitted or changed—due, it is thought, to the influence of Theodore of Mopsuestia, a very original and aggressive biblical scholar of Asia Minor in the early Christian centuries. Besides the biblical, there are extant some valuable apocryphal and pseudepigraphical manuscripts in the Syrian tongue.

73. The critical value of the Peshitta is not small, nor is it equal in every book, since they were manifestly the work of different translators. It does not reach the high standard of excellence of the Septuagint in its best parts, nor does it fall to the depths of some of the poorest parts of that version. Its readings almost always give good sense, which, if not

found in the original, have been touched up from tradition or some other source. The natural interchange between Hebrew and Aramaic idioms has likewise minimized its critical value. The freedom used by translators in the changing of suffixes and paradigm forms rather violates a modern critic's ideas of exactness. The dependence of the Peshitta on the Septuagint is often a difficulty in textual study. If both of them are against the Hebrew, it may be that the Syriac is merely a transcript of the Septuagint, hence greatly lowering the weight of authority against that original text.

The Syriac Pentateuch, like that of the Septuagint, is a fair translation of the Hebrew text. Certain books, as Genesis, Isaiah, the Minor Prophets, and the Psalter bear marks of the influence of the Septuagint. Ruth is a paraphrase, Job quite literal, while Chronicles is very like a Targum. Almost all the separate books of the Old Testament have been carefully studied, and their critical value estimated in monographs published by various Syriac scholars of modern times.

74. There are no wholly reliable printed editions of the Syriac Old Testament. The two chief editions or recensions are the Nestorian and the West-Syrian, represented respectively by the Urmia Bible of the American missionaries of 1852, and the text of the Paris Polyglot edited by Gabriel Sionita. This last recension, after the collation of additional manuscripts, appeared in the London Polyglot, and later,

Syriac Peshitta Text
Deut. 19 : 2-5

with few corrections, in Lee's text, issued by the British Bible Society in 1823. The Urmia edition is in reality a reproduction of Lee in Nestorian characters, with Nestorian vowels and better spellings. The three-volume Syriac Bible published (1887-92) by the Dominicans of Mosul is the latest edition of that work. Lagarde issued (in 1861) a Syriac text of the Apocrypha. Here is a large field for a few devoted scholars to investigate and issue a reliable text of the Syriac Old Testament. There is an announcement from Berlin (1905) that a new Syriac text of the Bible is now in the course of preparation by Beer and Brockelmann.

CHAPTER IX

THE TARGUMS—JEWISH PARAPHRASES

75. The peoples of Syria in pre-Christian times spoke a language closely related to the Hebrew. It has been named Aramaic, since its users were called Aramæans in the Old Testament. When a part of the children of Israel returned from the Babylonian exile they came into a land where Aramaic had made headway as the language of the people. This is seen in the fact that some portions of the Old Testament, written after the exile, are in the Aramaic tongue (see §16). It seems that either the Hebrew had degenerated, or that the Aramaic language had largely become the language of the common people. An evidence of this fact is seen in the public reading of the law by Ezra, in Nehemiah 8: 1-8, where it was necessary that interpreters follow him, and so put the words that he read into the language of the people as to make its meaning clear to them. This requirement for a people who were fast forgetting their Hebrew soon grew into the necessity for a regular "paraphrase," that is "Targum" of the books of the Jewish scriptures.

76. It is not known how early these paraphrases were written down. There are traditions that push them back into pre-Christian times. They are

thought to be the resultant accumulation of long years of oral interpretations that began in Ezra's day. Their present form was given them at some later date. It is noticeable that some of the quotations in the New Testament (Matt. 27: 46, with Psa. 22: 1) accord with the readings of the Targums, particularly among the spoken words of Jesus. These indicate that Aramaic was a common language among the peoples of Palestine in the first century, and also that it was freely used in connection with the Scriptures. Rules were given that one verse was to be read in the Hebrew, and then its Aramaic translation was to follow. This required rule seems soon to have produced a written Targum that was used on every public reading of the Scriptures. These Targums were first extemporaneous translations, then fixed written interpretations, for use in the synagogues and all public services where the Hebrew original was in use.

77. The first mention of a written Targum is found in a report (Bab. Shab. 115: 1) that a Targum of Job was confiscated in the first century A. D. Authorities, however, would not recognize the use of them as Scriptures, because they were not a translation, but a paraphrase of their sacred books. It is thought that Job could not have been the first of all the important Old Testament books to appear in this form, and hence that there must have been paraphrases of other books long before the first century. But all extant Targums are much later, perhaps none

dating back of the fifth or fourth century A. D.   It
is certain, however, that the Targums we possess are
based on material that stretches far back into the
centuries.   But the laboratory apparatus of the higher
critic cannot analyze it and point out the different
strata.   The Jewish schools of Babylonia and Jerusalem, while pursuing similar lines, have left us works
of two types, occasionally referred to below.

There are extant seven Targums or paraphrases of
the Old Testament.   These are as follows: (1) Three
on the Pentateuch; (2) one on the Prophets; and
(3) three on the Hagiographa.

78.   The Targums on the Pentateuch deserve the
most attention.   (1) The best known and the official
Targum is that attributed to Onkelos.   According to
the Babylonian Talmud he was a proselyte of the
first century.   But it seems that the names Onkelos
and Aquila (comp. §49) have been confused, so that it
is quite generally conceded that the author of this
famous paraphrase is unknown.   It is attributed in its
present form to later than the second century,
based, however, on earlier material.   It is also called
the Babylonian Targum on the Pentateuch.   Often it
is a beautifully literal and simple translation, rather
than a paraphrase of the Hebrew.   When the meaning is obscure some explanatory word or clause is
inserted, literal terms supplant figurative expressions
in the Hebrew, and the commonly accepted interpretation of disputed passages finds place in the volume.

(2)   A fragmentary Targum of certain parts of

From Erfurt Manuscript of the Hebrew Bible (Joshua 1: 2-5), showing Targum in alternate verses; formerly property of Johann Reuchlin

the Pentateuch, embracing about 850 verses, and known as Jerusalem Targum II. This Targum is thought to be due to the selection of certain passages designed to interpolate or fill out the so-called Targum of Onkelos. Its language is the Aramaic of Palestine, and its form quite paraphrastic. It is inferior to Onkelos.

(3) The Jerusalem Targum I, or Targum of Jonathan (pseudo-Jonathan). This complete Targum (only about a dozen verses lacking) on the Pentateuch seems to owe its origin to a kind of compilation of the above Nos. (1) and (2). The text is handled freely, and the Targum is replete with popular stories and marginal notes that have grown up around the text during the centuries. Figurative terms are displaced by literal, and all anthropomorphisms are thrown out. The religious and dogmatic conceptions of Judaism are prominent throughout this Targum. Targum No. (1) was first printed without vowels at Bologna in 1482 A. D., and with vowels in 1491. The first edition of No. (2) was printed in Venice in 1517, and the first of No. (3) appeared in Venice in 1591.

79. The one great Targum on the Prophets is attributed to Jonathan Bar Uzziel, a pupil of Hillel in the first half of the first century B. C. It is conjectured, but wrongfully, to be the work of Rabbi Joseph bar Hiyya. It is thought to have received its final form in Babylon in the fifth century. The similarity of the Targum of Jonathan to that of the so-called

Onkelos of the Pentateuch is striking. It agrees with the latter's method of avoiding figures, anthropomorphisms, and of toning down difficulties by the insertion of words and brief expressions. It gives a more literal rendering of the historical books than of the prophetic. Some of the difficult poetic passages are merely paraphrased. Occasionally a passage, like that of Hosea 1 : 3f., is turned wholly from the meaning of the original, and is devoted to a moralizing upon Israel's career. Thus Isaiah 5 : 1f. is not translated at all, but interpreted. Geographical names are often transferred into the later place-names. This Targum on the Prophets is about midway in faithfulness to the original, between the so-called Onkelos and Jerusalem Targum I on the Pentateuch. This Targum was first printed at Leiria, Portugal, in 1494 A. D., with the Hebrew text and a rabbinical commentary.

80. The Targums on the Hagiographa are all comparatively late in origin. They seem to have arisen almost after the need for such paraphrases had passed by. The earliest authentic mention of them is found in the eleventh century. The Hagiographa are divided into three groups: (1) Psalms, Proverbs and Job; Psalms and Job are very like in their translation; Job, however, has a double rendering of about fifty verses, and a few have a third explanation or translation. These additional renderings were added by some interpolator in the eighth or ninth centuries, for his language is late and artificial, and distinctly

marks his work as explanatory. Proverbs stands alone among the Targums. It is a strange mixture of Aramaic and Syriac. It is thought to have been made, not entirely from the Hebrew, but in large part from the Syriac version, for about one-third of it is almost identical with the Syriac version.

(2) The Targums on the Megilloth ("Rolls," that is, Song of Songs, Ruth, Lamentations, Ecclesiastes and Esther) are paraphrases rather than translations of the Hebrew. They abound in citations of historical parallels, reasons are given for the occurrence of certain events, words are philologically explained, etc. Ecclesiastes, Esther, and Song of Songs almost touch the limits in paraphrastic freedom. More than half of the so-called Targum of Esther contains legends about Solomon, the Queen of Sheba, etc. All these Targums were probably the work of different men.

(3) There were no known Targums of Chronicles until after the issuance of the Polyglot Bibles. Two very imperfect texts have been discovered and edited. Of Daniel, Ezra, and Nehemiah, no known Targums exist.

81. The Targums of the entire Old Testament preserve for us the earliest paraphrases and expositions of that part of Holy Writ. They give us the Jewish rendering of that text into Aramaic, presumably at a time when its meaning was comparatively well-known. Where their renderings pass beyond paraphrase into comment we are to remember that

the comments were by Jews who were sympathetic in language and thought with the Hebrew language, however fanciful now and then their interpretations may have been. These considerations give value to the Targums on the interpretative side, particularly of Jewish thought and life, of the Old Testament. Now on the text-critical side the value of these documents is not great. But there is a value which even the editors of the Variorum Teachers' Bible recognized, as will be seen by consulting the " variant readings " at the bottom of their pages. However, we are still in need of critical editions of these old texts before scholars can be sure of the accuracy of the text which is at their disposal.

CHAPTER X

82. Christianity was not limited in its adherents to the peoples who bordered on the Mediterranean sea-coast. Many important races and tongues whose boundaries lay next the coast-peoples embraced the teachings of the Bible of Christians. Such adherency soon called for the Bible of the new truth, translated into the various native tongues of the believers. Local scholars soon arose to perform this important task, so that each people or race sooner or later possessed a copy of the Bible translated into its own tongue. These translations were usually made from the version of scriptures which had been introduced to each individual province or race. Their value to the people for whom they had been translated was, of course, very great; but to us, of later times, it is only of comparative importance. For we must estimate it on the answer to several questions, such as: Who was the translator? How well equipped was he for that great work? From what version of the Bible did he translate? How faithfully has he translated the text before him? Did he use more than one version as the basis of his translation? Did he use any undue liberty with the text before him? We can scarcely expect an answer to all these questions, but enough can usually be

found to help us estimate, at least approximately, the value that we are to attach to these versions relative to the English Bible of to-day.

83. The Coptic Version: As soon as Egypt as a whole began to yield to the power of Christianity the country was filled with hermits and ecclésiastical officials. Early in the fourth century Pachomius, the founder of monastic life, was converted, and established a monastery (322 A. D.) in Upper Egypt. The necessities of this monastic community called for a version of the scriptures in their native tongue, the Coptic. Scholars find five or six Coptic dialects in the remnants of ancient literatures. Scripture versions of Coptic are classified as follows: Sahidic, Fayyumic and Bohairic.

The most important of these versions is the Sahidic, because of its greater age. It certainly reaches back to the sixth century, if not earlier, and had its origin in Upper Egypt. Its version of the book of Job is of especial interest, for it omits between three and four hundred lines or half verses that are supplied in Origen's Hexapla. Hence it is thought that the Sahidic version represents a pre-Origenistic text of the Septuagint, like the Old Latin. On the other hand, it is thought to be nearer the truth to regard the Sahidic Job as a translation of Origen's revised text of the Septuagint, with the omission of the second half of the verses under Origen's asterisk. There are several codices of Job, and some manuscripts that have value as aids in determining the Septuagint text.

The Bohairic version of the Old Testament probably dates from the sixth century. It is thought to have been of Alexandrian origin, for that language at a later time was the ecclesiastical language of Alexandria. The larger part of its text, viz., the Pentateuch, the Psalms, Proverbs and the Prophets, have been critically edited. This particular version is now used by the Coptic or Egyptian Christians, and is sometimes, though inaccurately, called the " Memphitic " version. The use of this version practically ceased in Lower Egypt after the Arab invasion. In fact, the Bohairic language yielded to the invaders, while the Sahidic was in use in Upper Egypt for several centuries later.

The Fayyumic version pertains almost exclusively to the New Testament.

84. The Ethiopic Version: The existence of Christianity in Abyssinia likewise produced a version of the Bible in the native tongue, the Ge'ez, or Ethiopic. Christianity in this country is thought to go back to the fourth century. But the current Ethiopic version cannot be traced back of the sixth or fifth. The translation was made from the Septuagint. The large collection of Ethiopic manuscripts in the British Museum was acquired at the time of the Abyssinian war in 1867. But these represent a late revision, made apparently from some Arabic or Coptic version, and even from the Hebrew, in the middle ages or later. We have the Bible of the Septuagint entire except Maccabees in this version. In addition

there are the Book of Enoch, Jubilees, 4 Esdras, Rest
of the Words of Baruch, etc.   There was no distinction between canonical and non-canonical books of
the Old Testament.   The number of Old Testament
books is usually 46, though there is some variation in
the figures.   Genesis-Kings, called the Octateuch,
was edited by Dillmann (1853) ; Psalms by Ludolf
(1701) ; Song of Songs by Nisselius (1656) ; Lamentations by Bachmann (1893).   The Ethiopic version
is usually a faithful translation of the Greek, but its
critical value must await the discussion of other and
more pressing versional questions.

   85. The Gothic Version : The Goths of Dacia in
Europe invaded Cappadocia in the third century.
Among the captives carried away were some Christians.   Ulfilas was born in Dacia, of captive Christian
parents, about 310 A. D.   His sturdy, aggressive
Christian character pushed him to the front, so that
about 340 he was consecrated bishop either at Constantinople or Antioch.   After maintaining his bish-
opric in Dacia for seven years he was driven to
Mœsia, the modern Servia and Bulgaria.   In this
country Ulfilas translated the Bible into the language
of the Goths, the captors of his parents.   He is supposed to have invented an alphabet before he could
undertake the immense task of translating the Bible
into the Gothic tongue.   His work was certainly done
about the middle of the fourth century, for he died
by 383.

   A contemporary, Philostorgius, states that Ulfilas

ወቶለ፡ብሲዉ፡እልባ
ሲሆዉ፡ወቶ፡ቀንጾዉ፡
ቅናታቲሆዉ፡ወትወ
ዴ፡ዴቤሆዉ፡ወዕፈ፡ር
11. ጾዉ፡ወይእውናሆዉ
ጨዉዎዕተ፡ሲቲ፡ለዳስ
ዉ፡ወትፈጾም፡እየዊሙ፡
ለእርን፡ወእየው፡ውሱዴ
10. ወቶቀርብ፡ሳህዉ፡ንበ
ኛንተ፡ይብይሪ፡ዘመር
ጡር፡ወያነብሪ፡እርን፡
ወይቂቁ፡እደዊሙ፡ዴ
ኩ፡ርእሱ፡በሀዉ፡በቅደ
ም፡እግዚእ፡ብሐር፡በ
ንቡ፡ኛንተ፡ይብተሪ፡
12. ዘመርጡር፡ወተሐርይ፡
ለህም፡በቅደዉ፡እግዚ
እ፡ብሐር፡በንበ፡ኛንተ፡
ይብተሪ፡ዘመርጡር፡ወ
13. ንሃእ፡እምውስተ፡ይወ
ለህዉ፡ወትወዴ፡ውክ
ተ፡ኣቀርንተ፡ቤተ፡ወ
ቅደኩ፡በእጀባዕት፡ከ
ወዘተርፈ፡ኩሉ፡ይም፡
ክዐው፡ጠቃ፡ቤቱ፡መቅ
14. ደኩ፡ወትንሡእ፡ኩሉስ
ብሐ፡ኣርው፡ወኣብዴ፡
ወክልኤ፡ኩለያ፡ቶ፡ወቶ
ንብ፡ር፡ውክተ፡ያሡዎ
ዕ፡ወሡጋ፡ለህዉ፡ወዉ
እሱ፡ወፅፉይ፡ታውዒ፡
እውዚ፡እክ፡እፉ፡እ፡እያ
ደብተ፡ሪ፡እከዉ፡ለንጢ
ራእት፡ውእተ፡ወትንሡእ፡
እሐዴ፡በግዐ፡ወያነብሪ፡
እርን፡ወይቂቁ፡እደዊሆ
ዉ፡ሳዕሰ፡ርእ፡ሰ፡በግዐ፡
16. ወተሐርዴ፡ለውእተ፡

በግዐ፡ወትኑሡእደዉ፡
ወትክዐ፡ውስተ፡ቤ፡ተ
17. መቅደ፡ከ፡ውስተ፡ክሩሉ
እውዴ፡ትነሡንሡ፡ወት
ጨብኛ፡በበ፡መሌቢ፡ቂ
ወተኃፅብ፡ንዋየ፡ወእ
ጡ፡ወእገሪሁ፡ወቶነብ
ር፡ርእሱ፡ውክተ፡ዘሌ
18. ቤ፡ከ፡ወቶዐርግ፡ኩሉ፡
በግዐ፡ውክተ፡መሡዎ
ዕተ፡ቆርበን፡ለእግዚ
እ፡ብሐር፡
19. ወንሃእ፡በግዐ፡ካልእ፡
ወያነብ፡ሪ፡እርን፡ወይቂ
ቁ፡እደዊሆዉ፡ሳዕሰ፡ር
20. እሱ፡ወሐርደ፡ወንሡኣ፡
እምደዉ፡ወኣንብር፡ው
ክተ፡ክተማ፡እዝኑ፡ለ
እርን፡እንተ፡የማን፡ወ
ውክተ፡ክተማ፡ኣጻባ
ተ፡እዴሁ፡ዘየማን፡ወዉ
ክተ፡ክተማ፡እጻበዕተ፡
እግሪ፡ዘየማን፡ወውክ
ተ፡ክተማ፡እዝኒ፡ወምስ
ለ፡ዴ፡ቂቀ፡እር፡ን፡ዘየማን፡
ወውክተ፡ክተማ፡እጻባ
ዕተ፡እደዊሙ፡ዘየማ
ን፡ወውክተ፡ክተማ፡እጻ
ባዕተ፡እገሪሆዉ፡ዘየ
21. ማን፡ወንሃእ፡እምው
ክተ፡ይም፡ዘመሡዎዕ
ት፡ወእምውክተ፡ቅብ
እ፡ቡሩከ፡ወትነሡ፡ሡ
ሳዕለ፡ኣርን፡ወሳዕለ፡
እልባሲሁ፡ወእንደነ
ሬሁ፡ሳዕለ፡ደቂ፡ወሳዕ
ለ፡እልባሲሆዉ፡ይት
ቀደኩ፡ውእቱ፡ወዳራ

translated "all the books of the Scripture with the
exception of the books of the Kings, which he omitted
because they are a mere narrative of military ex-
ploits, and the Gothic tribes were especially fond of
war." Only fragments of the Old Testament remain
among the about a dozen known manuscripts of the
Gothic Version. These fragments include parts of
Genesis 5, Psalm 52 and Nehemiah 5-7, and are
largely lists of names or numbers.

A study of the version shows that it is most closely
related to the Lucian text (comp. §55) of the Greek.
This would seem to be natural as that version of the
Greek was current in Asia Minor during the century
of Ulfilas' activity.

86. The Georgian Version: This, like the fore-
going version, arose in the fifth or sixth century on
the outskirts of Christianity. Armenian tradition
ascribes it to the work of Mesrop, who is said to have
invented the Georgian alphabet. There is in the monastery at Mount Sinai, a papyrus Psalter of the seventh or eighth century, and a copy of the Gospels and
a Psalter dated in the ninth century. A manuscript
of the whole Bible, with some omissions in the Pentateuch, is now preserved in two volumes in the
Iberian monastery on Mount Athos. A manuscript
of the Prophets at Jerusalem is ascribed to the eleventh century. The best printed edition seems to have
been that issued at Moscow in 1743. This copy of
the version has been supplied in certain gaps by the
use of passages translated from the Slavonic Bible.

Comparison of the different manuscripts shows that there have been frequent revisions and additions. This version, like the preceding, was doubtless made from the Greek, with some hints at the Syriac, though there is not as yet any critical edition which may be used as an aid in determining the original Greek text.

87. The Slavonic Version was the Bible of one of the great races contiguous to the centers of Christianity in the early centuries. Its origin is not traced back of the ninth century. The work is attributed to two brothers, Cyril and Methodius, sons of a Greek nobleman, whose relations to Slavonic neighbors gave them a knowledge of that tongue. Their first efforts are thought to have been bent towards translating such parts of the Bible into the tongue of the Bulgarian Slavs as would be of most use in church services. Later, the whole Bible was rendered into the tongue of these peoples. Some Slavic scholars maintain that the original tongue into which the Bible was translated was closely similar to the old Bulgarian.

Some of the manuscripts of this version date from the tenth or eleventh century. But the oldest manuscript of the whole Bible is very late, 1499, and is now at Moscow, known as the Codex Gennadius. Of the Old Testament manuscripts, the oldest are of the Psalter, reaching back to the eleventh or twelfth century. Special studies of several Old Testament books have been published in recent years. Greater facilities for travel and study in Slavic countries may

lead to the discovery of many more manuscripts of
this peculiar work.

The value of this version differs in different books

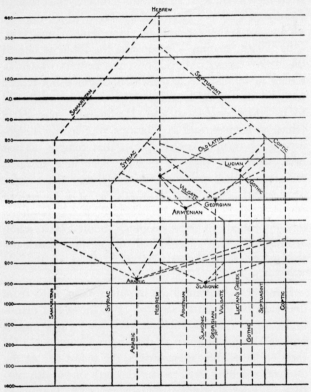

DIAGRAM SHOWING SOURCES IN GENERAL OF THE MINOR EASTERN VERSIONS (CHAP X)

of the Old Testament. The Pentateuch (the Law),
the " Prophets " of the Jewish canonical division, the

Psalter, Job, Ecclesiastes, Wisdom of Sirach, and Song of Songs were translated by different persons from the Greek. The Book of Esther was translated from Hebrew; Chronicles, Ezra, Nehemiah, and such other books as are found in the Latin Bible, were translated from the Vulgate, just before the date of the Gennadius Codex of 1499. This version, when critically edited, will be useful in ascertaining the readings of the Greek of the original text of such as were translated from the Greek, and of the Vulgate where that was the basis of a translation, and of the Hebrew of the Book of Esther.

88. The Armenian Version served the purpose of supplying with the Bible the Christian communities of Asia Minor. An Armenian church is mentioned in the third century. The Armenians seem to have been evangelized by Syrian Christians. Their Bible was a translation at the close of the fourth and beginning of the fifth century, as maintained by F. C. Conybeare, from the Septuagint. But its revision and correction seem to have been made by the use of the Syriac and Hebrew texts. It is noticeable that the chapters and verses of Jeremiah are arranged, not as in the Septuagint, but as in the Syriac and Hebrew. Where the Syriac and Hebrew differ, it usually follows the Hebrew. Such composite character of the Armenian Version is thought to be due to the use of Origen's Hexaplar text, whose symbols now and then seem to find place, in the addition from other versions, in Armenian manuscripts.

Conybeare says that the Armenian version is one of the most beautiful and accurate of all the versions. Its language is so closely allied, in grammar, syntax and idioms, to the Greek that its renderings very faithfully transmit the meaning of the original text.

The Armenian version contains the books of the Septuagint in the same order up to 1 and 2 Esdras (where the latter is Ezra in the Greek); Nehemiah (called 3 Esdras in the margin), Esther, Judith, Tobit, 1, 2 and 3 Maccabees, Psalms, Proverbs, Ecclesiastes, Song of Songs, Wisdom of Solomon, Job, Isaiah, the twelve Prophets, Jeremiah, Baruch, Lamentations, Death of Jeremiah, Daniel, Ezekiel and Death of Ezekiel. The following additional apocryphal books are found in the manuscripts: the Testament of the Twelve Patriarchs, the History of Joseph and his wife Asenath; and the Hymn of Asenath. These latter are not found in the printed editions of the Armenian Bible, nor are they in all manuscripts. There are also some further irregularities in the arrangement of these various books. Each Old Testament book has a preface containing an introduction and summary of contents. In addition to the usual preface some manuscripts have a special introduction, as a passage from David the Philosopher, from Athanasius, from Epiphanius of Cyprus. Daniel is a translation of Theodotion's version as found in the Septuagint (§50).

Printed editions of the Armenian Bible appeared first at Amsterdam in 1666; in Venice in 1733. The first critical edition appeared in Venice in 1805, edited by Zohrab, as a result of a collation of several manuscripts. A later edition appeared in Venice in 1860.

89. When the Arab invasion of Syria and Egypt had practically supplanted the native tongues by the Arabic, the Christians of these regions began to require and to secure the Bible in Arabic. Arabic versions of the Old Testament are based on several originals, Greek, Syriac, Hebrew and Samaritan. There are many manuscripts of various values, but scarcely utilized as yet for critical purposes. The whole Old Testament in Arabic appeared in the Paris Polyglot, and with slight variations in Walton's Polyglot. The Pentateuch was the translation of Sa'adya the Ga'ôn, a learned rabbi of the Fayyûm, in Upper Egypt, made directly from the Hebrew; Joshua was also translated from the Hebrew; Judges, Samuel, Kings, Chronicles and Job were made from the Peshitta; the Prophets, Psalms and Proverbs were translated from the Septuagint. This strange mix-up was found by the editors of the Polyglot in an Egyptian manuscript of the sixteenth century.

There are several manuscripts of the above translations, which are available for students. An Arabic translation of the Coptic version of the Septuagint is extant. There are also several manuscripts of an Arabic translation of the Samaritan Pentateuch. But the most interesting for textual study is the Arabic translation direct from the Hebrew. This portion of the Arabic Old Testament, however, agrees so thoroughly with the Hebrew that its variations are of slight textual value. Several individual portions of the Old Testament have appeared during the last three centuries, but much remains to be done to ascertain the real value of this version for the textual study of the Bible.

CHAPTER XI

OLD TESTAMENT MATERIAL SUMMED UP

90. In the preceding eight chapters (III-X) a bird's-eye view has been given of all the principal versions of the Old Testament except those in early English and the English language. We have seen that they stretch over a large area and have various values. Some are translations direct from the Hebrew, and thus bring us within one step of that early sacred text; others are translations of translations, and consequently are two steps distant from the Hebrew. If we should confine our attention only to translations direct from the Hebrew, our discussion would be either too brief or too technical for interesting reading. Such a restriction would rule out all early English versions, even down to Tyndale's work.

Though a translation of a translation may not be of great importance, still its evidence is valuable when we are seeking the true reading of a text whose original is irrecoverably lost, as is the Hebrew of the Old Testament. Therefore we have included in these chapters a brief description of several versions that are rarely treated in a popular work. These versions were prepared for peoples whose homes were on the outer borders of the nations where Christianity first made large conquests. The influence of such versions on the English Bible may be slight, but they are nevertheless worth our consideration. Such are the Coptic, Ethiopic, Gothic, Georgian, Slavonic, Armenian and Arabic.

91. The true relations of these versions may be best represented by the accompanying chart.

DIAGRAM SHOWING GENERAL RELATIONS OF THE ANCIENT VERSIONS TO THE HEBREW (CHAPXI)

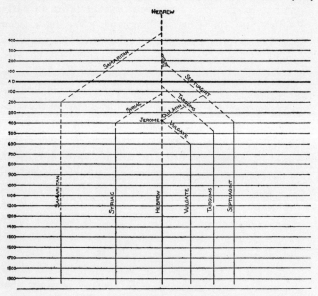

92. The central shaft of the chart is the Hebrew text, from which several of the greatest versions of the Bible have been translated directly. This Hebrew text itself has been multiplied by the same falli-

ble means as all other books of ancient times, by
scribes and copyists, who not only repeated the mistakes of their predecessors, but added thereto their
own errors. Such repetition of errors through centuries without a check of any kind would result in a
very corrupt text, for the tendency of errors to multiply is evident in every ancient manuscript whose
history we can trace.

Now the best kind of checks on errors, and the
best means of discovering them after they are made
are the several ancient versions that were a copy of,
or were translated directly from, the original Hebrew
or Massoretic text as it existed in those days. We
then have evidence that is valuable as to what the
Hebrew text was at the times when these several
translations were made from it. The degree of that
value is, of course, dependent on the purity of the
text that we possess of each several translation. For
example, the Septuagint was translated directly from
the Hebrew in the third and second centuries B. C.;
if our best text of the Septuagint is an exact reproduction of the first translation from the Hebrew it
can practically settle what the Hebrew text was at
that time. If the Septuagint text is not pure, then
the scholar's task is plain. By a study of every available manuscript of the Septuagint, and of all the
translations made directly from it, he must carefully
weigh the evidence and as approximately as possible
determine what that Septuagint original was.

This is precisely what must be done for every translation from the Hebrew, before we may be sure that we are making any real progress in finding out the state of the Hebrew text when such translation was made. The work requires long and patient study and research if it avails for the best results in Bible study.

93. The Samaritan Pentateuch (Chapter IV) is a version of, but not a translation from, the Hebrew. It was doubtless a copy of the Hebrew text of the fifth century B. C., written in old characters. When it broke relations with the text preserved among the Hebrews it soon began to bear marks of its independence. It contains the Pentateuch only, and its variations from the Hebrew are enough to stamp it as the Bible of the Samaritans. These variations, as we have already seen, are attributable to various causes. Those which have the most interest for Bible students are such as presumably preserve a better text than our present Hebrew itself. These are not many, but they are useful. The agreement of some of these variations with those of the Septuagint, and of the other Greek versions, is confirmatory both of the correctness of its own readings and of the versions with which it agrees. The fact that this is the earliest text of the Bible independent of the Hebrew makes it of interest to every one who not only visits Nablus, the home of a remnant of the ancient Samaritans, but delights in a study of every scrap of testimony to the early text of the Pentateuch.

94. The Septuagint is the first ancient translation made directly from the Hebrew of the Old Testa-

ment. It was made at Alexandria under the liberal-
izing influence of Greek thought and Greek civilization. It was made from the Hebrew text that was
current in those days (about 280-130 B. C.), by men
who were reasonably familiar with both languages.
But their style of Greek and their inability to render
certain expressions into an idiomatic Greek show that
the translators were probably Alexandrian or Egyptian Jews. We must not forget, too, that the Hebrew
at that time was probably not separated into words,
nor was it provided with vowel points. These facts
allowed the translators greater liberties in their use
of the text, and consequently afforded a larger liability to produce a version that should vary from the
next translator's rendering of the Hebrew. Now, we
must remember that the Septuagint started at this
time on a course of its own. It was copied and re-
copied over and over again during the succeeding
centuries, by scribes of varying intelligence. Errors
were made, re-made, and multiplied, as in the case of
the Hebrew text. Every such error in either case
carried the two texts farther and farther from each
other. Aquila, Symmachus, and Theodotion, rather
than attempt to harmonize the two versions, produced new translations into the Greek. Origen, however, undertook the colossal task of collecting into
one work the Hebrew, the three Greek versions
named above, and the Septuagint; the last he thoroughly revised on the basis of the Hebrew text.
Even in his day the variations between the two texts

were many. When we consider that the Hebrew and Greek texts used by Origen were divergences from the same original text in the second or third century B. C., we begin to appreciate how rapidly the errors of the scribes must have multiplied.

After Origen's time the Septuagint was several times revised in order to make it represent more faithfully the Hebrew text of the day. These revisions were made on the basis of the best texts available to the revisers.

Scholars at the present time are busying themselves about finding from all the Greek versions and parts of versions extant the true reading of the Septuagint in Origen's time, in the first century, and at such other times as its text can be fixed. The best text to-day, that of Swete, is the result of a comprehensive study of all the sources. A comparison with the Massoretic Hebrew will give us many readings, as seen in the margin of the Revised Version, that are preferable to those of the Hebrew text.

95. Jerome was a wise scholar. He soon saw that revisions of the Old Latin texts would be endless. And so he plunged into a most thorough study of the Hebrew original; and out of it produced the classical Latin version of the Old Testament (390-404 A. D.). Though ridiculed and condemned by many leaders in the church, he pressed on, smarting under their lashes, until the work was done. His translations were made from Hebrew manuscripts current in Palestine in his day. It is probable that they had been

guarded by one of the great Jewish schools in existence at that time, and hence may have been free from many of the errors found in manuscripts of other countries. At any rate, Jerome's work furnishes us a Latin version of the Hebrew text of his day, probably of the oldest and best manuscript that he could command. His translation then gives us a key to the condition of the Hebrew text at the beginning of the fifth century A. D. But before we can use Jerome's key we must ascertain as nearly as possible the very Latin text into which Jerome translated the Hebrew. To do this it is necessary to collect and compare all the Latin manuscripts extant, the Latin quotations of the church fathers, the modifications made in Jerome's text in later times, and any translations of that text made during the centuries.

Jerome's original Latin rendering has not yet been discovered. Scholars, however, are making progress, and the best Vulgate text is of some value, as seen in the marginal readings of the Revised Version.

96. The Syriac is closely akin to the Hebrew. When a Syrian translated the Old Testament into Syriac his task was not any greater than that of translating a German document into Dutch. We should then expect to find the Syriac a good representative of faithfulness to the original Hebrew. To a certain extent we are not disappointed. But another element enters into the work that somewhat discounts what ought to be a valuable aid. The Syrians were so close to the Hebrews in modes of thought and ex-

Complutensian Polyglot, 1514; Hebrew, Vulgate, Septuagint with interlinear Latin translation, Targum with Latin trans-
lation (§ 25), Genesis 1 : 1-12

pression that they did not hesitate, when they thought it would add clearness or conciseness, to change the readings of the Hebrew text as they transformed it into Syriac dress. This free handling of the Hebrew is further modified by some corrections, scholars discover, made on the basis of the Septuagint, and others are colored by the peculiar beliefs that soon sprung up in the Syrian communities.

But notwithstanding the variations due to the causes already enumerated, the Syriac text possesses a real value for the determination of the Hebrew text in the early Christian centuries.

97. The Jews themselves should be the best interpreters of their own Hebrew text. From the time that their own classical tongue, represented in the Old Testament Hebrew, began to degenerate, the reading of the Scriptures in the synagogues was accompanied by an interpreter who gave the sense in Aramaic, the spoken language of the common people. These oral interpretations gradually increased in importance, until somewhere in the early Christian centuries they were reduced to writing and indorsed by the authority of the rabbis. Just when this authorization was granted we are not certain. But these Targums, "interpretations," of some parts of the Old Testament possess both textual and exegetical value. They represent Jewish translations or paraphrases of the Hebrew text, and thus in many places indicate what must have been the true reading of that text when the Targum was prepared.

As in all other versions indicated above, we must guard against certain peculiarities of these Targums. They now and then depart quite markedly from a literal translation of the Hebrew, by expanding into a paraphrase, or by inserting words or phrases to complete what was supposed to be the sense. The gains from the Targums toward determining the Hebrew text of the early centuries, which is most valuable, are its confirmation of the readings of other versions.

CHAPTER XII

THE APOCRYPHA

98. The so-called apocryphal books cannot be overlooked in any discussion of the antecedents of the English Bible. They have formed part of the contents of the English Bible from Coverdale's edition (1536) down through the issuance of the Authorized Version (1611). They are also a constituent part of the Rheims and Douai version of the Roman Catholic church. The completed edition of Luther's Bible (1534) likewise made use of the majority of the apocryphal books. We find them embodied also in the edition of the Vulgate authorized and indorsed by the Council of Trent, and especially edited by papal authority in 1592. Still earlier, they are first found in connection with the sacred books of the Old Testament in the Alexandrian version. These peculiar books, which have come down through the ages in such close companionship with those now found as part of the Hebrew Bible, are full of interest. Bible students of to-day know too little about them, as they are not bound up either with the Revised Version or the American Revised Version.

This is not the place to go into a full discussion of the questions of the origin, character, and significance of these little books. But some items of each case will be mentioned, and a few points made that may be helpful to those who are seeking more light on this knotty little canonical problem.

99. The name "Apocrypha" (in Greek, ἀπόκρυφος), "hidden, concealed," is applied to certain books that have been incorporated for centuries among the so-called canonical books in several versions of the Scriptures. The original meaning of the word seems to have been entirely appropriate, for it was given to such works as were prepared for certain sects or companies of heretical believers, who carefully concealed them from the public. The evidence of this fact is seen in some of the titles of these sacred books ; for example, a papyrus of the first century has as its title, "A Holy and Secret Book of Moses, called the Eighth or Holy." So that the term " apocryphal " in its original sense was perfectly honorable, whereas in its later acquired sense it specifies books that have been rejected by the Protestant churches as spurious.

In the early lists of the sacred books of the church we find included all the books of the Septuagint. Hence the early significance of Apocrypha did not include what it was made to cover in later times. Its earlier meaning covered such works as the Book of Jubilees and the Book of Enoch. Jerome seems to have been the first to use it as applicable to all the books not found in the Jewish canon. He then classified as apocryphal all books found in the Septuagint which its translators did not find in the Hebrew Bible, from which they had prepared their version. In the

time of the Reformation Protestant churches adopted
as their Old Testament Scriptures the books that had
formed the Jewish canon, and thus threw out all other
books found in the Vulgate and the Septuagint versions. The Roman Catholic church, on the other
hand, declared the same books to be canonical as had
the Alexandrian Jews, and applied the word apocryphal to books outside those of the Vulgate and Septuagint versions, which were often included in some
versions. The Protestant churches designated the
latter, that is, those spurious books not contained in
the list of the Apocrypha, as Pseudepigrapha.

100. The books designated " apocryphal " by the
Protestant churches are those usually found in the
Greek and Latin, but not in the Hebrew Bibles. That
the reader may be able to locate them the following
list presents them in their relations to the Protestant
canonical books, remembering that our English order
is practically that of the Greek and Latin versions.
The books of Chronicles are followed immediately
by 1 and 2 Esdras (Ezra-Nehemiah) ; Tobit ; Judith ;
Additions to Esther, prefixed to, inserted in, and
placed after the canonical portions of the book of
Esther ; after the Song of Solomon, Wisdom of Solomon ; Wisdom of Jesus, Son of Sirach (or Ecclesiasticus) ; Baruch, with the Epistle of Jeremiah ; Story
of Susanna, prefixed to Daniel ; Song of the Three
Holy Children, inserted between verses 23 and 24 of
chapter 3, and Bel and the Dragon, appended to chapter 12 ; 1 and 2 Maccabees follow Malachi. In the

Vulgate these books follow Revelation, viz.: Prayer of Manasses; 3 and 4 Esdras. All the above except the last three are included among the canonical books of the Roman Catholic church.

The apocryphal books of the ancient church, now designated as the "Pseudepigrapha" by Protestant bodies, are very numerous. They cover a wide range of topics and reveal many literary peculiarities. Some of them are found in the best versions, and others are extant only as individual books. Search in European libraries and old monasteries of the East is frequently rewarded by the discovery of some new pseudepigraphical book or fragment of one. Direct references and hints in early ecclesiastical literature still point to others whose manuscripts have not yet come to light.

101. The books of the Apocrypha may be conveniently classified according to M. R. James, and described under the heads of (1) Narrative (historical and legendary); (2) Prophetic, and (3) Didactic. Of the Narrative there are (a) the historical and (b) the legendary.

(a) The Historical books are (1) 1 Maccabees, a part of the history of the Jews in the Maccabean period. The book is extant only in Greek and in translations therefrom, though it was originally written in Hebrew. (2) 2 Maccabees, claims to be an abridgment of a large five-volume work by Jason of Cyrene. It is extant in Greek, and is inferior in historical value to 1 Maccabees. It is prefaced by two

spurious letters to the Jews in Egypt. (3) 3 Maccabees, a fragmentary history of an attempt to mas-
sacre the Jews under Ptolemy Philopator (217 B. C.),
and their deliverance. It is found in the Septuagint,
but not in the Vulgate, or Roman Catholic canon.
(4) 4 Maccabees, is extant in Greek, and is a philosophical document discussing the superiority of mind
over matter by a concrete illustration. It is found in
some manuscripts of the Septuagint, but was not part
of its canon. (5) 1 Esdras (3 Esdras in the Vulgate), is extant in Greek, and includes a canonical re-
casting of Ezra-Nehemiah, to which is appended a
legend known to Josephus. The Vulgate embodies
this book in an appendix, and hence it is not one of
the canonical books of the Roman church.

(b) The Legendary are: (1) Additions to Esther;
in the Septuagint there are several letters, prayers and
visions, inserted at intervals, to explain and amplify
the story of Esther. In the Vulgate these are gathered together in an appendix, with an accompanying
note, stating that they are not in the Hebrew canon.
(2) Additions to Daniel are found in the Greek versions of the Septuagint and of Theodotion. A Hebrew original of the Song of the Three Children has
recently been found by Dr. M. Gaster in the Chronicle of Jerahmeel. (3) Tobit is a romance of the
captivity, extant in Greek and Aramaic, written not
later than the first century A. D. There are three
Greek and three Old Latin versions, besides Jerome's
version. (4) Judith is a romance in Greek, reciting

how the city of Bethulia was delivered from the Assyrians by the shrewdness of Judith, a Jewish widow. It is also one of the books of the Greek and Latin canons.

102.   (c)   The Prophetic are: (1) Baruch, a book ascribed to Baruch, the amanuensis of Jeremiah, originally writen in Greek, probably after 70 A. D.; is found in Greek and Latin Bibles.   To this is appended as chapter 6 (2) The Epistle of Jeremiah, a letter ascribed to the prophet, which was sent to the Jews in Babylon.   (3) The Prayer of Manasses purports to be the prayer of Manasseh while in prison (2 Chron. 33); it is found in many Greek manuscripts appended to the Psalms; in the Vulgate it follows the New Testament, as do 3 and 4 Esdras, and is not in the Roman Catholic canon.   (4) 4 Esdras, called 2 Esdras in the Authorized Version, but 3 Esdras when Ezra and Nehemiah are counted as one book, as in the Greek.   The original Greek of this book is lost.   But it is found in Latin, Syriac, Arabic, Ethiopic and Armenian.   It was relegated by the Roman church to its appendix as not canonical.

(d) The Didactic are: (1) Wisdom of Jesus, Son of Sirach (commonly called Ecclesiasticus) is found in the Greek Bible, was written by a Palestinian Jew, and was translated from a Hebrew original.   The Syriac version of this book was likewise made from the Hebrew.   Some portions of the Hebrew text have been recently discovered.   (2) Wisdom of Solomon is found in the Greek Bible, and was probably written

ותגעל מות נפשי · · · · · · וזיתי לשאל תחנותי
ואפטר מבכבאין עזר לי · · · ואצפה סוכר דאיף
ואזכרה את רחמייי · · · · · · וחסדין אשר עשלם
המצל את חוסי בו · · · · · · ויגאל זמכל רע
וארים מארץ קולי · · · · · · · ומש ברי שאול שועתי
וארומם ייי אב אתה · · · · · · כי אתה גבור ישעי
אל תרפני ביום צרה · · · · · · בים שואה ונמשואה
אהללה שמך תמיד · · · · · · ואברך בתפלהי
או שמע קולי ייי · · · · · · · ויאין אל תושני
ויפני כל רע · · · · · · · · · · ומלטו ביופ ימו
לכן הודיתי ואהללה · · · · · · ואברכה את שמיי
הודן לייכי טוב · · · · · · · · בלעולם חסדו אפי
הודן לאל התשבחות · · · · · · כי לעלם אסדו
הודן לשומר ישראל · · · · · · כי לעולם חסדו
הודן ליוצר הכל · · · · · · · · כי לעולם חסדו אי
ר ל גאל ישראל · · · · · · · · כי לעולם חסדו אי
לעק ישראל · · · · · · · · · · כי לשעולם חסדו
אדרו לבועה שדן ומקדשן · · · · כי לעולם חזהדי

Hebrew fragment of Ecclesiasticus. Taylor-Schechter collection of the
University Library, Cambridge, England
Ecclesiasticus 51 : 6c-12

by an Alexandrian Jew in the first century, if we are to pass on the literary character and content of that wonderfully clever book of Jewish philosophy.

103. The above-named Protestant apocryphal books are those most familiar to us from their presence in many old English editions of the Authorized Version, and in large family Bibles. But besides these there is a continually growing collection of pseudepigraphical books which Bible students must take account of. At least one of these, the Book of Enoch, is quoted in Jude (14b), and others are quoted in some of the church fathers as if authentic and authoritative.

There are various classifications of these books, but that of M. R. James (in Encyclopædia Biblica) is comprehensive, and followed for the main part here. This literature is (1) Legendary or Haggadic Narrative; (2) Apocalyptic; (3) Poetical; (4) Didactic.

1) The Legendary: (1) The Testament of Adam, extant in Greek, Latin, Syriac, Arabic and Ethiopic; (2) The Book of Jubilees (or Apocalypse of Moses), a commentary on Genesis, extant in Ethiopic; (3) Testaments of Abraham, Isaac and Jacob, found in Greek, Slavonic, and Roumanian; (4) Apocalypse of Abraham, extant in Slavonic, from the Greek; (5) Testaments of the Twelve Patriarchs, extant in Greek and Latin; (6) Life of Aseneth (wife of Joseph), extant in Greek, Syriac and Latin; (7) Testament of Job, extant in Greek; (8) Testament of Solomon, extant in Greek; (9) Book of Noah, a fragment found

in the Book of Enoch; (10) Penitence of Jannes and Jambres, extant only in Latin and Anglo-Saxon fragments.

2) Apocalyptic: (1) Book of Enoch, originally written in Hebrew or Aramaic, extant in Greek, Ethiopic and Latin; (2) Secrets of Enoch, extant in Slavonic only; (3) Sibylline Oracles, extant in Greek and Latin; (4) Assumption of Moses, extant in Latin, quoted in Jude; (5) four Apocalypses of Baruch, extant in Greek, Slavonic, Ethiopic and Syriac; (6) The Rest of the Words of Baruch, or Paralipomena of Jeremiah, extant in Greek and Ethiopic; (7) Prophecy of Jeremiah, attached to the Epistle of Jeremiah in Ethiopic manuscripts; (8) Ascension of Isaiah, extant in its entirety only in Ethiopic, but fragments exist in Greek, Latin and Slavonic; (9) Apocalypse of Elijah, extant in Coptic; (10) Apocalypse of Zephaniah, extant in Coptic; (11) A Revelation of Moses, extant in Hebrew; (12) An Apocalypse of Esdras, extant in Syriac; an Ethiopic manuscript of a book by the same name is in the British Museum; there are several other books of less note under this classification that are either quoted or referred to in various ancient authors.

3) Poetical: (1) Psalms of Solomon, eighteen psalms in Greek that were once translated from Hebrew; (2) Additions to the Psalter: Psalm 151 in the Greek; three apocryphal psalms in Syriac—all probably of Jewish origin.

4) Didactic: (1) Magical Books of Moses, ex-

tant in papyri found in Egypt; (2) The Story of Achiacharus, the cup-bearer, steward, signet-keeper and overseer of accounts to Esarhaddon (Tobit 1 : 21f.).

The above list, though it does not contain all known pseudepigraphical books, is being increased almost annually by the discovery of other books quoted and referred to by early ecclesiastical writers, These works are becoming more and more essential for Bible students, because they give many reflections of the pious mind of Jew and Christian in the early centuries of Christianity.

104. The books of our Revised Version are identical with those that made up the ancient Hebrew Bible. All the Apocrypha and Pseudepigrapha were produced between about 250 B. C. and somewhere in the early Christian centuries. They were written by persons who doubtless had a pious turn of mind, but who wished to palm off on a credulous public, or credulous church, works which were intended to promote some religious or philosophical idea. To get their works adopted and indorsed they gave them some title that carried the name of a glorious patriarch or personage in early Jewish history. Such works appealed more readily to the non-Palestinian Jew, as we see in the translation and adoption of several non-Jewish documents in the Alexandrian or Septuagint translation. We have seen how these same books have been carried into the numerous editions of the Septuagint, into the Vulgate, and into several

other versions of later date. The church fathers now and then quoted from these extra-canonical books, and the Roman church formally adopted many of them as part of their biblical canon. Somehow or other the spread of learning, and the quickening of a spiritual life in reformation times cut down the biblical canon of the Protestant churches to the limits of the ancient Hebrew canon. This determination won its way until to-day we find no apocryphal book either in the Revised Version or the American Revised Version.

In 1892, the Rev. C. J. Ball issued the Variorum Apocrypha, the Authorized Version with variant readings, after the manner of the Variorum Teachers' Bible. The Revised Version of the Apocrypha appeared in 1895.

105. Why were the apocryphal books not received into the biblical canon of the Old Testament? What constitutes the real difference between the two classes of literature? Who decided what should be Bible and what should not be Bible? How many times these questions have been asked and remained unanswered!

Answers to these questions are not easy to find. In the first place, no man and no body of men, so far as recorded, formally decided what should be the fixed canon of the Old Testament. There seemed to be a kind of unanimity of opinion, doubtless based on common grounds, why such and such a book should be valid for Scripture and another should not. Westcott, Canon of the New Testament, says rightly, p. 346f.: " The collection of sacred books was brought about gradually, spontaneously, silently." "The judgment appeared as a natural manifestation of the life of the Christian body, and not as a logical consequence of definite principles."

Scholars have been searching far and wide for a statement of the reasons inquired after. Some of the reasons produced for the acceptance of any book into the canon have been, (a) its antiquity, it must be known to be ancient; (b) its authenticity, it must have been regarded as authentic by those of early days; (c) its authorship, each book must be connected with some great name; (d) its purpose, each book must present some distinct phase in religious thought and life; (e) its temper, each book must be in harmony with the already accepted biblical books; (f) its religious tone, each book must make a religious impression that will be a determining element in its location.

On the other hand, there were certainly many reasons why a book was not accepted as canonical. Some of them, as seen in a study of the temper of scholars in the early Christian centuries are: That book was rejected (a) whose ethical teachings were contrary to those of the accepted books; (b) which contained manifest errors of history and geography; (c) whose contents embodied silly, ridiculous, or trifling statements or stories; (d) which was largely compiled or made up of imitations of other writings; (e) which lacked the spiritual element; (f) which was not accepted by the early Christians or Jews; (g) which appeared after the closing of the canon, and whose internal and external evidence locates it after the beginning of the Christian era. There are many statements in rabbinical writings that limit the canon to the regular books of the Hebrew Bible, and reject, as did the early Syriac version, every book not contained therein. Thus in this day we estimate that the partition between the two classes of literature was specifically set up and maintained.

Part II. The New Testament

CHAPTER XIII

WRITING AND MANUSCRIPTS IN GENERAL

106. The story of early Old Testament versions is a long one, for it deals with documents in many languages that stretch over a large area of time. The composition, canonization, and early translations of the Old Testament are veiled in the mists of history. The meagerness of the manuscripts, the policy pursued in the multiplication of versions, and their value for critical study, are problems which confront every thorough student of the Old Testament. The present stage of Old Testament study is still far from satisfactory to those who are desirous of securing a good text, built on an abundance of early manuscript authority.

On turning to the New Testament, however, we find an opposite condition of things. There is an abundance of manuscripts, several of them reaching to the fourth Christian century. They have been deposited in many of the largest libraries of Europe, and are most valuable testimony. Besides these numerous witnesses, the versions of the New Testament are several centuries nearer the original than are those of the Old Testament; or, in other words, the space of time between the date of the composition of the New Testament books and the earliest translations of those documents, is very much shorter than between similar documents of the Old Testament. This fact gives the versions of the New Testament much larger value than can be credited to those of the Old Testament. On the other hand, the larger number of early and valuable manuscripts of the New Testament rather discounts the comparative value of the versions.

107. The books of the New Testament come down to us in Greek, most if not all of them written in the first century. Most of the Epistles of Paul, the earliest of the books, were written as letters to the churches which he had founded and fostered, and not one of them was by him intended to be preserved as a permanent part of a collection of sacred books. Indeed, Paul does not seem to have given any directions regarding his letters, except that occasionally he requested that they should be read before a church or interchanged with that sent to some other church (cf. Col. 4: 16). They preserve the epistolary form even when, as in the case of Romans, the treatment is more elaborate and systematic than usual with him. The individuality of the writer stands out in greater boldness, and the familiar handling of themes in such direct address, gives a certain personal touch and interest not found in formal literary documents.

These letters of Paul are our earliest records of the progress and expansion of Christianity. Paul's intimate relationship with the early churches, and his daily burden of soul for them (cf. 2 Cor. 11: 28) give them a special value. From hints and direct statements in these letters Paul must have carried on an extensive correspondence with his churches (2 Thess. 3: 17; Phil. 3: 18). He received letters or messages from his churches (1 Cor. 16: 3; 7: 1) and sent to them other letters (cf. 2 Cor. 10: 10; 1 Cor. 5: 8) besides those preserved to us in the New Testament. The so-called Catholic Epistles, James, 1 and 2 Peter, 1, 2 and 3 John, and Jude have more of the form of literary epistles. Some of them were evidently intended, if not for general Christian reading, at least for large numbers of persons.

The Gospels are the written reports of the facts known or gathered by their authors concerning the life of Jesus on earth. They used written records in their compilations, as direct discourse is introduced as if it were the identical words of the speakers. John's Gospel stands quite alone, and presents a phase of the life of Jesus distinct from the first three —the Synoptics. Luke's narrative in the Acts is a setting forth in their order of events connected with the beginnings of the church and stretching to the arrival of Paul at Rome. Of all these the Gospels and the Acts seem to have been the only books of the New Testament that were obviously records intended to be of permanent and historical value.

108. After the books of the New Testament were written they were scattered all over the Roman em-

pire. The Christians everywhere took care of them, copied and multiplied them in the century immediately following their production. Marcion, who was a devout teacher during the reign of Antoninus Pius (138-161 A. D.), makes appeal to a rule of faith which consisted of " the Gospel " and " the Apostolicon." This latter is known to have contained ten epistles of Paul, which were recognized by Marcion as authoritative. Soon after this date other writers, especially of the church fathers, quote and refer to various books of the New Testament as if they constituted an authoritative collection of sacred documents.

But we do not possess one of the original manuscripts either of Paul's letters or of any other one of the books of the New Testament. They were doubtless multiplied by Christians who copied them privately, and by slaves, professional scribes and monks in many places in the Christianized world. Scholars such as Origen, Eusebius and Jerome greatly stimulated biblical learning, and caused the multiplication and preservation of its sacred manuscripts. That sacred calling was later confined almost exclusively to monasteries, of which there were hundreds in the Orient. The profession of scribe was so revered that a writer of the sacred books was exempted from working in the gardens of a monastery, lest the skill of his pen be marred by injury to his hands.

109. Since these original manuscripts have been lost, how shall we proceed to recover their contents?

The process will be substantially that followed in restoring the text of the Old Testament (Chapter II). In this case, however, we shall not be obliged to employ such a wide range of matter. Here we shall examine the earliest extant manuscripts of the Greek, the versions which were translated directly from the Greek, and the quotations in the writings of the church fathers and others. The earliest extant Greek manuscripts date from the fourth century (not more than three centuries after the writing of the New Testament books) down to the invention of printing in the fifteenth century. In fact, a few were copied after the printer began his work. The versions began to be made in the second century, and continued to multiply until the tenth. Their evidence, however, in each case depends largely on the antiquity of the manuscripts still extant of such version. The use of the New Testament made by the church fathers either in quoting from the original Greek or from one of the versions, is valuable evidence for the reading of that text at the given date. On the other hand, the carelessness that some of the church fathers manifested in their quotations or references to current versions often diminishes their value for the textual critic. The diligent student of the text will, however, gradually discover the relative value of these ancient witnesses, and accord them their meed of regard.

110. The known manuscripts of the New Testament, produced prior to the invention of printing, now number several thousands. They are found in public

and private libraries and collections in almost every civilized country. They are divided according to the character of the writing into two classes: (1) Uncials, that is, those written in capital letters, and (2) Cursives, those written in a running hand. The former include for the most part the oldest manuscripts down to the ninth century, and the latter those written from the ninth to the fifteenth century. Besides the New Testament manuscripts, properly so-called, there are over four hundred Lectionaries, or service books, in which are found selections from some parts of the New Testament for use in church services.

The oldest uncials are written on expensive and durable vellum or parchment; on leaves about quarto or folio size, usually in two and occasionally in three or four columns on each page. They have as a rule no space between the words, no accents, and few pausal marks. There are no marks to indicate the end of sentences, except paragraph extensions. There are certain words that admit of an abbreviation, such being indicated by a superlinear stroke. The following in English letters will illustrate about the appearance of an early uncial manuscript (from John 1: 1-4):

INTHEBEGINNINGWASTHEWORDAND T H E
W O R DWASWITHG̅D̅ANDTHEWORDWASG̅D̅
THESAMEWASINTHEBE G I N N I N G W I T H
G̅D̅ A L L THINGSWEREMADETHROUGHHIM
ANDWITHOUTHIMWAS N O T A N Y T H I N G
MADETHATHATHBEENMADEI N H I M W A S
LIFEANDTHELIFEWASTHELIGHT O F M E N

Codex Vaticanus (B) (§§ 120, 121).   Fourth Century

This method of writing gave to subsequent scribes and copyists considerable liberty as to the divisions of words and sentences. In this very quotation there happens to be a case of this kind. In the margin of the Revised Version we find: " Or, was not anything made. That which hath been made was life in him; and the life, &c." The text's reading puts the period after "that hath been made." This illustrates how the copyist, as soon as he should begin to depart from this endless-chain method of writing, could, by separating his words at different places, produce a different sense from the original. Just this thing occurred in numerous places in the New Testament, and it was perpetuated until we have a multitude of variant readings collated from the different groups of manuscripts. Another class of variants consisted of expansions of the text in order to explain certain events mentioned; particularly is this frequent in the Gospels and the Acts.

Again, it is evident that the same kinds of errors already enumerated in the Hebrew Old Testament (Chapter III) were operative in producing variant readings for the Greek manuscripts. Different schools of believers, located in different sections of the Christian world, likewise perpetuated manuscripts that became tinged by their marginal notes which contained either their doctrinal tenets, their corrections or their deliberate alterations. These items crept into the text, and thus spread the error. The amount of such doctrinal variation, however, was relatively small.

These and other circumstances fostered a tendency to multiply variants, and thus complicate the problem of restoring the original text.

111. No manuscript earlier than the ninth century carries a date. The time of the writing of any particular undated document is determined in one or more of several ways. Some of the means of fixing the date are (1) the material on which a document is written, (2) the form of the letters, (3) the style of writing, (4) the use or absence of the Ammonian sections of the Gospels, (5) the Eusebian references to the sections of Ammonius, after 340 A. D. (the year of Eusebius' death), (6) the system of Euthalius in the Acts and Epistles.

Apparently the earliest extant attempt in Greek manuscripts to break up the text into paragraphs is found in the Vatican manuscript. Tatian, however, in his Diatessaron seems to have divided the Gospels into larger sections or "titles," to whose numerical designation was appended a summary of contents, either at the beginning of the Gospel or at the top or bottom of the pages or both.

Ammonius of Alexandria, about 220 A. D., adopted a novel method of harmonizing the Gospels. He took Matthew as his standard, and marked off therein 335 sections; in Mark he noted 236; in Luke 342, and in John 232. These sections were marked by Greek letters with a fixed numerical value. To make practical his plan, ten lists were made, to which another letter written under the designation of the section referred. In these lists all the parallel passages were classified. The first list contained all the passages common to the four Gospels; the second, those common to the first three of them; the third, those common to Matthew, Luke and John; the fourth, those common to Matthew, Mark and John; the fifth to the ninth lists, those common to different twos; and the tenth, those found in one only. Such designations introduced into manuscripts set one stake for the age of that manuscript.

Eusebius adopted certain modifications of the Ammonian method. The use of these devices in a manuscript would place its production not earlier than the date of Eusebius' death (340 A. D.). In 458 A. D. Euthalius of Alexandria introduced into Acts and the Pauline and General epistles certain divisions which he called stichoi. These were indicated by a mark set at every fiftieth line. Though they were arbitrary divisions they served as guides and checks for the copyist. The same term stichoi was later applied to another division, called also comma or colon, which was made according to the sense.

These devices, however, were not universally adopted, nor are they present in any of our modern Bibles. Their use, however, for a considerable time, supplies us with a useful key for ascertaining the date of some of the uncial manuscripts. Nestle catalogued 127 such manuscripts in 1901.

112. The cursive manuscripts were produced from the ninth to the sixteenth century. They number

thousands, every great library possessing one or more, and copies being found even in some small public libraries. Some of these are only second in value to the uncials, but many of them are relatively unimportant. They seem to have been written in great numbers by the monks in the middle ages. Every monastery, and there were hundreds of them, had its scribe or scribes, whose chief business was the copying of the sacred Scriptures. So many of these copies have been carefully preserved that we have on our catalogues 3,702 (Nestle in 1901). Only a small proportion of them has been fully collated. They are designated by numerals in distinction from the capital letters that mark uncials. Some of the most valuable of these cursives will be indicated in a subsequent chapter. The accompanying cut is from the first page of a beautiful manuscript of the fifteenth century, now preserved in the library of the University of Chicago.

First page of a manuscript of the Gospels in the Library of the University of Chicago. About A.D. 1500. Matthew 1 : 1-4a

CHAPTER XIV

SOME GREAT NEW TESTAMENT MANUSCRIPTS

113. Uncial Greek manuscripts are assigned to dates from the middle of the fourth century to the ninth. At the present time only one hundred and twelve such documents are known; and of that number two only contain the entire New Testament. It seems that before the collection of all the New Testament manuscripts into a single volume, there were four groups of those books: (1) The Gospels; (2) the Acts and Catholic Epistles; (3) the Pauline Epistles, and (4) the Apocalypse. A large number of the manuscripts now reflect this method of grouping. The uncial manuscripts are designated by the capital letters of the Latin, Greek, or Hebrew alphabets. Students of the footnotes of the Variorum Teachers' Bible are familiar with such alphabetical designations. Many manuscripts, both uncial and cursive, have names as well as symbols.

Cursive manuscripts are dated from the ninth to the sixteenth centuries. Of these there are about 3,500 known and catalogued, not by letters, but by numerals. The group system noted above is observed in this method of enumeration, that is, each group has its own system of successive numbers. They are indicated in lists of manuscripts as Evan. (the Gospels);

Act. (the Acts and Catholic Epistles); Paul. (the Pauline epistles); and Apoc. (the Apocalypse). Regarding the Lectionaries, we find these abbreviations: Evst. (the Lectionary of the Gospels), and Apost. (the Lectionary of the Acts and the Epistles). The cursives, as a rule, occupy a small place in the considerations of the textual critic. Their evidence is mainly valuable when the sum total of testimony is collected, coming into prominence only where two great authorities disagree on a reading.

114. Among the most fascinating stories in biblical lore are those connected with the discovery, transmission, and preservation of early manuscripts. Their production was sometimes a matter of imperial edict, as when Constantine the Great ordered from Eusebius, the famed historian and Bible scholar of the fourth century, for the churches of Constantinople, the preparation of fifty manuscripts of the Bible, to be written "on artificially wrought skins by skilful calligraphists." The persecutions and wars of the middle ages destroyed such documents in large numbers. Fire, flood and fanaticism combined to wipe out these perishable treasures of Christendom. But some were sheltered in out-of-the-way fastnesses, in monasteries upon the mountainside, in the sacred precincts of carefully guarded churches, and in the palaces of kings. They were given as presents, they were borrowed, bought, and stolen. Their intrinsic value was almost always underestimated, and they were subjected to inexcusable risks of being hopelessly lost.

Fortunately, however, there were some haunts unreached by the demons of destruction, wherein these treasures were preserved. Large-hearted benefactors and long-headed Christian statesmen secured many of these documents and deposited them where they are safe, and can be available for scholars through all time. In the succeeding sections a few only of these invaluable manuscripts will be described, and these, too, practically in the order in which they appear in the catalogues of manuscripts.

115. Codex Sinaiticus (S, generally designated, X) was in the monastery at Mt. Sinai, but is now in the Imperial Library at St. Petersburg. The story of its discovery and acquisition by Constantine Tischendorf of Leipsic is one of the most fascinating in the history of biblical manuscripts. Tischendorf set out in 1844 to make a tour of the Orient, particularly of monasteries, in search of biblical manuscripts. One of the out-of-the-way places visited by him was the monastery of St. Catharine, located at the base of Mt. Sinai. The monks graciously showed him their ancient library. In glancing around he noticed in a basket, evidently for waste paper, a considerable quantity of leaves on which were written Greek inscriptions of a more ancient character than any he had ever seen. A brief examination showed that they were parts of the Bible. In this batch he found forty-three leaves, and was told by the librarian that two basketfuls of such leaves had already been used to kindle the fire. He was readily given permission to carry

away what he had found, but was not allowed to see the remainder of the book from which these had been taken. Tischendorf told the monks their value, and then left for Europe. He presented the forty-three leaves to King Frederic Augustus of Saxony, who deposited them in the court library at Leipsic. Tischendorf published their contents (1846) under the title of Codex Friderico-Augustanus. These leaves contained parts of 1 Chronicles and Jeremiah, with Nehemiah and Esther complete.

In 1853, Tischendorf returned to the monastery at Mt. Sinai, but without securing any further manuscripts. With unquenchable zeal he made a third trip to the same place in 1859, with the sanction and support of Czar Alexander II. At first he was met with the same kind of refusal that defeated him in 1853. Finally (on February 4), a few days before he left the monastery, he showed the steward his recently published edition of the Septuagint. At this the official said that he also had a copy of the Septuagint. Thus Tischendorf was led to the steward's room, where a bundle of loose leaves of parchment wrapped in a cloth were unfolded and set before him. There was the treasure he had so long sought for! The dream of days, months and years materialized now before his eyes. With pent-up feelings he coldly examined the leaves, and soon saw that it contained not only part of the Old Testament, but the New Testament entire. He was permitted to examine it in his own room that night. He says: " In the presence

Convent of St. Catharine, Mount Sinai. Where Tischendorf found Codex Sinaiticus (§ 115)

of the found treasure it was not possible for me to sleep." He discovered in the mass parts of the Old Testament, including the poetical books entire, the New Testament entire, the Epistle of Barnabas, and part of the Shepherd of Hermas. He saw that if he could not get possession of the original he must copy the whole document.

116. Just at this point the influence of the Czar proved to be of immense advantage. Tischendorf showed the monks how gracious an act it would be to present this precious biblical document to the supreme head of the Greek Church. He was so far successful as to secure a "temporary loan" of the document. It was carried by Bedouin on a camel's back from Mt. Sinai to Cairo, Egypt. At this place he, with the help of two of his countrymen, copied the 110,000 lines of the Codex, and noted the more than 12,000 changes by later hands. In October of the same year (1859) he was permitted to carry it to Europe as a "conditional present" to the Czar, merely for the purpose of publication. Tischendorf, while on his way to Russia, showed it to several royal heads of Europe, including the Emperor of Austria and the kings of Saxony and Prussia. In November he was permitted to lay it before the Czar of all the Russias and the Holy Synod at St. Petersburg. Tischendorf himself was then permitted to make use of it in Leipsic in the preparation of his full edition of the Codex. Finally it was returned (in 1869) to the Imperial Library in St. Petersburg, where, in return for imperial presents

to the monks at Mt. Sinai, it found a permanent home, and may be seen to-day as the most precious biblical treasure of the Russian Government.

The text of this great manuscript was printed at Leipsic, and published in four folio volumes at St. Petersburg at the cost of Czar Alexander II, as a celebration of the first millennium of the Russian Empire. The types were especially cast to bring out practically a photographic imitation of the original manuscript. The New Testament text, with the Epistle of Barnabas, and the Shepherd of Hermas, was issued in a separate volume in Leipsic (in 1863) in smaller type, in four columns, and an octavo edition in ordinary type (in 1865).

117. This Sinaitic Codex consists of 346½ leaves of vellum, made from the finest and best quality of antelope skins. The leaves are 13½ inches wide by 14⅞ inches high, written in large uncials, with four columns of forty-eight lines each. It is the nearest complete, and the oldest, with the exception of the Vatican manuscript, among all the ancient Greek manuscripts of the New Testament. It is assigned by Tischendorf to the middle of the fourth century, or about the time of the death of Eusebius, 340 A. D. Part of the evidence for this assignment is the presence in the margin of the Gospels of the marks of the so-called " Eusebian sections," " written in a hand evidently contemporaneous with the text." Tischendorf thought it entirely possible that this might have been one of the fifty copies which Constantine had

ordered for the churches of Constantinople in 331 A. D. and that it might have been sent by the Emperor Justinian to the convent at Mt. Sinai, which he founded.

As almost every ancient manuscript, the Sinaitic Codex has been corrected and modified by several later writers. (See cut facing p. 16.)

This codex, in addition to being one of the most ancient, is at the same time one of the most valuable of New Testament manuscripts. It often agrees with the Vatican Codex as against the readings of many later manuscripts. A few of the most notable readings in which this manuscript and the Vatican Codex agree are in John 1: 18, where these codices read "God only begotten," for the usual "only begotten son;" Acts 20: 28, "church of God" for the usual "church of the Lord;" the omission of Mark 16: 9-20; the omission of John 7: 53 to 8: 11, the account of the woman taken in adultery. Sometimes it is in agreement with the Old Latin version. In other passages it supports the readings of other texts, thus proving its independence as an authority. Its great importance will be recognized at once by any one who makes use of the variant readings printed in the New Testament in the Variorum Teachers' Bible.

118. Codex Alexandrinus (A) is the name given to the greatest biblical treasure of the British Museum. So much of its history as we know is not so romantic as that of the Sinaitic Codex. This manuscript was offered (in 1624) by Patriarch Cyril Lucar,

of Constantinople, to Sir Thomas Roe, British Ambassador to Turkey, to be presented to King James I. This sovereign having died before it reached England, it was formally presented to Charles I (in 1627). It remained in the royal library until that was made a gift to the National Library in the British Museum. Visitors to the manuscript room to-day may see the New Testament volume open under glass.

The previous history of this manuscript is slightly known. Patriarch Cyril Lucar carried it to Constantinople from Alexandria. A preliminary note to the manuscript, written in Arabic, and signed by "Athanasius the humble" (thought to be Patriarch Athanasius III, whose death occurred in 1308), claims that the manuscript was presented to the official ecclesiastical cell of that town. A Latin note dates the gift in 1098. Cyril Lucar stated that it was written by Thecla the martyr, a noble lady of Egypt, just before the Council of Nicea (325). These statements, however, are only traditional. The fact that the document has attached to it some of the work of Eusebius and Athanasius (who died 376) would locate it probably in the fifth century. The style of writing seems at least to be more elaborate and ornamental than that of the Sinaitic or Vatican Codex.

119. Codex Alexandrinus is written on 776 leaves, each $10\frac{1}{4}$ inches wide by $12\frac{3}{4}$ inches high, and carrying two columns of uncial writing (whereas the Sinaitic carries four). It contains the Old Testa-

Codex Alexandrinus (A). Fifth Century (§§ 118-119)
1 John 5 : 9 to 2 John 13

ment and the New Testament, except the following passages, which are lost: Matthew 1: 1 to 25: 6; John 6: 50 to 8: 52, and 2 Corinthians 4: 13 to 12: 6. It contains also at the end the Greek Epistle of Clement of Rome, of which one leaf is lost, and a fragment only of the second Epistle.

The New Testament portion of this codex was published in uncial type by C. G. Woide (London, 1786), and by B. H. Cowper in common Greek type (London, 1860). The trustees of the British Museum issued the whole manuscript in a magnificent photographic facsimile in 1879-1883, under the editorial oversight of Sir E. Maunde Thompson, principal librarian of the Museum.

This was the first uncial manuscript that was used by biblical scholars. It stands about third or fourth in importance among the great uncials. In the Gospels it is thought to occupy a peculiar position, that of a revised text that was most circulated in the fourth century, whose readings are more in agreement with the Authorized than the Revised Version. In the remainder of the New Testament it stands next to the Sinaitic and Vatican codices, except in the case of the Apocalypse, where it is pre-eminent. It is provided with the Eusebian sections (§111), but not with those of Euthalius, hence it is located before the middle of the fifth century. Its agreement with the Vulgate in several respects led Dr. Hort to infer that Jerome made considerable use of a text related to A.

120. Codex Vaticanus (B) is a manuscript of the Greek Bible now preserved in the Vatican Library àt Rome. It was brought to Rome by Pope Nicholas V in 1448. It was entered on the first catalogue of the Vatican Library in 1475. Its earlier history is mere conjecture. Its real character and value were unknown for centuries because it was not accessible to scholars. The Roman church guarded it so closely that no Protestant scholar of ability was allowed to study it for any adequate length of time until the middle of the nineteenth century. This codex (B) was first made known in 1533, when Sepulveda called the attention of Erasmus to it. In 1669, Bartolocci, librarian of the Vatican, made a collection of some of its variant readings, which remained unpublished. Abbate Mico collated it for Richard Bentley in 1720 (published in 1799) ; and Andrew Birch, of Copenhagen, in 1781 (published in 1788, 1798, 1801). Napoleon took this treasure to Paris, where Hug carefully examined it in 1809, and was the first to make known its great value and supreme importance (1810). In 1815, it was restored to Rome, and became practically inaccessible to scholars. Tischendorf in 1843, after several months' delay, was permitted to look at it for six hours. In 1844, de Muralt was allowed nine hours to examine it. In 1845, the English scholar Tregelles, even with Cardinal Wiseman's introduction, was not allowed to copy a word. His pockets were searched and all writing material taken from him. If he looked too intently

at any passage the two attendants would snatch the volume from him. Other scholars who had traveled far, and were thoroughly competent to estimate its value, suffered the same disappointments in their efforts to examine it.

In the meantime, Cardinal Angelo Mai printed (Rome, 1828-38) this manuscript, but it was not published until 1857 (in five volumes). The inaccuracies of the edition discounted its value from the first. In 1866, Tischendorf made a third attempt to see it, this time applying for leave to edit the document. He secured permission to study it under the supervision of C. Vercellone, for three hours a day. By the end of the eighth day he had, contrary to the conditions on which he was to use the manuscript, copied out bodily twenty pages. His permission was revoked, but upon entreaty he was given six more days. As a consequence of this opportunity, Tischendorf was able, in 1867, to publish, up to that time, the best edition of the text. Vercellone and his successors published a very complete edition in six folio volumes (Rome, 1868-81). But the best edition of all was a photographic facsimile of the entire work, issued in 1889-90, by which the manuscript itself is now made accessible to the scholars of the world.

121. Codex Vaticanus (B) was written in uncials on fine vellum, of three columns (of forty-two lines each) to a page 10 inches wide by 10½ inches high. The character of the writing is plain and simple, such as leads scholars to locate this manuscript in the first

half of the fourth century. It contains no enlarged letters, no pauses, no divisions into chapters or sections. Tischendorf· thought that the scribe of the New Testament was the same one who wrote a part of Codex Sinaiticus. This supposed identity of one of the scribes is evidence of contemporary character. There are corrections by several hands, some of which are of real value.

This codex originally contained the whole Greek Bible. In its present state, after all the ravages of time and use, it lacks Genesis 1: 1 to 46: 28; Psalms 106-138; all of Hebrews following chapter 9: 4; the Catholic Epistles and the Apocalypse.

But there are some marked differences between the two great manuscripts (S and B), just described. These consist in the character of the corrections found in the manuscript and the notable difference in the order of the books of the New Testament (in Codex Sinaiticus, Paul's Epistles precede the Acts, and Hebrews is found between 2 Thessalonians and 1 Timothy; in Codex Vaticanus the Catholic Epistles are between the Acts and Paul's Epistles, and the Hebrews precedes the Pastoral Epistles).

Most New Testament textual critics agree that B is, upon the whole, the best and oldest of the known manuscripts, but it must not be given absolute authority over all others. Westcott and Hort made large use of it in their text of the New Testament. In fact, both the Sinaitic and the Vatican codices until very recent times have not been accorded their full

meed of authority. The Alexandrian codex had so
long held the field almost alone, that only the strong-
est of arguments could win for these new documents
in the field of New Testament criticism their proper
places. B gives us, as does S, "the simplest, short-
est and concisest text." The charge that many important words are omitted is imaginary, say Westcott and Hort (p. 557). If B and S agree there is
usually strong evidence for the genuineness of a reading; if it is supported by ante-Nicene testimony it is
conclusive. Such concurrent testimony gives us the
most ancient readings, that may be traced to within
a century of the time when the original autographs
were penned.

122. Codex Ephræmi Syri (C), or Codex
Ephræm, is found in the National Library in Paris.
It was brought to Europe by Johannes Lascaris. At
his death in Rome, in 1535, this codex, with his whole
library, was purchased by Pietro Strozzi. The Medici family later bought it to add to their treasures.
Catharine de Medici carried it with her to Paris in
the first half of the sixteenth century, that she might
read in it, as she could, the sermons of St. Ephræm.
This codex is a palimpsest (that is, "rubbed off
again"). Its original writing had been partly rubbed
off, and over it had been written the sermons of
Ephræm. Near the end of the seventeenth century
Peter Allix, a student in the Royal Library, thought
he could see traces of a text underneath the sermons
of Ephræm. Careful investigation proved the truth

of his discovery. A few pages were made out and used in Mill's Greek Testament (1710). But not until 1834 was any good progress made in reading the underlying text. The application of specially prepared acid brought it out more clearly. But Tischendorf (1840-41) was the first to read in a successful manner the basal text. In 1842, he published his results, having read almost every word, and even having discovered the notes of several correctors of the text.

Codex Ephræm is a manuscript of the Greek Bible of the fifth century almost entirely erased by some scribe, probably because of the scarcity of vellum, and the small regard for this copy of the Bible, and he had written over it somewhere about the twelfth century, the works of the Syrian father, Ephræm. It is written in medium-sized uncials on pages 9½ inches wide by 12¼ inches high, one wide column to the page. The original manuscript presumably carried the entire Greek Bible. But its present contents preserve only sixty-four leaves of the Old Testament, and 145 out of an original 238 of the New. Parts of every New Testament book are found except 2 Thessalonians and 2 John. The "Eusebian sections" and the division into chapters appear in the Gospels, but in no other books. Scholars generally locate the writing of this manuscript in the fifth century. As an aid to the textual study of the New Testament this codex is very valuable. Dr. Scrivener set it about "midway between A and B, some-

Greek Bible. Codex Ephraem. Fifth Century. A palimpsest—Syriac written over the Greek in the Twelfth Century.
Matthew 20 : 16-23

what inclining to the latter." It does not belong to any one of the great families of texts, but rather partakes of the peculiarities of several of them. Reference to the Variorum Teachers' Bible shows how frequently textual critics make use of its readings as of real textual value.

123. Codex Bezæ (D) is now in the library of the University at Cambridge. Theodore Beza, the disciple and friend of Calvin, procured it from the monastery of St. Irenæus at Lyons, in 1562, but made little use of it because of its wide variations from other manuscripts. Beza presented it to the University of Cambridge in 1581. It was first published in facsimile type in 1793 (Cambridge) by Kipling, in two folio volumes. Dr. Scrivener issued it in common type with full introduction and critical notes in 1864.

This codex dates from the fifth or sixth century, and was written probably in France (Gaul). Its pages are eight inches wide by ten inches high. It carries a single wide column of Greek on the left-hand page, and facing it on the right hand a column of Latin. This is the oldest known manuscript on which two languages are found. The script of the two tongues is very similar, both being in large uncials. The lines are of uneven length, because of an. attempt to make each line conclude a sentence, phrase or clause. Several correctors have left their notes on this manuscript, some of whom were nearly contemporary with the time of the production of the manuscript itself.

The presence of the Latin text on this codex is evidence to scholars that this manuscript was written in western Europe, where Latin was the ruling tongue. Indeed, such a manuscript would have been of little use in the East. But what relation do these texts bear to each other? Is the Greek a translation of the Latin, or vice versa? Or are they independent texts? Or was one modified to suit the other? Opinions are divided on these points. Dr. Scrivener and most modern scholars have held that the Latin was modified to suit the Greek; but Professor Harris now maintains that the Greek has been changed to suit the Latin, and therefore has slight value in Greek textual work. Its text is then of a peculiar kind. It often agrees with the Old Latin and Syriac versions, in that it has some bold additions, modifications and interpolations. Dr. Hort says (Vol. 2, p. 149) : " At all events, when every allowance has been made for possible individual license, the text of D presents a truer image of the form in which the Gospels and Acts were most widely read in the third and probably a great part of the second century than any other extant Greek manuscript."

124. There are still more than one hundred uncial manuscripts, of secondary importance, dating from the fifth to the ninth and tenth centuries. These are mostly defective and fragmentary. No one of them is thought to have formed part of a complete Greek Bible, and only six of them contain more than one of the groups of New Testament books, if the Acts

and the Apocalypse be reckoned as two groups,—as held by the majority of New Testament scholars.

The cursive manuscripts, dating from the ninth to the fifteenth century, form a great collection. About thirty of them contain the whole New Testament. There are more than 600 cursives of the Gospels; more than 200 of the Acts and the Catholic Epistles; about 300 of the Pauline Epistles; and about 100 of the Apocalypse. A full catalogue both of uncials and cursives is found in Mitchell's Critical Handbook of the New Testament (1896); and a brief description by Dr. Ezra Abbott of many of the most important may be consulted in Schaff's Religious Encyclopædia (Vol. 1); and a more detailed and critical estimate in C. R. Gregory, Prolegomena to the eighth edition of Tischendorf's Greek Testament, published more recently in a revised edition in German. Prof. H. von Soden, of Berlin, has issued the first part of an elaborate work entitled, "Die Schriften des Neuen Testaments," which gives a fresh and complete survey of the material of New Testament text criticism.

CHAPTER XV

125. The last three chapters have treated the subject of the Greek manuscripts of the New Testament as the principal bases of our present day Greek Testament. These do not exhaust our sources, as we have already seen in the various references to the church fathers. Very early in the history of the Christian church the New Testament was translated into the tongues of the peoples who inhabited and bordered on the Greek-speaking world. As rapidly as Christianity pushed into these outer regions, the gospel had to be presented in the language of its converts. To do this most effectively it was translated from the Greek into the languages of several of the most influential peoples.

These several versions or translations furnish us only indirect evidence as to the readings of the original text. But the fact that some of them were made in the second century, almost two centuries back of the oldest Greek New Testament manuscript, gives them added value. They therefore stood nearly two hundred years closer to the autographs than Codex Vaticanus, our oldest manuscript, and were made, in fact, no more than a century, and perhaps a generation, after the penning of the latest New Testament books. In order, then, to make proper use of them in textual work, one must re-translate them into Greek, to see what the basis of their translation was.

But difficulty faces the scholar who attempts this kind of work. He must remember that these versions have been subject to the same kind of scribal errors and corruptions as those found in Greek and all other manuscripts. If now we had the first translation of each separate version from the Greek we should have a prize for determining the original Greek from which the translation was made. But we have neither this nor any manuscript of any of the versions reaching back of the fourth century. Of several of the versions there is not as yet any reliable critical edition. Scholars must either make scant use of what we have, or at great pains produce a text that gives us a consensus of the best readings of all the best manuscripts.

The most valuable of the versions of the New Testament are the Latin, the Syriac, the Coptic, the Ethiopic, the Gothic and the Armenian.

126. The Latin Bibles of the Old Testament were discussed somewhat in detail in Chapter VII. We observed there that the Old Latin was a translation, for the Old Testament, from the Septuagint, while for the New it was made directly from the original Greek. Of the Old Testament, the Old Latin text exists only in fragments, but in the New Testament the text is substantially complete. The Vulgate of the New Testament is a revision of the Old Latin

that was made by Jerome, one of the greatest biblical scholars of the early church, who did his work near the close of the fourth century.

From quotations in the writings of the Latin church fathers, such as Tertullian, Cyprian, Lucifer of Cagliari, Hilary of Poitiers, Ambrose, Jerome, Rufinus, Augustine and Pelagius, the Old Latin New Testament can be almost entirely recovered. The prevalence of this version in the second century is unquestioned. It was doubtless modified and often corrected to bring it into harmony with some of the variant readings of the Greek manuscripts found in the different provinces and dependencies of the Roman Empire. It was just these wide divergencies that led to the revision of the Old Latin version by Jerome in the latter part of the fourth century. Thus scholars find three groups of the Old Latin texts: (1) African, or N. African; (2) European; and (3) Italian.

The history of the origin or growth of these different families of texts is but imperfectly known. They are classified and arranged largely on the basis of the quotations of the fathers.

127. As the Vulgate superseded the Old Latin versions, the latter lost their authority in the Church. As a consequence the manuscripts of these versions fell into disuse, and in course of time largely vanished from sight. But there are about forty manuscripts and fragments of manuscripts of the Old Latin New Testament extant to-day. Some of them are so frag-

mentary as almost to be counted out. Of the Gospels there are no more than twenty-eight, fragments and all; of the Acts, seven; of the Catholic Epistles, five; of the Pauline Epistles, nine, and of the Apocalypse, three. Manuscripts of the Old Latin text are indicated by small Roman letters of the Latin alphabet, a, b, c, etc.

Some of the most notable of these manuscripts are: Codex Vercellensis (a), which contains the Gospels, with lacunæ, or gaps, in the Western order; that is, Matthew, John, Luke, Mark. It is written in silver letters, two columns to a page, on fine vellum. It is supposed to have been written by Eusebius, bishop of Vercelli, about 365 A. D., and is thus equal in age to the Greek New Testament manuscripts. It is now in the cathedral of Vercelli, Italy.

Codex Veronensis (b), contains, with some lacunæ, the Gospels, and belongs to the fourth or fifth century. It is of great value, and is preserved in Verona, Italy.

Codex Colbertinus (c), contains the Gospels in Old Latin, and the rest of the New Testament in the Vulgate. It was written in the eleventh or twelfth century in Languedoc, where the Old Latin was used down to a late period in history. It is a valuable document, and is preserved in Paris.

Codex Bezæ (d), compare §123.

Codex Brixianus (f), contains the Gospels, with a few lacunæ. It seems to be an Italian text. It dates from the sixth century, and is now at Brescia.

Codex Palatinus (e), a mere fragment, but African in type, of the fourth or fifth century. It is now in Vienna.

Codex Bobiensis (k), a fifth or sixth century form of the African text. This and the preceding text(e) were pronounced by Tischendorf to have remarkable value.

The manuscripts of the Gospels mentioned above and others in the list extant can be classified under the three texts already mentioned, viz.: the African, European and Italian; some, however, are so mixed as to be indeterminate.

128. The Acts is represented by Codex Bezæ (d) (§123); by the Latin text of the bilingual Codex Laudianus (e), which has the Latin text on the left and the Greek on the right-hand page, the reverse of Codex Bezæ. It is written in large uncials in lines of uneven length, some of them containing no more than one or two words. The text is admittedly Western, sprinkled with Alexandrian readings. It dates from the sixth century, and was presented by Archbishop Laud to the library of Oxford in 1636. It is by far the most valuable biblical manuscript possessed by that library. Codex Gigas Holmiensis (g), said to be the largest manuscript in the world, contains the Acts and Apocalypse in the Old Latin, and the rest of the New Testament in the Vulgate, also some fragments of a palimpsest of the fifth or sixth century.

The Pauline Epistles are represented by Codex

Old Latin Gospels.   Codex Vercellensis.   Late Fourth Century.
John 16 : 23-30

Claromontanus (d), a bilingual text after the style of D (§123), which holds an important place in the estimation of textual critics. It may belong to Codex Bezæ, and is here classified under the same but with a small letter indicative of its relative position among manuscripts.

The seven Catholic Epistles, which usually follow Acts in the Greek manuscripts, were not all incorporated into the Latin canon until the fourth century. 1 Peter, 1 John and Jude were the only ones previously recognized and received. One of the best representatives of this division of the New Testament is Codex Corbeiensis of James (ff), a manuscript of the tenth century. This text is now in St. Petersburg. This translation is thought to be as old as the early part of the fourth century. Cyprian supplies numerous quotations from what appears to be the African text of these epistles.

The Apocalypse formed part of the Old Latin New Testament as far back as we can trace it. The African text of the Apocalypse does not seem to have been revised in the fourth century as were other parts of the New Testament except Acts. Hence the text found in Primasius' commentary of the sixth century differs only slightly from the text quoted in Cyprian. The quotations from the Apocalypse in the writings of the church fathers are so numerous as almost to determine with certainty the character of the text from which they quoted.

Of the manuscripts and fragments named in these

two sections, two are bilinguals, Codex Bezæ (Evan. d), and Codex Claromontanus (Paul. d); four, as well as Evan. d, viz.: Codd. Vercellensis (Evan. a), Veronensis (Evan. b), Palatinus. (Evan. e), and Bobiensis (Evan. k), are dated in the fifth or fourth century, when they were in use in the Christian church.

129. The above mentioned manuscripts were doubtless written just as the Old Latin was gradually receding from its position of influence and power in its competition with the revised New Testament of Jerome. The fact that the two versions existed side by side for a couple of centuries—the fourth to the sixth—contributed toward an intermixture of the two texts. Scholars and scribes who either studied the two translations or copied them, were not always careful to refrain from either inserting on the margins or incorporating into the text, familiar expressions or explanations from one or other of the texts. Such simultaneous use of two similar Latin versions led to a larger mixture of the two versions in the case of the New Testament than in the Old.

The superiority of Jerome's translation of the Old Testament doubtless led scholars to look with greater favor on his revised New Testament. Not only the faithfulness of its revision on the basis of the Greek, but its harmonistic character—an attempted union of the different Old Latin texts—also gave Jerome's work a larger place in the thoughts of leaders in the church.

Another fact in its adoption is significant: " in the

Greek
Codex Claromontanus (d) (§ 128). Fourth or Fifth Century
Romans 7 : 4-7

Latin

sixth century, in Gaul, most of the books of the Old Testament are quoted from Jerome, while for the New Testament the Old Latin holds its own " (White, Hastings' Dict. of the Bible, iv. 877). The sixth century saw the almost universal adoption of the Vulgate by the leaders in the church, except in Africa. The real victory for the Vulgate was achieved when Pope Gregory the Great (590-604) put the new revision on a par with the Old Latin text. In his commentary on Job he even expresses a preference for Jerome's revision.

130. This substantial endorsement of Jerome's work by the Roman pontiff radiated its influence throughout the Roman Empire and gave it an impetus that it had never before received by any high authority. Such supreme recognition, however, could not at once cast into the background a text revered like the Old Latin. In fact, Jerome's text in some provinces, notably in Gaul, had become distressingly corrupt, while in Italy it was kept comparatively pure. Among our minor sources of information, such as the late manuscripts, Lectionaries, quotations and selections in service books of the church, we learn that the Old Latin text held its own for several centuries. One old manuscript from the ninth century (St. Germain) retains the Old Latin text of Judith, Tobit and Matthew. Codex Colbertinus (c), already noticed (§127), of the twelfth or thirteenth century, has the Gospels in Old Latin, and the rest of the New Testament in the Vulgate. The Perpignan manuscript

(of Paris) of the thirteenth century, has Acts 1 : 1 to
13 : 7, and 28 : 15-31 in Old Latin, but the Gospels in
the Vulgate.

Christianity's conquest of Great Britain and Ireland took place while the Old Latin still held sway.
Augustine's mission to England introduced there the
Vulgate. The scholars of Northumbria soon adopted
this improved text, and later secured the great
Codex Amiatinus, already mentioned (§67), one of
the best manuscripts of the entire Vulgate now extant.

The Irish, too, until after Columba's time, used the
Old Latin ; a single almost pure Old Latin text of the
Gospels is extant in Codex Usserianus (r). After the
year 700 the Vulgate text gained an increasingly
strong foothold among the Irish, with the result that
the Latin Bibles of Ireland and North Britain partook
of a mixed type of manuscripts of which the Book of
Armagh is an example. A discussion of the early
texts in England is reserved for Chapter XIX.

131. There were early attempts to arrest the corruptions of the Vulgate,—to purge from it the arbitrary interpolations of scribes and scholars. Within
about 150 years after Jerome's day Cassiodorus made
a serious attempt to revise the current text of Jerome. The bulk of our information regarding his
work is found in his own instruction to the younger
brethren in the monastery at Vivarium, about 544.
He desires that they study their Bibles in the
" emended codices," and says that his nine codices,

quia inpotestate erat
sermo ipsius
et in synagoga erat homo habens
daemonium inmundum
et exclamauit uoce magna
dicens
sine quid nobis et tibi ihu
nazarene uenisti perdere nos
scio te quis sis scs di
et increpauit illi ihs dicens
ommutesce et exi ab illo
et cum proiecisset illud
daemonium inmedium
exiit ab illo nihil que
illum nocuit
et pae tus est pauor in omnib
et conloquebantur
adinuicem dicentes
quod est hoc uerbum
quia inpotestate et uirtute
imperat spiritibus
inmundis et exeunt
et diuulgabatur fama de illo
in omnem locum regionis
surgens autem de synagoga
introiuit indomum simonis
socrus autem simonis
tenebatur magnis febrib
et rogauerunt illum pro ea
et instans super illam impera
uit febri et dimisit illam
et continuo surgens
ministrabat illis
cum sol autem occidisset
omnes qui habebant infir
mos uariis languoribus
ducebant illos ad eum
at ille singulis manus impo
nens curabat eos
exiebant etiam daemonia
amultis clamantia et di
centia quia tues filius di
et increpans non sinebat
ea loqui

quia sciebant ipsum esse xpm
facta autem die egressus ibat
indesertum locum
et turbae requirebant eum
et uenerunt usque ad ipsu
et detinebant illum
ne discederet ab eis
quib ille ait quia et aliis ciui
tatibus oportet me euan
gelizare regnum di
quia ideo missus sum
et erat praedicans in syna
gogis galilaeae
factum est autem cum
turbae inruerent in eum
ut audirent uerbum di
et ipse stabat secus stagnu
genesareth
et uidit duas naues stantes
secus stagnum
piscatores autem discende
rant et lauabant retia
ascendens autem in unam
nauem quae erat
simonis
rogauit autem a terra
reducere pusillum
et sedens docebat
denauicula turbas
ut cessauit autem loqui
dixit ad simonem
duc in altum et laxate retia
uestra in capturam
et respondens simon
dixit illi
praeceptor per totam
noctem laborantes
nihil cepimus
in uerbo autem tuo
laxabo rete
et cum hoc fecissent
concluserunt piscium
multitudinem copiosam
rumpebatur autem rete cor

Codex Amiatinus (⅔ 67, 130). Seventh Century. Leading Manuscript of
the Vulgate
Luke 4 : 32b to 5 : 6

covering the whole Bible, were revised by him " with the collation of early codices," and that he left them a Greek pandect, or whole Bible, by which, as Jerome had done, they could correct the errors in their Latin version. We have no list of the corrections of Cassiodorus, nor have we any fragment of his work, unless it be part of the great Codex Amiatinus (of the eighth century), already described. The divisions of this codex and its introductory matter accord with Cassiodorus' own account of his work.

The Vulgate carried to England, and thence also into Ireland, in Augustine's day and immediately thereafter, becoming somewhat modified by the Old Latin, was later carried to the continent, to France, Switzerland and Germany. It was copied and multiplied by Irish and British monks in continental monasteries, and further changed to accord with other texts found in these several countries. To this condition of things we are indebted for the prolific crop of manuscripts from the ninth century.

The Moors practically shut up northwestern Spain to itself. Closed in their mountain fastnesses the Spanish monks perpetuated their own Old Latin Bible, which they added to, interpolated, expanded to suit their fancy until their text became exceedingly corrupt. The Irish manuscripts that had been brought to Europe and the Spanish documents met in Gaul or France, and presented a double confusion to Bible students. This condition of things invited correction.

132. Charlemagne was fully aware of the existing confusion and set about to find a remedy, that the church might have a unified or uniform standard Bible. The records tell us that in 797 he put the task into the hands of an Englishman, Alcuin, abbot of St. Martin at Tours. Having at hand both Spanish and Irish manuscripts, he sent to his native place, Northumbria, for additional documents, and documents of a less corrupt character. On the basis of these manuscripts, regardless of the Greek, Alcuin revised the current Latin Bible. On Christmas, 801, Alcuin presented to Charlemagne his revised edition of the Latin Bible. This is most nearly represented to-day in the fine Codex Vallicellianus at Rome.

Others besides Charlemagne became conscious of the need of a revision of the Bible. Theodulf, bishop of Orleans (787-821), through his acquaintance with southern France and northern Spain; put himself in possession of both Irish and Spanish manuscripts. By a study of all these texts, with commendable zeal and industry, Theodulf produced a revised text of the Vulgate. But his revision is not of much critical value, because of its unevenness, and of his method of putting in the margin the variants which he had collected, and of thus giving a permanent place to many corruptions of the Spanish texts. This revision is best represented by a Latin Bible in the National Library at Paris, numbered Lat. 9380. Theodulf's privately undertaken revision exercised little influence on the history of the text.

INCIPITLIBER
ISAIAE·PRO
PHETAE ▾

Cap. I.

ISIOISA
IAEFILII
AMOS·
QUAM·UI
DITSUP
IUDAM·
ETHIERU
SALEM·IN
DIEBUS·O
ZIAE·IOATHĀ

achaz ezechiae regum iuda· Auditecaeli
etauribuspercipite terra qnm dns locutus
est filios enutriui etexaltaui· lpsiautem
spreueruntme· Cognouit bos possessorē
suum etasinuspraesepedominisui· lsrahel
noncognouitme· populusmeus nonintelle
xit· Uaegentipeccatricipopulograui·Ini
quitate semini nequam filiis sceleratis·

133. The monastery of St. Gall, near Lake Constance in Switzerland, was the home of a particularly zealous and active school of Bible students in the ninth century. Irish monks flocked to its retreat and took with them their own style of writing. Under the great scholar Hartmut, in the ninth century, this school produced many biblical manuscripts written by Irish scribes, and in imitation of the Irish style of script, by native scribes. This peculiar style seems to have prevailed in the upper Rhine valley. The text, however, perpetuated at this place came from Italy and Spain.

But the close of the ninth century saw the decline of Charlemagne's influence, the deterioration of the biblical texts copied in the monasteries, and the decadence of the power of Christianity in France. The invasion of the Normans crushed the school at Tours, and the Danes broke up the famous schools at Wearmouth and Jarrow in England. By these calamities, biblical scholarship of every kind received almost a death-dealing blow. Efforts to regain a footing seemed to be almost in vain. Lanfranc, the archbishop of Canterbury (1069-89) is said to have done some correcting of all the books of the Bible and to have taught his pupils the same. But unfortunately nothing of these labors remains. Stephen Harding, abbot of Citeaux, about the middle of the twelfth century collated good Latin and Greek manuscripts and made a revision of some considerable value that is now preserved in four volumes in the library at Dijon,

France. Cardinal Nicolaus Maniacoria likewise issued
a revision, now extant in a manuscript at Venice.

134. The thirteenth century was marked by an
astounding spirit of revision in France, due in the
main to the influence of the king, St. Louis, and to
the vigorous scholarship generated by the new University of Paris.   There was most extraordinary
activity in the production of new Latin Bibles. Roger
Bacon tells us that theologians and booksellers combined to produce a fixed type of text, which he calls
Exemplar Parisiense.   The fame of the University
created a large demand for these books, and they
went far and wide.   But the Exemplar Parisiense
was a corrupt text which Bacon deplored. This de-
fect scholars attempted to remedy by uniting their
researches in the production of a list of corrections
based mainly on Latin and Greek manuscripts and
called Correctoria Bibliorum. Four separate bodies
of men or individuals prepared as many lists of corrections to be employed by the Bible students and
copyists in Paris and in Rome. These counters to
the multiplication of degenerate texts of the Vulgate
furnished a partial remedy to the growing evil. The
most important contribution to the form of our Bible
that sprang out of the Paris activity was the formal
division of the Bible into chapters. Paragraph and
section divisions had already existed for centuries.
But Stephen Langton, a doctor in the University of
Paris, and later archbishop of Canterbury, made the
divisions of our Bible known as chapters, about 1228.

135. The masses of corrections that had been collected were put to good use before the Vulgate was put into permanent form by the printing press. When the literary revival of the fifteenth century struck the various national coteries of biblical students, strenuous effort was made to find the best possible text of each version. At the invention of printings steps were taken to put the Latin Bible into permanent form. The first complete book to be issued from the printing press was a Latin Bible—the Vulgate—printed in two volumes by Gutenberg and Fust, at Mayence (Mainz), in 1455. It is commonly known as the " Mazarin Bible," for it was first found in recent times in the library of Cardinal Mazarin. It was made, however, from some inferior manuscripts, and, with all its beauty as a piece of mechanism, it is full of errors. Thenceforth Latin Bibles poured forth in profusion from the press. It is said that during the first half century of printing 124 editions were published. In 1514 ff. the Complutensian Polyglot presented as one of its texts the Vulgate revised with the aid of several ancient manuscripts. In 1528, Stephanus' Vulgate Bible, a critical text based on three manuscripts, was issued at Paris; later (1538-40) a larger edition appeared, which had been prepared on the basis of seventeen manuscripts. This is in reality the foundation of the official Roman Vulgate, adopted at the Council of Trent, April 8, 1546. The first Latin Bible to contain the modern verse divisions was a small octavo edition of Stephanus, dated 1555.

The authority granted by the Council of Trent for the publication of an official Vulgate was not immediately put to use. Professor John Hentenius, of the University of Louvain, by the use of thirty-one manuscripts and two printed copies, prepared a private edition (1547) that was often reprinted. Several of the popes bestirred themselves to prepare an official edition that would answer the requirements of the church. The oldest and best manuscripts were collected and a commission was appointed to edit an official text. The work lagged, however, until Sixtus V came to the pontificate in 1585(-90). With great zeal and diligence both he and his commission pushed forward the work. Manuscripts, printed editions, and the original Hebrew and Greek were taken into consideration, the readings which agreed with the Hebrew and Greek receiving the preference where there was disagreement between authorities.

The edition produced by the commission was printed and published by the Vatican press in three volumes in 1590, and was designated the " Sixtine Edition." It bore on its title page: " Biblia Sacra Vulgatæ Editionis, tribus tomis, distincta Romæ, ex Typographia Apostolica Vaticana, M. D. XC." On the second page we meet the papal designation: "Biblia Sacra Vulgatæ editionis ad concilii Tridentini præscriptum emendata et a Sixto. v. P. M. recognita et approbata." This edition was intended to be that authorized by the Council of Trent; and by the bull recited in the preface it was to be used in all the churches in the Christian world. No other edition should be published without the permission of the Apostolic See, nor should this " Sixtine Edition " be reprinted in any other place than the Vatican for the next ten years. Such editions as should appear subsequently should be carefully collated with the Sixtine edition, should be accompanied with an official attestation, and should have "no variant readings, scholia or glosses printed in the margin." Violation of these orders was to be punished by the greater excommunication.

136. This first official Vulgate, the Sixtine edition of 1590, did not meet with a universal and enthusiastic reception. Its requirements and its new translations were unpopular, and the death of its great projector, Pope Sixtus V, in the same year were distinct setbacks to the dissemination of the new edition. In January, 1592, after the death of a number of popes, Clement VIII occupied the pontifical seat. Having called in the Sixtine edition of the Vulgate, he published another official edition, claiming as a pretext that Sixtus V had intended both to recall the 1590 edition because of its many typographical errors, and to issue another in its place, but death had prevented it. In reality, his claim was only a pretext, for the Sixtine edition had been carefully printed and published. The reasons for the publication of the Clementine text of 1592 are thought to have been either hostility to the author of the 1590 edition or a desire to produce a more faithful text as authorized

by the Council of Trent. The text of this new edition of 1592 contains about three thousand variations from that of 1590, and leans toward the text issued privately by Hentenius in 1547. H. J. White (Hastings' Dict. of the Bible, Vol. iv. p. 881) concedes the superiority of the Clementine text. Pope Clement VIII avoided the penalties of the Sixtine edition preface by inserting on the title page the name of Sixtus V, thus in reality issuing it as a new Sixtine edition. After 1604 Clement's name appears on the title page conjointly with that of Sixtus V. This Clementine Vulgate of 1592 is to-day the standard edition of the Roman Catholic church. The few modern editions that have been issued contain slight variations only from this Clementine text of 1592. Hetzenauer has published an edition of the New Testament Vulgate (1899) that correctly represents its great predecessor, the Clementine text.

137. The importance of the Vulgate in the history of Bible translations and of the church cannot be overestimated. It has occupied the first place in the Roman church since the sixth century. It was early carried to England and was the basis of the Christianity that took such deep root in that rich soil. Charlemagne made it his personal duty to scatter it far and wide in his realm. The monks of the middle ages multiplied its copies by the hundreds, so that manuscripts reaching into the thousands are found in numerous private and public libraries of Europe and the Orient. The invention of printing began to

fix certain texts, and the process culminated in the Clementine edition of 1592, the official Bible of the Roman church. The first English Bible—that of Wycliffe—was translated from the Vulgate. This version was the basis of the Rheims and Douai translation of 1582-1610, the official English Bible of the Roman church. There were later revisions of this version under the care of Challoner (1750 and later), of the Douai institution, and of archbishop Troy (1791 and after), of Dublin. These editions were current in Great Britain about 1800. Slightly variant editions of these have held the field of the Roman church in America down to the present day.

138. Protestant scholars have expended long years in an attempt to construct a critical text of Jerome's Latin. They have carefully studied and collated thousands of manuscripts, and many printed editions that thereby they may ascertain the original of that great version. Some of the most active in this research have been Richard Bentley, in the eighteenth century; Bishop Wordsworth and H. J. White, in the nineteenth century—all in England; Samuel Berger, in Paris, France, and P. Corssen, in Berlin, Germany. The contributions of these five scholars are monumental. The prosecution of just such work by many other devoted students of the multitude of manuscripts now available will go far to ascertain the original version of the revered scholar, Jerome.

CHAPTER XVI

THE SYRIAC AND OTHER EASTERN VERSIONS

139. The Syriac Old Testament occupied our attention in Chapter VIII. One of the first requirements of the Syrian converts to Christianity was an edition of the New Testament in their native tongue. Just how early it was made is not known. Indeed, there are many questions regarding the origin of the Syriac New Testament which still remain unanswered. This chapter can give only in outline some of the most interesting points in the discussion.

The easiest method of presenting the facts regarding the earlier Syriac texts will be to take up the usual divisions of the New Testament one at a time.

THE GOSPELS.—The earliest editions of the Gospels in Syriac that are now known to biblical scholars are (1) the " Diatessaron " of Tatian; (2) the Old Syriac Version or "Gospel of the Separated;" and (3) the " Peshitta." Just when, where, how, and why these versions came to be, are the puzzling questions that confront us. The existence of some of these texts was not known in Europe until the sixteenth century. Some of them have even come to light within the last seventy-five years, showing us that there is still a great branch of biblical literature comparatively unknown and uncultivated.

176

(1) The earliest version of the Syriac Gospels current in the early centuries of Christianity was the so-called Diatessaron of Tatian, who was a pupil of Justin Martyr (martyred about 165). This Diatessaron was a composite Gospel based on the four Gospels, to which the Syrian church became so wedded that the bishops in the fifth century took vigorous steps to get rid of it. They were apparently entirely successful, for there is no known copy of this Syriac Diatessaron in existence to-day. Our chief authorities for the text of it are (a) the Arabic translation of it, of which there are two manuscripts in Rome, and (b) the commentary of Ephræm Syrus (died 373), found only in an Armenian translation. A few quotations of this Syriac Diatessaron are found in some Syriac commentaries on the Gospels,—enough to indicate somewhat the character of the version.

140. (2) The second version of the Syriac Gospels used in the early church was the " Gospel according to the Separated (Evangelists)," according to Burkitt's rendering (Ency. Biblica, col. 4999). This version is known to-day in two codices: (a) The manuscript found at the Convent of St. Mary Deipara in the Nitrian Desert in 1842-47, now in the British Museum, and published by Cureton in 1858, and since known as the "Curetonian Syriac." (b) The palimpsest discovered at the Convent of St. Catharine at Mt. Sinai by Mrs. Lewis in 1892, and only partially transcribed in the next year by Messrs. Bensly, Harris and Burkitt. The " Cureton " text is assigned

to the middle of the fifth century, and contains the
Gospels with many omissions in the order of Matthew, Mark, John, and Luke.   The Sinai palimpsest
is thought to be a half century older than the " Cureton."   Its contents are about three-quarters of the
whole material, and supplement " Cureton," and parallel it in such a manner as to give us a reasonably
good text, with variations, of course, of the " Old
Syriac."

(3)   The Peshitta, " the simple," version of the
New Testament has been in use in the Syrian church
continuously from the fifth century.   This name,
however, is not traced farther back than the ninth
century.   It has been conjectured that the name arose
in order to distinguish the Syriac version proper from
that version translated from Origen's Hexapla by
Paul of Tella (§70).

This version is extant in some manuscripts that are
dated in the fifth century.   These manuscripts differ
slightly, however, from the texts of modern editions.
The first printed edition was issued in Vienna, 1555, at
the expense of the emperor, Ferdinand I, by Albert
Widmanstad.   The latest and best edition appeared at
Oxford, 1901, edited by Pusey and Gwilliam.   Westcott and Hort called this version the " Syriac Vulgate."

Each new discovery of Syriac manuscripts of the
Gospels has shifted the discussion as to the relation
of these three versions.   Burkitt (Ency. Biblica)
now concludes, though all scholars do not agree with

him, that the Diatessaron of Tatian was the original form in which the Gospel circulated in Syria. The "Gospel according to the Separated," that is, the second early Syriac Version, is supposed to have been translated from the Greek about the year 200. The third of the three early versions, the Peshitta, is regarded as an edition of the "Gospel according to the Separated," "revised in closer conformity with the Greek," and published with authority, probably in the beginning of the fifth century (411 A. D.), with the purpose of superseding both the Diatessaron and all other Syriac texts. Both of those purposes were accomplished with such thoroughness that no Syriac version of the Diatessaron, and only two copies of the "Gospel according to the Separated," or Old Syriac, are known to-day.

141. The Acts and the Epistles. Up to the present time there is no manuscript or even text of the so-called "Old Syriac," of the Acts and the Pauline Epistles. There is no doubt that there was such a version, for it is distinctly confirmed in the quotations of Aphraates, and in the commentaries of Ephræm. These letters are current only in an Armenian translation, for the supremacy of the Peshitta must have forced out of use all rival Syriac texts. These portions of the New Testament are found, however, in the Peshitta version. The Gospels and the Acts and Epistles formed the entire New Testament of the early Syriac church.

The Catholic Epistles and the Apocalypse, therefore,

were not found in the Old Syriac version. Addai
gives orders as follows : " The Law and the Prophets . . . and the Epistles of Paul . . . and
the Acts of the Twelve Apostles . . . these books
read ye in the churches of Christ, and with these
read not any other, as there is not any other, in which
the truth that ye hold is written " (quoted by Nestle
in Hastings' Dict. of Bible, Vol. iv. p. 647.)   It is
regarded as fixed that the Syriac canon in the middle
of the fourth century contained neither the Catholic
Epistles nor the Apocalypse.

A list of the canonical books recently discovered
at Mt. Sinai gives an arrangement that differs from
that in the Peshitta.   We find here Galatians at the
head of Paul's letters as follows : Galatians, Corinthians, Romans, then Hebrews.   Ephræm seems to have
had the same order.   Another interesting item in
Ephræm's day is that the church at Edessa had in
its canon of the Bible the " Apocryphal Correspondence of St. Paul and the Corinthians," which is now
known to have belonged to the Acta Pauli.   It is now
certain that the four Antilegomena of the Catholic
Epistles and the Apocalypse were never a part of
the Peshitta and never appeared in a printed edition
of the Syriac New Testament until 1630.

142. The Peshitta was the supreme version in the
Syriac churches in the fourth century ; and since the
Nestorian schism (about 431) has continued to
be the New Testament of that body of believers.
The Jacobite branch of the Syrian church, on the

other hand, was not satisfied with the current authoritative version. There were at least two attempts to carry over into the Syriac canon the full list of books found in the Greek New Testament, and used by the Greek-speaking churches.

The first attempt to revise the Peshitta was made in 508, by Philoxenus, bishop of Mabbogh (485-519) in Eastern Syria, with the assistance of Polycarp. They endeavored to translate the whole Bible into Syriac. Authorities disagree as to whether any of this version is still extant, though the versions of 2 Peter, 2 and 3 John, and Jude, that are now bound up with the Peshitta are thought to owe their origin to Philoxenus. A manuscript of the Apocalypse of this version was discovered by Gwynn and published in 1897.

The Philoxenian version of the New Testament was revised in 616 by Thomas of Heraklea (Harkel) in Mesopotamia, and of the Old Testament by Paul of Tella (compare §70). This translation is excessively literal and well supplied with critical notes. The work of Thomas of Heraklea was based on some Greek manuscripts found in Alexandria, and the notes contain important variants in some of these documents. Apparently the Greek manuscripts used by Thomas were late, and belong to the Western type.

Some of the manuscripts of the Harkleian version lay claim to a considerable antiquity. There are at least thirty-six of them. Two in the British Museum date from the tenth century. Cambridge University

·has one dated 1170. Rome has one of the seventh and one of the eighth century. Florence has one dated 757. Both of these revisions contained all the books of the New Testament except the Apocalypse.

Though there is scarcely a Syriac manuscript in all Europe that contains the twenty-seven books of the present New Testament, there are some manuscripts which contain books not found in our Greek New Testament. Codex 1700 in Cambridge University library contains " The Epistles of St. Clement to the Corinthians in Syriac." These Epistles stand between the Catholic and Pauline Epistles, and have the same notations for use in church services. Other manuscripts contain Clement's de Virginibus, or de Virginitate. These instances show the unique development of the Syriac church and scholarship.

143. The above noted versions complete the genuine Syriac texts of the New Testament. There is another fragmentary version, however, that is classified as Syriac, on about the same grounds that the Targums are counted as Hebrew. The Aramaic language is divided into the classical Edessene, or Eastern Aramaic, and the Western Aramaic, covering Jewish Aramaic, Samaritan, etc. This version is used by the Malkite (Greek) church in Palestine and Egypt. It was discovered in a Lectionary in the Vatican library, and described by Assemani and Adler (1789), and published in two volumes by Count Erizzo (1861-64), and by Prof. Lagarde (1892). Those two learned English women already referred to, Mrs. Lewis and

Codex of the Old Syriac Gospels over which was written in A. D. 778 a
narrative of the Holy Women. Found at Convent of
St. Catharine in 1892. Matthew 1 : 1-17a

Mrs. Gibson, republished (1899) the known fragments of the Gospels on the basis of two new manuscripts found at Mt. Sinai.   Fragments of Acts and the Epistles of Paul, with James and Hebrews have also been added to the known fragments of this version.

The relation of the fragments of the so-called Palestinian version or Jerusalem Syriac, to the other Syriac versions is apparent.   It contains a text that has been influenced by the Peshitta, but follows quite faithfully the Greek text.   It is thought to have arisen in the sixth century, when an attempt was made by Justinian to root out the Samaritan beliefs and replace them by supplying a version of the New Testament in the vernacular of the Jews of Palestine.   It is even asserted by some scholars that the language of this version is probably closely identified with that spoken by the peoples of Palestine in the time of Christ.

144.   The Egyptian or Coptic versions of the Old Testament were noticed in §83.   The three branches of the Egyptian versions of the New Testament are (1) the Sahidic, or dialect of upper Egypt; (2) the dialect of middle Egypt, as seen in the Fayyûm; (3) the dialect of Alexandria, the Bohairic.

The Sahidic was the dialect of the Christian community whose headquarters was at Thebes.   At the end of the eighteenth century (1799) Woide published the known fragments of the Sahidic New Testament. Within recent years large numbers of fragments have been discovered, almost enough to complete the New

Testament. Some of these reach back to the fifth and possibly to the fourth century. They are very numerous in Paris, and when critically edited will form a useful apparatus in determining the character of the Greek New Testament from which they were translated, somewhere back in the fourth century.

The second Coptic dialect is the Bohairic, the primitive Christian language of lower Egypt after the decline and disappearance of the Greek in the early Christian centuries. Its central city and home was at first Alexandria, and afterwards Memphis, hence this dialect has been called, though improperly, Memphitic. This was the literary language of Alexandria, expressing with remarkable precision such ideas as may be translated from the Greek. While its age relative to the Sahidic is in dispute, Burkitt (Ency. Bibl., col. 5008) and many others are convinced of its late origin. Its artistically complete language rapidly gave it supremacy throughout all Egypt, so that " Coptic " to-day means the " Bohairic " dialect. The oldest known codices of this tongue that can be certainly dated belong to the twelfth century, though there are some fragments that reach back to the ninth (888). Of the Coptic dialects, the Bohairic is the only one which preserves a complete New Testament. Of this version Horner issued Vol. I, the Gospels, in London, 1898. Burkitt describes the peculiarities of the Bohairic as (1) greater faithfulness to the Greek; (2) a different choice of Greek words to be transliterated; (3) when it has a different Greek reading from others, it is almost always a specifically "Alexandrian" reading.

Both Sahidic and Bohairic carry the full Greek canon of the New Testament, though the Apocalypse seems to have been regarded as non-canonical, for it is not part of these manuscripts of the New Testament.

The existence of an Egyptian version occupying a place midway between the Sahidic and Bohairic is fully established. This seems to have been current in the Fayyûm, just west and southwest of Memphis and south of the delta. Large numbers of manuscripts from this district have reached Europe in recent years. When these shall have been carefully edited, and a new text of the Sahidic New Testament published, we shall know where the Fayyûmic version stands in the Coptic group.

145. The Armenian version of the New Testament originated somewhere about 400 A. D. The earliest translations of the Gospels and the Epistles into Armenian were made from the Syriac, not from the Peshitta, but from the Old Syriac. About the middle of the fifth century this translation was so thoroughly revised by the use of a Greek text that we can scarcely recognize at its base, the first text. This Greek text was probably that of the Vatican and Sinaitic, or one closely related to them.

Armenian manuscripts of the Gospels usually lack Mark 16: 9-20. Those that contain these verses have a break after 16: 8, in which the colophon, "Gospel of Mark," is inserted, and it appears again after

16: 20. One manuscript, dated 989 A. D., contains
the doubtful verses, with a heading ascribing them to
the presbyter Aristion. It is thought that the scribe
of the manuscript had authority for attributing the
story of the resurrection to the presbyter who added
it to the Gospel of Mark. This same manuscript likewise, among all old Armenian manuscripts, is the only
one that contains the story of the woman taken in
adultery (John 8: 1-11). The oldest manuscript of
the Armenian version is dated 887 A. D., and two
others belong to the same century, while a half-dozen
originated in the tenth century.

The best critical edition of the Armenian version is
that of Zohrab (Venice, 1789).

146. The Ethiopic or Ge'ez version is that used by
the Abyssinians. While Christianity secured a foothold in this country as early as the fourth century, the
Ethiopic version probably does not reach back beyond
the fifth century. There are traces of an older Ethiopic version of the Gospels made from the Old Syriac,
as was the case in the Armenian version. But the
version now current was made from the Greek. There
are many manuscripts of a late date, representing
later revisions, which were made from the mediæval
Arabic text current in Alexandria. The Ethiopic New
Testament was first printed in Rome in 1548-9, and
was reprinted in Walton's Polyglot. The British and
Foreign Bible Society issued (1830) an edition that
had been prepared by T. P. Platt. This was reprinted
at Basle in 1874. It has no critical value for

Gothic Gospels (§§ 85, 147)
Mark 7 : 3-7

scholars. But it is ascertained at least that it is related to the Vatican and Sinaitic manuscripts in the type of text. It is colored also by Alexandrian and Western elements. These, however, cannot be correctly estimated until we shall have a critical text.

147. The Gothic version prepared by Ulfilas has already been referred to in §85. The New Testament fragments of this translation show that it was made directly from the Greek. The remnants that we possess seem to have belonged to northern Italy, somewhere about the time of the Lombard conquest in the sixth century. The largest fragments that we possess are portions of the Gospels preserved in a superb manuscript at Upsala, Sweden, written upon purple vellum in letters of silver and gold, and dating from the sixth century. Portions of the Pauline Epistles are found on a palimpsest in Milan. The remainder of the New Testament is lost. The Greek text from which Ulfilas made his New Testament translation was mainly of the so-called Syrian type. Westcott and Hort (N. T., vol. 1, p. 158) conclude in these words : " The Gothic has very much the same combination as the Italian revision of the Old Latin, being largely Syrian and largely Western, with a small admixture of non-Western readings."

148. There are several other versions that may be mentioned by name only. The Arabic versions of the New Testament have been made, some from the Syriac and some from the Greek, in the eighth and ninth centuries. The current Arabic New Testament

is a translation in the main from the Bohairic dialect, with corrections and additions from the Greek and Syriac.

The Georgian New Testament was translated from the Greek, but at so late a period as to be of slight critical value. The Slavonic version exists in a goodly number of manuscripts. The New Testament is preserved both in manuscripts and in Lectionaries. These do not seem to reach back earlier than the eleventh century. While the best text of the Slavonic or Russian points to a Greek-text basis, that basis does not contain the readings of the oldest and best manuscripts. Hence this version has no considerable value as a critical aid in determining the original readings of the New Testament.

No other versions of the New Testament are of sufficient value to deserve mention at this point.

CHAPTER XVII

GROUPING AND CLASSIFICATION OF MANUSCRIPTS, VERSIONS, AND OTHER WITNESSES

149. As soon as modern scholars began to compare different manuscripts, and to note the variations of each from the other they were obliged to adopt some one text as a standard. This necessity brought about the adoption of what has been known as the " received text," or " Textus Receptus."

The earliest printed edition of the Greek New Testament was that incorporated in the Complutensian Polyglot, printed in 1514-17 and published in 1522. Its text, however, was based on many manuscripts, put at the disposal of Cardinal Ximenes by the papal authorities at Rome. Erasmus, the Dutch scholar, was the editor of the first Greek New Testament published (1516). His text was based chiefly on two inferior manuscripts, preserved in Basle, Switzerland, one of the Gospels, and one of the Acts and the Epistles, and only one manuscript of the Apocalypse. None of them was complete, so that Erasmus was obliged to translate Latin into Greek to fill up lacunæ in the Apocalypse. The first edition was full of errors; but it was quickly succeeded by a second, third, fourth, and fifth, each presenting a better text than its predecessor, though Erasmus never had more than eight manuscripts at his disposal.

The famous printer and scholar, Robert Stephanus (or Estienne), of Paris, published several editions of the Greek New Testament. His text was based on Erasmus (editions of 1527 and 1535), the Complutensian Polyglot, and fifteen manuscripts in the Paris library. The third edition, a Paris folio, issued in 1550, is practically the "Textus Receptus" of the Greek New Testament, which has held its place in England from that day to this. The "Textus Receptus" on the continent has been the Elzevir edition printed at Leyden in 1624. It was based on Stephanus, revised by the use of texts published by Beza in 1565-1611. The name "Received Text" is due to a statement in the preface to the second Elzevir edition, 1633, where it is claimed that this is the text now "received by all."

The period of the dominion of the "Textus Receptus" extends from the Reformation down to the middle of the eighteenth century. Its text then is that of Erasmus (based on eight manuscripts), improved by Stephanus (on basis of the Complutensian Polyglot and fifteen manuscripts) and Beza as printed in England. On the continent the Elzevir edition based on Erasmus and Stephanus constitutes the "Textus Receptus."

Scrivener republished the "Textus Receptus" at Cambridge in 1859; and a new edition (1877) with variations of Beza (1565), of the Elzevir edition (1624), of Lachmann, Tischendorf and Tregelles.

150. It is plainly evident that such a text, based

Greek
Codex Bezae (D) (§ 123). Fifth or Sixth Century
Latin
Luke 6 : 1-9

on a few comparatively late manuscripts, was not likely to be a very exact reproduction of the original autographs of the New Testament. As the years went by manuscripts of earlier dates were discovered on every hand. Documents reaching back to the sixth, fifth and even fourth century were brought to light. They stood several centuries nearer the originals than any of those that formed the basis of the " Textus Receptus." Necessarily there would grow up a dissatisfaction with the basing of so important a work on such defective sources. Lachmann, Tischendorf, Tregelles, Scrivener and others had paved the way for the construction of a new text of the New Testament, based on the latest and best evidence. When Westcott and Hort began their work they had some severe opposition. The " Textus Receptus " had won almost a sacred place in the hearts and minds of some of the biblical scholars of the day. To set this aside, required a bold, heroic move. But it was done, and done in a scholarly, loyal and Christian manner.

The great mass of Greek New Testament manuscript material at their disposal for the work they had in hand complicated their problem. Their first task was to find out just what available manuscripts were of sufficient importance to form a basis for a grouping or classification. They built more or less on previous classifications, but outstripped all other critics " in tracing the transcriptional history of the text and in the application of the genealogical method as the only way to rise up to the autographic fountainhead " (Schaff, p. 271). After carefully noting their characteristics and value, they decided to classify the documents, irrespective of any printed editions, into four great groups: (1) the Syrian or Antiochian; (2) the Western; (3) the Alexandrian; and (4) the Neutral.

151. The Syrian group. The early church fathers, such as Clement, Origen, Tertullian and Cyprian, have embodied numerous New Testament quotations in their writings, but none is a certain representative of Dr. Hort's so-called Syrian Greek (or Græco-Syrian) text. It seems to have been produced by the Greek and Syrian church fathers at about the close of the fourth century. Dr. Hort maintains that the so-called Syrian readings have been the result of combining non-Syrian readings; in other words, the Syrian group is representative of a text that originated in a revision of existing texts in the vicinity of Antioch in the beginning of the fourth century. This text then originated later than those of the other groups, and consequently is not of equal authority with them. The uncial Codex A (§§ 118, 119) is a good representative, in the Gospels, as is the Syriac Peshitta (as revised). Chrysostom, archbishop of Constantinople (died 407) made use of it in his extensive homiletical works. The later Greek fathers, including even the great biblical scholar, Theodore of Mopsuestia (died 429) made liberal quotations from this text. The large mass of cursive Greek manuscripts (mainly written in Constantinople) also belong to this group.

BISHOP B. F. WESTCOTT

Finally it is the text which is largely reproduced in the " Textus Receptus." " It is an eclectic text, which absorbs and combines readings from the early texts of different lands " (Schaff, p. 272).

152. The Western group, so-called, but inappropriately, is made up of that body of texts which have been handled with great freedom. " Words, clauses, and even whole sentences, were changed, omitted, and inserted with astonishing freedom, whenever it seemed that the meaning could be brought out with greater force and definiteness" (Hort. vol. 2, p. 122). This text seems to be most readily recognized in the Old Latin version, and in the bilingual uncials which were written in the West (cf. D §123). This text seems to have had its origin very early, before the copying of a text was done with adequate care, before it was regarded as wrong to interpolate, expand, contract, or omit at will such passages as to the scribes seemed best. The Greek text used by the ante-Nicene fathers, where they did not come into contact with Egypt, was Western. These manuscripts contain many old and important readings, but the critic must carefully weigh every item of evidence before he can feel free to adopt them. Every mark of the characteristic license taken by the writers of this text must be purged ere it can be used as an authority. The scribes exercised the same freedom in their handling of the Western text as they had done in such " post-apostolic writings, as the Epistle of Barnabas, the Shepherd of Hermas, and the Ignatian Epistles." Therefore the

care exercised by critics had to be scrupulous and far-reaching.

153. The Alexandrian group or text is found in great abundance in the New Testament quotations of the church fathers of Alexandria, such as Clement, Origen, Dionysius, Cyril of Alexandria, Eusebius in part, and the Memphitic branch of the Coptic version. These readings are quite distinct from either the Syrian or the Western texts. They present a clean-cut Greek scholarship, such as might be expected to emanate from Alexandria, as a center of Greek learning. There is an entire absence of such extraneous additions as one finds in texts that have been treated like those of the Western group. There is still, however, a lack of those elements that would designate this as one of the earliest forms of the text.

154. The Neutral group is the purest text extant. It is almost entirely free from corruption and mixture with other texts, and is thought to represent the nearest approach, at the present time, to the New Testament autographs. Its best representative is Codex Vaticanus (B), lacking the Pastoral Epistles, the Apocalypse, and four chapters of Hebrews, and its second best is Codex Sinaiticus (S) which contains the whole New Testament. These two codices, the oldest and best extant, were apparently derived independently from a common original, at no great distance from the autographs. When the readings of these two texts agree, their evidence is conclusive against overwhelming numerical evidence of later

Fenton John Anthony Hort

texts, unless internal testimony contradicts. This text then had no home. It belonged to the entire Eastern world of Christianity.

Dr. Hort conjectures (vol. 2, p. 267) that both of those great manuscripts (S and B) were written in the West, probably at Rome; " that the ancestors of B were wholly Western (in the geographical, not the textual sense) ; and that the ancestors of S were partly Alexandrian." The corrections of these texts by later hands likewise have an important textual value. Among the church fathers the pre-Syrian and Neutral text elements are most numerous in Origen, Didymus, Eusebius and in Cyril of Alexandria. The relation of this neutral text to the " Textus Receptus," or Syrian text, is about that which exists between the Revised Version and the Authorized Version. Drs. Westcott and Hort were both members of the British Revision Committee, and by their textual experience succeeded in establishing as the basis of the translation of the Revised Version a purer text than any other, ancient or modern.

155. The above grouping of the Greek manuscripts of the New Testament, as proposed by Dr. Hort was made the basis of his and Dr. Westcott's Greek New Testament. Though it has been severely, and perhaps justly, criticized, no superior scheme for classifying New Testament manuscripts has been proposed. It gave us the best text of the New Testament (1881) ever printed or published. It was received almost universally with favor and gratitude, as the first suc-

cessful breaking away in England and America from the traditional "Textus Receptus," and was a decided advance toward the reconstruction of a text that stands but a few generations at most from the New Testament autographs.

Since the issuing of this text in 1881 several minor editions of the Greek New Testament have appeared, abundantly supplied with variant readings. Dr. Scrivener again published, in 1882, the "Textus Receptus," with the variant readings of Lachmann, Tischendorf, Tregelles, Westcott and Hort, and the Revised Version of 1881.

For the English Bible student there is no edition of the New Testament that so inducts him into the value of ancient manuscripts as the Variorum Teachers' Bible. Its variant translations, and the best readings of different manuscripts and versions are admirably gathered together at the bottom of the pages. Authorities are so cited as to give the reader assurance that the best that can be afforded is set before him.

CHAPTER XVIII

HOW MANUSCRIPTS AND VERSIONS ARE USED

156. In the preceding chapters we have briefly described scores of manuscripts, versions, and quotations. This material is now available for biblical scholars and students. By the judicious use of them they can gradually detect and count out scribal errors, they can eliminate what were originally marginal notes made by copyists and ecclesiastics, which have since been incorporated into the text. By a careful comparison and weighing of the evidence at hand they can, as it were, rub off the excrescences of the true text, and give us almost the polished shaft of the original, the very writings of the apostles and evangelists.

This is the use that scholars are making of the invaluable biblical treasures that are found carefully preserved in the great libraries of the world. There are certain principles, on which they work. They lay down certain rules, and by these rules every fact concerning a manuscript, its history and its readings, is judiciously investigated and weighed. The evidence for the readings of the versions is likewise tested in the same mental crucible and the refined resultant incorporated in the purest text. This branch of biblical research is called "Textual Criticism."

157. This textual criticism is usually looked upon as a dry and uninteresting study. But the science of biblical criticism is one of the most fascinating of all branches of investigation. Its importance for the Christian church and for Christian truth is beyond computation. For all Christian doctrines and teachings are based on the exegesis of the Scriptures. The character of this Scripture is then all-important. The careful student will not rest until he knows that he has the best and purest text possible, in order that what he extracts from it may be wholly reliable for the foundations of his beliefs.

This criticism of the text, or textual criticism, which aims to secure as near as can be, the words of the original writers, or the lost autographs, is distinct from " higher criticism." This latter, more properly termed historical and literary criticism, deals with such problems as the origin, composition, authenticity and literary characteristics of any document. It does not trespass upon the province of the interpreter, but deals with matters that are preliminary to his work.

Its field is that broad one of history, literary methods, individual characteristics, all such questions as aid in the determination of the general character of any document, and its proper place in the general literary material of any given period of history.

158. Enough has been said of the great variety of texts and versions to show the necessity of textual criticism. Chapter I discussed several kinds of varia-

tions that are found on the margins of our Revised Version. These variants are a few of the thousands that are found in the manuscripts and versions which formed the basis of our English Bible.

The methods or accidents which gave rise to these variants in the Old Testament were mentioned in §21. Practically the same reasons would obtain in the case of the variants of the New Testament. Such variants began to exist very early in the history of the biblical texts, probably with the very first copyist. And they never ceased to multiply until the printer's art once for all did away with the very fallible work of the copyist. Origen and Jerome were greatly disturbed by the evident corruptions of the biblical texts in their days. After their times, as we pass on down through the middle ages, we find that copies prepared for private individuals, and for ecclesiastical use and authorities, had been written with a good degree of care—with more faithfulness than characterized the work of the first four centuries. It is ascertained by scholars that the changes of the later centuries are comparatively unimportant, and that these manuscripts perpetuate, on the whole, only such erroneous readings as arose from one cause or other in the preceding centuries. For example, when Erasmus first printed the New Testament, he stereotyped a text that practically agreed with a text that was current in Antioch at the close of the fourth century (Schaff, Companion, p. 175).

As we have already seen, Origen (§§ 52-54) was

one of the first, followed by Hesychius (of Egypt), and Lucian (of Antioch), to attempt to restore a pure text, by a comparison of the different manuscripts. With their pioneer methods they took a step in the right direction, and noted the character of the variants found in the texts at their disposal.

159. As scholars began the more carefully and systematically to examine the sources, they made collections of the variant readings. Those found in the Old Testament manuscripts and published have been already referred to in §26. The variants in the New Testament manuscripts were estimated by John Mill, in 1707, to be about 30,000. Scrivener in 1874 stated that they would not fall far short of 150,000. This estimate includes such variants as the manner of spelling, the order of words, and the order of sentences. There is no other ancient book, even of the famed Greek and Roman classics, that is current in so many manuscripts, nor that presents such a mass of variant readings.

The mere existence of such an enormous number of variations in the readings of the text of the New Testament has rather startled some Christians. They fear that such a colossal list of variants throws the whole question of the discovery of the true text of the New Testament into hopeless confusion. On the other hand, these witnesses simply point out that the tremendous importance of the New Testament in the early centuries caused the production of this treasure-house of manuscripts, which certainly does not impair, but rather guarantees, the integrity of the text. Only about 400 of the almost 150,000 variations materially affect the sense. Of these 400 only about fifty are of real significance for one reason or other. And still, again, not one of these fifty " affects an article of faith or a precept of duty, which is not abundantly sustained by other and undoubted passages, or by the whole tenor of scripture teaching " (Schaff, Companion, p. 177). Richard Bentley, the ablest of the classical critics of England, affirmed that even the worst of manuscripts does not pervert or set aside one article of faith or moral precept (Schaff, p. 175f.).

160. Since the presence of a large number of variants in the manuscripts and versions necessitates textual criticism, scholars have laid down certain principles or rules along the lines of which this science proceeds. The following statements of the rules embody substantially the principles generally adopted by New Testament critics down to the present day, as set forth by Schaff in the Introduction to the American edition of Westcott and Hort's New Testament in Greek:

(1) Before proceeding to critical work with any manuscripts the scholar must have acquired a general knowledge of what must be looked for in order to make a choice of readings; in other words, his training must have been such as to have prepared him to weigh evidence as between the value of the variants that he discovers. This rule emphasizes the fact that only men of scholarship who have especially trained

minds are capable of prosecuting this close critical work.

(2)   Every kind of evidence, internal and external, concerning a manuscript must be taken into account according to its intrinsic value. The place where a manuscript was discovered, the conditions under which it was found, the probable conditions under which it was preserved, the character of the writing, and the material upon which the writing was done—these and many other evidences must be carefully considered by the textual critic, and be given due weight in the important work that he has before him.

(3)   The internal evidence or sources of the text must be sifted and classified, and the authorities for variant readings must be weighed rather than numbered. One independent manuscript may be worth a score which were copied from the same original. More careful scrutiny may discover that the witnesses fall into certain groups or families, and that they represent certain tendencies.

(4)   The restoration of the pure text must be founded on the history and genealogy of the textual variations. In other words, before the pure text can be determined scholars must carefully trace as far as possible the ancestry of the manuscripts. This may be a very simple or a very complex matter. It may be found, as an example, that ten manuscripts may be traced to one and the same original; and that one hundred manuscripts were copied from a second original of good character. It would not be just to

give the hundred manuscripts ten times the weight in evidence as to variant readings as the ten manuscripts. At first thought we should say that the evidence in the two cases is about equal. But before reaching a conclusion we should be required to examine with great care all other available evidence bearing on the question of the readings.

161. (5) Briefly speaking, the reading of an older manuscript is preferable to that of a later, because it is presumably nearer the source. Now and then, however, later copies may represent a more ancient reading, for their descent may be through an entirely different genealogical line.

(6) In general, the shorter reading is preferable to the longer, because insertions and additions are more probable than omissions. Many illustrations of this case may be seen in the margin of the Revised Version. In Mark 3: 14, after "And he appointed twelve," the margin says, "Some ancient authorities add, whom also he named apostles;" in 9: 49, after "For every one shall be salted with fire," the margin says, "Many ancient authorities add, and every sacrifice shall be salted with salt;" to 11: 25 the margin reads, "many ancient authorities add ver. 26, But if ye do not forgive, neither will your father who is in heaven forgive your trespasses." By this rule scores of readings are counted out as indicated by the statements in the margin of the Revised Version.

(7) The more difficult and obscure reading is preferable to the one that is more easy and simple in

construction. This is seen in many New Testament passages where an insertion or addition is made to explain an otherwise obscure passage, or one difficult to understand, or hard to believe to be true. In Luke 12: 31 we find, "Yet seek ye his kingdom," to which the margin remarks, intending to clear up the obscurity, "Many ancient authorities read, the kingdom of God." Romans 8: 28b reads, "all things work together for good," but the margin contains this: "Some ancient authorities read, God worketh all things with them for good." This latter is easier to believe and understand than that severe truth contained in the text of the Revised Version.

(8) The reading which best explains the origin of the other variations is preferable; or, in other words, that reading is to be preferred, from which all the other variations may have been derived, though it itself could not have sprung from them.

162.   (9) That reading is to be preferred which best suits the peculiar literary style of the author, for copyists usually disregard the idiosyncrasies of an author. This is a difficult rule to make use of, for an author does not always express himself in a uniform manner, nor should we be required to rule out an expression because he uses it but once. Even the expert critic may abuse the license granted under this rule.

(10) That reading which bears the ear-marks of doctrinal controversy should be ruled out in favor of one to which no such suspicion is attached. In Mat-

thew 1 : 16 the Revised Version reads, "and Jacob begat Joseph, the husband of Mary, of whom was born Jesus, who is called Christ;" the Curetonian Syriac is biased toward the miraculous conception, for it reads, "And Jacob begat Joseph, to whom was betrothed Mary the Virgin, who bare Jesus Christ;" the Sinaitic Syriac, on the other hand, denies such conception, for it reads, "And Jacob begat Joseph, and Joseph, to whom was betrothed Mary the Virgin, begat Jesus, who is called Christ." Both of these quotations reveal changes and insertions that were made for doctrinal or controversial reasons, and they are rejected in favor of that text to which no such suspicion can be attached.

(11) The agreement of the most ancient witnesses of all classes decides the true reading against all mediæval copies and printed editions. If all ancient testimony, manuscripts, versions and quotations agree on a certain reading, no mediæval or modern witnesses can rule it out of court.

(12) "The primary uncials, the Sinaitic (S), the Vatican (B), the Ephræm (C), and the Alexandrian (A) codices—especially S and B—if sustained by ancient versions and ante-Nicene citations, outweigh all later authorities, and give us presumably the original text."

163. The application of these rules in dealing with manuscripts, versions, and quotations has given us the best texts in use to-day. They have ruled out, in the main, the Greek text of Textus Receptus, which was

the basis of all Protestant versions of the New Testament, in favor of another text based on the great uncial manuscripts above referred to. As we have already noted, the Textus Receptus was based on a few late cursive manuscripts, employed by Erasmus, Stephanus and Beza, before the discovery of the wealth of early documents which we now possess. The great New Testament critics of the nineteenth century, Griesbach, Lachmann, Tregelles, Tischendorf, Scrivener, Westcott and Hort, have had at their disposal all the wealth of documents now preserved in our great libraries. By the careful construction and application of the rules above recited they have been successful in giving us a Greek text that reaches back at least one thousand years before the date of the manuscripts that formed the basis of the Textus Receptus. We now have a Greek text of the New Testament dating at least from the fourth century, and representing the best that modern scholarship has been able to produce.

Part III. English Versions of the Bible

CHAPTER XIX

EARLY ENGLISH MANUSCRIPTS

164. Christianity was introduced into Great Britain as early as the second century. Its progress was comparatively slow before the sixth century, but in Ireland it had taken deep root. This Irish acorn grew to immense proportions, until in the sixth century it extended to Scotland and northern England, where the invasions of the Teutons largely crushed out its earlier gains. The landing of Augustine at Kent, in 597 A. D., gave a new lease of life to the struggles of the few remaining Christians. The vigorous efforts of that giant saint soon pushed the gospel to the front. In spite of his rather irascible temper and occasional unwise movements, Christianity made decided steps in advance, particularly in southern England. And by the loyalty of one of his own converts especial favors were granted to missionaries in Northumbria.

Almost the entire progress of Christianity throughout Great Britain was due to the active preaching of the gospel. Few could read, and there were fewer copies of the Bible to be read. Therefore the most effective and rapid method of spreading the good news of the kingdom was through the heralding of the truth by the missionaries of the Christian church. The mingling and commingling of languages on the isles of Britain placed a barrier to the early translation of the Bible into anything that could be popularly recognized as the one language of the country. The version of the Bible in use was, of course, the Latin; and the preachers who traveled everywhere declared the truth in the tongues of their listeners. These preachers were usually the educated monks, or their pupils, who were able to interpret the Latin Bible to their auditors.

165. But the vigorous Briton mind very soon began to put its thoughts into writing. That quaint Celtic-Saxon poet-singer Cædmon began to attune his words to his native harp about the middle of the seventh century. At first merely a farmer, he was transformed, through a vision of the night, into a forceful poet. When the monks translated narratives out of the Latin Bible, Cædmon, with a sparkling genius, put them into a charming poetic paraphrase. These specimens of our earliest English literature are also the first known attempts to put the Bible into English dress. Its character and form give it no claim to be regarded as a translation of the Bible, but its antiquity and subject matter attract particular attention, for it is one of the forerunners of the English Bible.

All that we know of Cædmon has been preserved by Bede. He tells us that this poet was an ignorant farmer of Northumbria, who worked for an official of the abbey of Whitby. At the festive gatherings in the great hall it was the custom to pass around the harp, requiring each one present to play and sing. For several years Cædmon had left the hall just as his turn came, for he could not sing. One night, after he had thus gone out to care for his horses and cattle, he fell asleep in the stable; and as he slept he heard a voice saying," Cædmon, sing to me." And he said, " I cannot sing, and for that reason I have come away from the feast." Again the voice said, " Sing to me." And he answered, " What shall I sing?" "Sing to me the first beginning of created things." Thenceforth words came to his lips, and he sang in his dreams a hymn of praise to God his maker. The next morning the story of his dream brought him before the Lady-Abbess, and he was found to be possessed of a divine gift. For as soon as the monks translated any portion of the Bible story out of the Latin text he immediately sang it to the accompaniment of his harp in short lines of Saxon verse. Cædmon's paraphrase appeared about 670, just as Christianity is said to have won marked triumphs in the conversion of England.

166. South England at about the same time was receiving religious instruction through popular poetry attuned to the harp of Aldhelm, abbot of Malmesbury. This shrewd official observed that the usual sermon had little attraction for the ordinary run of Englishmen. Being a skilful musician, he put on the garb of a minstrel, and took up a position on a bridge over which many people were obliged to pass. His

artistic playing soon attracted a group of listeners. As soon as he had thus collected an audience he gave his music and words a religious turn, and by the strains of his splendid instrument and the persuasive form of his attractive language won many to Christianity.

This same Aldhelm, later bishop of Sherborne, who died in 709, was the first known translator of the Psalms into Anglo-Saxon English. There is a manuscript in Paris which is thought by some scholars to be the Psalter of Aldhelm; but this document was written in the eleventh century, and bears on it some ear-marks of a later time. About the same time, it is thought, and at Aldhelm's request, Egbert, bishop of Holy Island, produced a translation of the Gospels. This particular document is represented by a copy in the British Museum.

These two bishops, one representing the Old Testament and the other the New, are two important forerunners of the complete manuscripts of the whole Bible in early English.

167. The most renowned Christian and scholar of this period was Bede, born 674, died 735. He is called the brightest light in Western Europe in the eighth century. He is the head of the long procession of translators of the Bible, stretching from the eighth to the twentieth century. One of his followers, Cuthbert, has left us the story of the death of this good old monk of Jarrow. All through the day before Ascension Day, A. D. 735, he had been dictating his

translation of the Gospel of John. For he said, " I do not want my boys [monks] to read a lie, or to work to no purpose after I am gone." On the evening of that day one chapter only remained untranslated. The great scholar seemed very near to death. Early on the morning of Ascension Day his amanuensis said, " Dear master, there is one chapter yet to do." " Take thy pen and write quickly," said Bede. All through that day, interrupted by saying farewells to the brethren of the monastery, he painfully translated on. Just as night began to wrap the earth in her shroud, his sobbing scribe leaned over, and whispered, " Master, there is just one sentence more." And he said, " Write quickly." The scribe wrote on, and then said, " See, dear master, it is done now." " Yes, you speak truly ; it is finished now." Then, by his request, they laid him down on the pavement of his cell, and he departed with the " Gloria " on his lips, to be with the dear Master whom he had so faithfully served during a long and devoted life. Of this translation, however, there is no trace left. It is supposed that it perished, with many other treasures of Northumbria, when the country was laid waste by the Danes. But the part that the Venerable Bede had in the early translations of the Latin Bible into the vernacular language of England in the eighth century is undisputed. And his profound influence upon the Christianity of England in its formative period cannot be overlooked.

168. One of the greatest patrons of religion and biblical learning in these centuries was King Alfred

(848-901). His name stands with the best of England's kings, as one who planned and promoted the intellectual. and moral well-being of his subjects. Though Christianity was on the wane, he quickly instilled new life into it, and gave the use of the Bible a new impulse. He was so convinced of the genuine value of it that he translated, or caused to be translated, and placed at the head of the laws of his country, a copy of the ten commandments; to these he added other laws of the Pentateuch. His activity did not cease here, for he seemed to have regarded himself as one in the succession of Aldhelm and Bede. He is said to have produced, or to have caused the production of, a translation of the Psalter. But there is no known copy of this work in existence, though there is a manuscript in the British Museum which carries the name, King Alfred's Psalter. This copy contains the Latin text with an interlinear English translation; but it is now generally conceded to belong to the eleventh century. There is, however, another Latin Psalter in the British Museum, thought to have been written about 700 A. D., which, was supplied with a word-for-word translation in the dialect of Kent at about the close of the ninth century.

169. This same period is thought to have produced our earliest translation of the Gospels into English. One would suppose that the earliest portion of the Bible to be put into English would be the Gospels, but no version is known older than that of the Psalter just mentioned. The so-called Cotton manu-

Cotton Manuscript (⅔ 169). Seventh Century, and inter-linear Anglo-Saxon paraphrase of about A.D. 950. A summary prefixed to the Gospel of John

script of the British Museum is a Latin version of the Gospels copied toward the end of the seventh century by Eadfrith, bishop of Lindisfarne, from a text which Adrian, friend of archbishop Theodore, had brought to England in 669. About 950 Aldred, a priest, prepared and wrote between the lines of this Latin text, his Anglo-Saxon paraphrase. This is the earliest known version of the Gospels in the English language; but its dialect is that of Northumbria. This text is now known under the names of "The Lindisfarne Gospels," "The Book of Durham," and "The Gospels of St. Cuthbert."

The Bodleian library at Oxford possesses another interlineated copy, a gloss of the Lindisfarne version, known as "The Rushworth Gospels," which had its origin a little later in Ireland.

The Latin text used in all these interlinear versions was not that of the Vulgate, but of the Old Latin, already described in Chapter XV.

170. The earliest copies of translations of the Gospels, with no accompanying Latin text, are found in the tenth century. There are six known copies of such translation, varying slightly the one from the other. Of these, two are found in each of the libraries of Oxford, Cambridge, and the British Museum. The oldest of them, at Cambridge, was produced by abbot Ælfric, and written at Bath about A. D. 1000. The variants of these manuscripts may point to the same original text, whose identification is not yet made out. It is known, however, that one of these manu-

scripts represents a text that was in general use in Wessex. This same Ælfric, later archbishop of Canterbury, made an Anglo-Saxon version of the Pentateuch, Joshua, Judges, Esther, Job, a part of Kings, and the apocryphal books of Judith and Maccabees. He left out what he regarded as of least importance. Judith and Maccabees seem to have been included to fire the patriotic spirit of his countrymen against the invading Danes. One of the interesting phases of Ælfric's work is the fact that he says that he made use, in his translation, of older versions. Thus far, however, no such works have been discovered. The lack of any such versions to-day may be due to the terrific destruction which the Danes visited upon the country, and to the devastations of the Normans. Of Ælfric's work there is one manuscript in Oxford and one in the British Museum.

171. In about a half-century after Ælfric's day came the Normans (1066) to crush the Saxons and plant their scepter on the isles of Briton. Their invasion meant the dethronement of the Anglo-Saxon language and the substitution therefor of the Anglo-Norman. The Anglo-Saxon tongue was ostracized from the court, from books, and from schools. It was turned out of doors by royal decree, to find a refuge only with the cloistered monk, the priest, and the peasant. Its prohibition banished it from writing, and hence from a literary use. But its flavor could not be entirely destroyed. The new tongue, brought in by the conquerors and authorized by royal edict,

slowly but gradually percolated the conquered realm. The confusion of tongues thus brought about prevented the production of anything that could claim the name of literature until the thirteenth century. All activity, too, in the production of Bible translations suffered almost extinction during this period of literary chaos.

But we have one notable piece of Scriptures from the early part of the thirteenth century (1215). An Augustinian monk by the name of Orm made a metrical version of parts of the Gospels and the Acts for use in church services, which is known to-day as "The Ormulum." This version is not a translation, but a paraphrase, accompanied with brief explanatory notes, designed for use in that day. The language of this version is a peculiar compound. Its vocabulary is Teutonic, but its cadence and syntax are colored by Norman characteristics. The " Ormulum " is preserved in a fine manuscript of 20,000 lines in the Bodleian library at Oxford. It seems to have been easier to make a paraphrase than a translation in the early thirteenth century. Following the Ormulum some one put Genesis and Exodus into verse for general use.

172. There was also produced, a little later, by an unknown author, a version of the Psalter, metrical in form, and almost a translation in its faithfulness to the original. It is curious, and yet explicable, that there was no real translation-version of any book of the Bible after the Norman conquest until about the middle of the fourteenth century, except of the Psal-

ter. Of it there were two prose translations that require especial notice in any discussion of this period.
So general was the use of the Psalter, and so universal its character, that for more than a century it
seems to have almost monopolized the attention of
leading Christian scholars, and evangelical authorities.
One notable translation sprung up in south England,
and the other in the north. The translation attributed
to south England is credited to the skill and scholarship of William of Shoreham, in Kent, and located in
time about 1320. This man Shoreham was a poet of
no mean proportions. His poems are in the Kentish
dialect, while his Psalter is in the dialect of the West
Midlands. The north England translation was produced in about the same period by Richard Rolle, the
so-called "Hermit of Hampole," near Doncaster, in
Yorkshire. In Rolle's translation each verse is followed by a commentary in order thereby to make it of
the utmost value to the common preacher of his day,
who might not completely understand the significance
of the translation. The original from which they
translated was the Latin Vulgate, and their work furnishes us to-day admirable specimens of the English
language of that time.

The time of the work of these two biblical scholars
falls before the middle of the fourteenth century.
They are located by some students at 1320 for William
of Shoreham and 1340 for Richard Rolle. In other
words, their translations were completed, distributed,
and in full use, about the time of the birth and youth

of Wycliffe, about 1320-40. These translations of the Psalter, widely sown and known in England, created a thirst for larger portions of God's Word, and thus prepared the soil for the large service of Wycliffe, whose work will engage us in the next chapter.

173. The spread of the Shoreham-Rolle versions of the Psalter was the beginning of the conquest of the English language proper. The old Anglo-Saxon gradually faded out before the newcomer, which was given grace and favor through the Psalms that were so well beloved by the people at large. Political concessions to the common people had opened up before them the beauties of a liberty and independence that filled life with a new impetus and new inspiration. The production of such English literature as that of Langland, Gower and Chaucer presented a new side to the life of the awakening Englishmen of the fourteenth century. These productions, together with the Psalters already noted, stirred up the appetite of the English nation intellectually and religiously, so that Wycliffe, by his mental and religious instinct, could rightly divine the moment when a new translation of the Bible would satisfy the intellectual and spiritual hunger of a people.

CHAPTER XX

174. John Wycliffe stands out as one of the most illustrious figures of the fourteenth century. He was born in Yorkshire about 1320, and completed his education at Oxford. He is said to have become Master of Balliol College, and to have won a high place among the scholars of his day. In 1361 he resigned the arduous post of Master, and settled on a living at Fillingham, Lincolnshire. This mode of life gave him more leisure for the production of pamphlets and addresses on the stirring questions of those troublous days. With Oxford and its attractive circle of scholars close at hand, Wycliffe became deeply interested in the great ecclesiastical controversies of the times. His own personal knowledge of the conditions and needs of the common people, as seen among his parishioners, and his thorough acquaintance with the intellectual life of Oxford, prepared him for doing a large service for the people of his day. Wycliffe's public life may be divided for convenience into three periods: (1) His education and training at Oxford, and the beginning of his ecclesiastical activity (1336-66); (2) his semi-political and anti-papal, as well as purely ecclesiastical, work (1366-78); and (3) his open war against Rome, and his preparation from the Latin

JOHN WYCLIFFE

Vulgate of a translation of the Bible for the common people (1378-84).

175. The fourteenth century was a period of transition. It was neither the middle ages nor the reformation. It was a kind of middle ground between the two. Politics, society, and the church were struggling to hold on to the old order, and at the same time to make friends with new thoughts, ideals, and progress. The "hundred years' war with France" had just been concluded, and had left on the country all the countless fruits of such bloody struggles. The papal quarrels at Rome, and lavish expenditures, had so depleted that central ecclesiastical treasury that the Pope issued demands for funds on the Britons. Parliament refused to accede to such orders, and Wycliffe stood by the government. The immense wealth of the great dignitaries of the church and the organized corporations through which they constantly added to their accumulations were the objects of some of Wycliffe's most determined assaults.

The power of his attacks lay not so much in his enthusiasm as in the purity, spirituality, and unselfishness of his character, in his determination to crush the wrong and enthrone the right; in his broad views of the questions of the day and the best method of solving them in the interests of the common people as over against the oppressions of church and state.

176. Wycliffe had reached middle life before he struck the keynote to his great life-work. In 1366, when he was forty-six years old, he publicly justified

and approved Parliament's action in refusing to hand over money at the demand of the Pope. This act soon drew him into the center of the fight against Rome. In 1371 he was the most prominent reformer of the religious and social forces in England. Papal encroachments and abuses of wealth in church quarters were vigorously exposed and resisted. As an inspiration to him, Wycliffe had the University of Oxford at his back, except when he promulgated some doctrine distinctively heretical. Since Oxford had become, or was popularly regarded, the center of liberalism in thought for all Europe, Wycliffe could cut a wide swath without losing its moral support. With keen, logical argumentation he met and defeated his papal opponents. He had no peer in the lecture hall or the pulpit, and was the terror of the corruptionists and the promoters of the papal church. But Wycliffe's logic and metaphysics, his scholasticism and political views, are not the outstanding characteristics for which he is most largely remembered and honored in the church to-day. These were only elements of his symmetrical mind that helped him to divine the crying need of his times. He perceived that there was a gulf between the common people and church authorities, and that it should be bridged; that they should be brought together on the Word of God. He saw, too, that the surest method of defeating Rome would be to put the Bible into the hands of the people. The version current in that day, except a few scattered fragments from earlier centuries, was the Latin Bible, which was used only by the clergy and high church officials. The learned only could make intelligent use of this text; and those whose duty it was to teach it and interpret it were indolent and careless, or haughty and exclusive so far as the common folk were concerned.

177. Wycliffe "came to the kingdom for such a time as this." He saw that the true emancipation of the soul of man lay in his opportunity to read the Bible in his own tongue, in his own home, that such a reversal of the prevalent condition of the people would mean the loss of Rome's power. The perception of this method of procedure led Wycliffe to turn his whole attention to the work of putting the Bible into the language of the every-day man and woman,— the common people who had been spiritually fed, so far as they had been fed at all, by a careless, indolent and haughty priesthood. Wycliffe had already shown himself to be an open antagonist to the methods and officials of the church; and this resolve on his part made him still more unpopular, even an object of attack by the influential ecclesiastics of England. Though a schoolman, Wycliffe laid supreme emphasis on the Scriptures as a basis for a religious life, and thus had no hesitation in throwing the weight of his energies into the production of a version of the Bible that could be read by the simplest peasant.

178. Wycliffe conceived the idea of translating the whole of the Latin Bible or Vulgate into the English of his time. Just when and where he began the

work is not known. But the New Testament was finished about 1380; and within two years (in 1382) the whole Bible appeared in English dress. Wycliffe, of course, did not do all the work himself. As rector of Lutterworth, in Leicestershire, he sustained close relations with the great centers of intellectual and spiritual thought, particularly of Oxford and London. He called into service other scholars whose sympathies and abilities were in accord with his own. Ample evidence is at hand to show that most of the Old Testament work was done by one of his devoted disciples and fellow workers, Nicholas of Hereford. There is a manuscript now in the Bodleian Library, at Oxford, which was doubtless written under the direction of Hereford; for its break in the middle of Baruch 3: 20 is thought to point to the time when he was suddenly summoned to London to answer to the charge of heresy. Hereford was excommunicated and Wycliffe is supposed to have completed his work on the Old Testament. Hereford's own work was scholarly, exact, and often stiffly literal. His training and surroundings made him rather unpractical, put his results in a rather stilted style, designed far more for scholars than for the ordinary, every-day reader. Wycliffe, on the other hand, had been trained in the practical field of the parish, had become accustomed to the plain, every-day parishioner and his needs ; and thus he strove so to translate the Latin into good every-day English that his translation could be read and understood by any plowboy. There is, therefore,

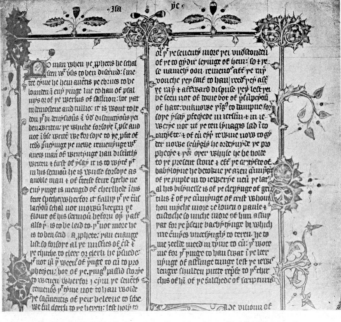

Wycliffe's Bible, before 1397. Introduction to Isaiah and part of
chapter 1 : 1

a very noticeable contrast between the styles of the two translators. Hereford's dialect, so far as his work reveals one, is that of south England, while Wycliffe's is that of east-Midlands and of the north.

179. As soon as Wycliffe had issued his translation he organized a kind of religious order of poor, though not mendicant, preachers to preach and teach the English Bible to the common people. These were voluntary workers, not church clergy, who co-operated, when possible, with the clergy. If these church authorities opposed them, they carried on their work independently, and with all the vigor of their consecrated leader, Wycliffe. His disciples or followers were called "Lollards," and increased so rapidly that one of his sharpest opponents said, "You cannot travel anywhere in England but of every two men you meet one will be a Lollard." This illustrates the immense popularity that soon greeted Wycliffe, and made him the chief advocate of personal religion and of loyalty to the Scriptures. This fact, too, gave him great influence with the church authorities, and made him the most successful reformer on English soil. The culmination of his translation marked the first serious defeat for the church's complete control of the people of England, and the beginning of the end of the rivalry between the Norman-French and English languages. Henceforth the former waned and the latter increased in popularity and strength until it became established as the language of England.

Wycliffe did not live to see the best fruits of his

translation. Two years (1384) after its completion (1382) he died of a stroke of paralysis, brought on by continuous and heavy work. But he had planted a tree whose fruits, spiritual and literary, would be the joy and the exaltation of the common people down through the centuries.

180. The disparity between the style of Wycliffe's and of Hereford's work in the English Bible required some harmonizing version. Within a short time after Wycliffe's death this work seems to have been undertaken by some of his followers or disciples. For such a revision appeared in 1388. It is not known definitely who did the work, but it has been attributed, in part at least, to John Purvey, Wycliffe's former curate at Lutterworth. The prologue tells us on what principles the revision had been made, but omits all names of revisers, except to say that the writer was " a simple creature." A few lines out of this prologue in modern spelling read: " Though covetous Clerks are mad through simony, heresy and many other sins, and despise and impede Holy Writ as much as they can, yet the unlearned cry after Holy Writ to know it, with great cost and peril of their lives. For these reasons, and others, a simple creature hath translated the Bible out of Latin into English. First, this simple creature had much labor, with divers companions and helpers, to gather many old Bibles, and other doctors and common glosses, and to make a Latin Bible somewhat true, and then to study it anew, the text with the gloss, and other doctors, especially

Lire [Nicolaus de Lyra] on the Old Testament, who gave him great help in this work." This prologue shows that the "simple creature" attempted to establish a Latin text on the basis of all the Latin versions and authorities that he could consult, and then to translate his corrected text—a good case of textual criticism at work.

181. This revision of Wycliffe's Bible soon took the place of the first translation. Within less than a century it became the regular edition of Wycliffe's Bible. Its popularity grew rapidly. It was eagerly sought for, and large sums were paid for it by the rich. Multiplied by transcription only, a copy was worth a large sum of money. Early in the fifteenth century a complete copy would have brought, in our money, about one hundred and fifty dollars. Foxe reports that a load of hay was given for the use of the whole New Testament for one day. Wycliffe's Bible was proscribed by archbishop Arundel in 1408, when he made it a penal offense to read any of Wycliffe's writings or translations within the province of Canterbury. In 1414 a law was enacted that all persons who should read the Scriptures in the mother tongue should "forfeit land, catel, lif, and goods from their heyres for ever." Such prohibition could not smother the fire. There are now known to be in existence about one hundred and seventy manuscript copies of Wycliffe's Bible. Of these less than thirty contain the original translation of 1382, while the remainder are copies of Purvey's version,—all written before

1430. Many of these copies were written in a small hand without ornamentation, and were used by private individuals or in families. Some of the finest copies known have been traced to the possession of such royal personages as Henry VI, Henry VII, Richard, Duke of Gloucester, Humphrey, Duke of Gloucester, Edward VI, and Queen Elizabeth.

With all its popularity and treasured value, Wycliffe's Bible did not appear in printed form for almost 500 years after its first appearance in 1382. It was in 1850, when two hard-working English scholars, Forshall and Madden, after twenty years' labor on 170 manuscripts, published in four large quarto volumes a work with the title: "The Holy Bible, containing the Old and New Testaments, with the Apocryphal Books, in the earliest English Versions made from the Latin Vulgate by John Wycliffe and his followers, edited by the Rev. J. Forshall and Sir F. Madden."

182. The production of the first translation of the whole Bible into English for the use of the common folk of England is to be accredited to the foresight, insight, and energy of John Wycliffe. Dr. Gasquet, an English Roman Catholic scholar, has recently (1894) challenged the authenticity of the Bible attributed to Wycliffe; but the evidence in favor of the great reformer's origination and completion of the work in 1382 is too specific and convincing to admit of such doubt. It is true that his translation was made, not from the original languages of the Bible, but from the Latin Vulgate current in England in his

day. Nevertheless, it provided an easy entrance into
the secrets of the divine Word for all who could read;
and gave uneducated preachers and teachers an un-
failing source of divine truth to set before those who
could not read it for themselves. Wycliffe's work,
and that of his co-laborers, has indelibly stamped itself
on our present-day Bible. Some of the permanent
words and expressions that are first found in his version are: " strait gate," "make whole," " compass land
and sea," " son of perdition," " enter thou into the
joy of thy Lord." Some compact methods of expression also have remained with us: " I wente, and
waisehid, and sai " (John 9: 11); " all things ben
nedeful to me, but not alle thingis been spedeful "
(1 Cor. 6: 12).

The great service done the English language and
the English people by Wycliffe's combination and crystallization of the various dialects of England in his
translation cannot be overestimated. He practically
unified the various related tongues of England, and
made them one for the future use of the English
speaking and writing world.

183. It is a matter of interest to make some comparisons between the language of King Alfred's day
(871-901) and of Wycliffe's time (1382), and of this
time—three dates about 500 years apart. This may
best be done by giving in the three dates the so-called
Lord's Prayer; giving the earliest, that of King
Alfred's day, first, Wycliffe's second, and the American Revised Version third:

Uren Fader dhic art in heofnas
Our Fadir that art in heuenes
Our Father who art in heaven

Sic gehalyed dhin noma
Halewid be thi name
Hallowed be thy name

To cymedh dhin ric
Thi Kingdom comme to
Thy Kingdom come

Sic dhin willa sue is in heofnas and in eardhs
Be thi wille done as in heuen so in erthe
Thy will be done, as in heaven, so on earth

Vren hlaf ofer wirthe sel us to daeg
Gyve to us this dai oure breed ouer other substance
Give us this day our daily bread

And forgef us scylda urna
And forgive to us oure dettis
And forgive us our debts

Sue we forgefan sculdgun vrum
As we forgyven to oure dettouris
As we also have forgiven our debtors

And no inleadh vridk in costung
And leede us not in to temptacioun
And bring us not into temptation

Als gefrig vrich fro ifle
But delyvere us fro yvel
But deliver us from the evil

This prayer breaks off where it does in Matthew in the King James Version, and where the Revised Version closes it, giving an interesting comment on the relation of the text used by Wycliffe to that one finally adopted by the Revisers of 1881-85.

CHAPTER XXI

TYNDALE'S VERSION OF THE BIBLE

184. Wycliffe died in 1384. The translation of
the Bible that he undertook, with Nicholas de Hereford's assistance, was completed in 1384, and its un-
likenesses harmonized and revised in 1388 by John
Purvey. This stupendous task was undertaken and
completed without any reference to the original languages of the Bible. It was a translation of the Latin
Vulgate current in that day. Its clothing was the first
dawnings of the English language in anything like
popular form. It took up and crystallized the somewhat volatile form of the English tongue that was
used at that time, and so made it semi-literary in character. Wycliffe's work, however, was reproduced
only by that slow, laborious and fallible method of
the pen. Copies made by hand were expensive, rare,
and not widely circulated until the lapse of years.
Thus the natural antipathy of the ecclesiastical ma-
chine of the country gradually waned, and the version
was partially tolerated by the authorities. In convocation at Oxford in 1408, action was taken warning
the people against a private translation, thus: " we
therefore decree and ordain that no man hereafter
by his own authority translate any text of the Scripture into English, or any other tongue, by way of a

WILLIAM TYNDALE

book, pamphlet, or treatise; and that no man read any such book, pamphlet, or treatise, now lately composed in the time of John Wycliffe . . . upon pain of greater excommunication, until the said translation be approved by the ordinary of the place, or, if the case so require, by the council provincial."

In 1412 a more stringent law was enacted against heresy, and the Lollard party was apparently crushed. But Wycliffe's Bible was slowly, gradually, disseminated, even without an act of approval as required in the convocation of 1408. Its distribution was, of course, very limited after the Lollards were suppressed. Its matter, being a translation of a translation, in the English tongue, gave it popularity with certain classes down to the time of Tyndale.

185. The fifteenth century—the next after Wycliffe's day—was full of the most astonishing surprises, of epoch-making events. Political, national, and material questions were to the fore, while the religious remained in the background. The intellectual world suffered an upheaval, for the cloistered learning of the monasteries had to yield to the liberalism and freedom of the schools and universities. The fortified faith and civilization of the middle ages was forced to recognize a newer and wider basis of thought and ideas. We face here the breaking down of the faulty methods of the dark ages and the inception of revolutionary principles and practises. It was the renaissance, the regeneration of the nations of Europe. It was the emancipation of the mind, of

thought, and of literature. It was the unshackling of
the soul, the beginnings of the reformation, penetra-
ting every country of Europe.

186. Some of the great facts that helped to usher
in that marvelous century must be enumerated and
kept constantly before the mind. In 1453 the Turks
captured Constantinople, and thus drove out scores
of Greek and Christian scholars who fled westward
and took refuge in the various countries of Europe.
Their learning and presence became forceful elements
in the intellectual and religious awakening of the fifteenth century. In 1455 Gutenberg printed from
movable types the first complete Bible, the Vulgate,
later called the Mazarin edition. In 1458 the Greek
language was first taught in the University of Paris.
The first Greek grammar was published in 1476, and
the first Greek lexicon in 1480. In 1488 the first
printed Hebrew Bible appeared. In 1492 Grocyn became the first teacher of Greek in Oxford. The first
Hebrew grammar appeared in 1503, and the first lexicon in 1506. Erasmus edited the first Greek New
Testament in 1516; and in 1514-17 the great Complutensian Polyglot, edited by Cardinal Ximenes and
printed at Alcala, Spain, made its appearance in six
magnificent volumes. Before the end of the fifteenth
century it is asserted that no less than eighty editions
of the Vulgate were printed in Europe alone. Besides
this enormous growth and popularity, there were versions translated and printed in the languages of the
chief countries of Europe, and circulating more or

less freely among their population. Some of these were: German, Russian, Slavonic, Bohemian, Italian, Spanish, French, Dutch and Danish. But no one had yet printed a Bible in the English language.

In this same period there was great enterprise and activity in material things. The printing press began its work in Germany in 1454, and in 1470 Caxton first introduced it into England. In 1492 Columbus discovered America; in 1497 Vasco da Gama rounded the Cape of Good Hope; and in 1520 Magellan sailed around the world. In 1473 Copernicus was born, and his epoch-making work, revolutionizing the science of astronomy, was finished in 1530, though not published until 1543, the year of his death.

These intellectual, literary and material advances gave a new impetus to life and living and so stirred the progressive peoples of that day as to provoke the most vigorous research into many and hitherto unknown realms of knowledge.

187. Such marvelous progress in intellectual and material lines inspired the forces of the religious and spiritual spheres. New motives and new men arose who championed with vigor the cause of religious living. Just about one hundred years after the appearance of Wycliffe's translations and his death (1384) William Tyndale was born (1484). A native of Gloucestershire, " about the borders of Wales," Foxe says he was " brought up from a child " in the University of Oxford, and was " singularly addicted to the study of the Scriptures." He studied in Mag-

dalen Hall under the famous classical teachers, Grocyn, Latimer and Linacre. Somewhere about 1510 he left Oxford and went to Cambridge, probably to study under Erasmus, the renowned Greek New Testament scholar. His university career seems to have covered about ten years, for about 1520 he returned to his native heath, and for two years was a tutor in the family of Sir John Walsh. The inspiration that he had received at Oxford and Cambridge fired his soul to action, for during these years he carried on vigorous thinking and discussion with the conservative and unthinking clergy regarding the work of the church. In one of these controversies with a churchman, according to Foxe, Tyndale said, " if God spare my life, ere many years I will cause a boy that driveth a plough shall know more of the Scriptures than thou doest." Tyndale's thorough preparation for handling the Greek of the New Testament, for Erasmus' Greek New Testament appeared in 1516, while he was still studying at Cambridge, and his familiarity with the needs and requirements of the times, furnished him the stimulus and inspiration to produce an English Bible translated directly out of its original languages.

188. When his opponents became too numerous, and even began to endanger his life, Tyndale went to London. Here he sought out Tunstall, bishop of London, of whose love of learned pursuits he had heard through Erasmus, to secure, if possible, his approval and support for his plan of translating the

Bible into English. But the bishop discovered ex-
cuses enough not to receive him. Tyndale, however,
soon found a friend and helper in Humphrey Monmouth, an alderman of London, who for his favor to
Tyndale was afterward incarcerated in the Tower of
London. This Monmouth gives a description of Tyndale in which he says: "I took him into my house
half a year; and there he lived like a good priest as
methought. He studied most part of the day and
of the night at his book; and he would eat but sod-
den meat by his good will, nor drink but small single
beer. I never saw him wear linen about him in the
space he was with me. I did promise him ten pounds
sterling, to pray for my father and mother, their souls
and all Christian souls. I did pay it him when he
made his exchange to Hamburg" (Demaus, p. 103).
His life of almost a year in London was an eye-opener
to Tyndale. Brought up comparatively in the country, he soon learned that the city was cosmopolitan
in character. Here he met tradesmen and merchants
from many countries, and through them secured much
valuable information regarding the progress of
thought in political and religious lines. Doubtless he
learned the possibilites, too, of finding a place where
he could put into print the translation that he was
making. His experiences with churchmen and poli-
ticians in London for almost a year seem to have
driven him to the following conclusion: "I understood not only that there was no room in my lord of
London's palace to translate the New Testament, but

also, too, that there was no place to do it in all England."

189. Though he left London practically as an exile, he was given assurance that means would be provided to print his translation, and that it would be secretly imported into England, and distributed where it would serve its high and noble purpose. In the springtime of 1524 he went to the free city of Hamburg. Contemporary evidence goes to show that the most of the year following the spring of 1524 was spent in Wittenberg, in close relations with Luther, the giant reformer of Germany. Early in the spring of 1525 he returned to Hamburg to receive a remittance of funds from his London friend, Monmouth.

In April, 1525, he went to Cologne to put into print his completed translation of the New Testament. Here he found Quentel, an expert printer, who undertook the work. But the enemies and spies of the anti-reformation party were busy, especially in Germany. Cochlæus, an open enemy of Luther and the reform movement, was now in Cologne, carrying a book through the same press as that where Tyndale was at work. By some accident he heard the printers boasting of the new successes about to be won for Lutheranism in England. To be certain of his ground, he invited to his home, and dined and wined, these same printers until they talked freely, and gave away the secret, viz., that they were printing 3,000 copies of the New Testament in English for Tyndale,

to be secretly distributed throughout England. Cochlæus immediately informed the authorities at Cologne,
who put a stop to the work. Tyndale, however, with
Roye, his amanuensis, took their printed sheets and
escaped by boat on the Rhine up to the city of
Worms, already famed for its Lutheran strength.

190. Tyndale found a welcome refuge in this hos-
pitable city, and also put his work into the hands of
the printer Schœffer. Cochlæus had already sent to
England a description of the work done in Cologne,
so Tyndale laid it aside temporarily, it being quarto
in form, with marginal notes, and first issued an
octavo edition of 3,000 copies, without either introduction or notes. This edition was soon followed by
the completed quarto begun in Cologne. Both editions were shipped into England hidden away in cases
of merchandise, so that they might be successfully
distributed from the very first. Being completed late
in 1525, it is probable that they reached England early
in 1526. Henry VIII had been informed by Lee (December 2, 1525), later archbishop of York, who was
then on the continent, "that an Englishman, at the
solicitation and instance of Luther, with whom he is,
hath translated the New Testament into English, and
within few days intendeth to return with the same im-
printed into England." A German scholar, Spalatinus, records in his diary of August, 1526, some interesting facts regarding Tyndale. Among other
things he says that Tyndale "was so skilled in seven
languages, Hebrew, Greek, Latin, Italian, Spanish,

English, French, that whichever he spoke you would
suppose it his native tongue " (Demaus, William Tindale, p. 153). He further adds : " that the English,
in spite of the active opposition of the king, were so
eager for the Gospel as to affirm that they would buy
a New Testament even if they had to give a hundred
thousand pieces of money for it."

191. As soon as Tyndale's English New Testament reached England there was a rushing demand
for it by the common people, that they might read it,
and by the ecclesiastical authorities, that they might
burn it. Archbishop Warham issued a decree for its
destruction. Bishop Tunstall added fuel to the fire
by saying that he could find 2,000 errors in it. Decrees and denunciations, however, were of little avail
to stay its popularity. By order of the ecclesiastical
authorities the books were bought up and burned in
London, Oxford and Antwerp. No attempt to check
the printers succeeded. An effective organization of
distributers in England was supplied by numerous
clandestine shippers from the continent. The fight
was desperate on both sides, one to disseminate Tyndale's New Testament as widely as possible, the other
to annihilate it. The bishops liberally contributed to
buy up whole editions to consign to the flames. Packington, an English merchant at Antwerp, was a friend
both of Bishop Tunstall and of Tyndale. The bishop
made a contract with Packington to buy all the books
he could, at any cost, send them to him and he would
burn them at St. Paul's Cross. Hall, the chronicler,

crōmes/which fall from there masters table.Then Jesus an
swered and sayde vnto her.O woman greate is thy fayth / be
hit to the/even as thou desyrest.And her doughter was ma
de whole even at that same tyme.

¶ Then Jesus went awaye from thence / and cam nye vnto
the see of galyle/and went vppe in to a mourayne/and sat do
une there. And moche people cam vnto hym harynge with
them/halt/blynde/dōm/maymed/ and other many: and cast
them doune at Jesus fete. And he healed them / in so moche
that the people wondred / to se the dōm speake / the maymed
whole / and the halt to go / the blynde to se/ and gloryfyed the
god of israhel.

Mar.
viij. ¶Jhesus called his disciples to him and sayde: I have com
passion on the people/be cause they have contynued with me
nowe iij. dayes/and have nothinge to eate:and I wyll not let
them departe fastinge leste they perysshe in the waye. And his
disciples said vnto him:whēce shuld we get so moche breed in
the wyldernes as shulde suffyse so greate a multitude:and Je
sus saide vntothē: howe many loves have ye ? and they seyde:
sevē and a feawe fysshes. And he cōmaunded the people to syt
doune on the grounde. and toke the sevē loves/and the fysshes
and gave thankṣ/ and brake them/and gave to hys disciples/
and hys disciples gave thēto the people. And they all ate/and
were suffysed. and they toke vppe of the broke meate that was
lefte vij. basketṣ full. They that ate were iiij. M. men/besyde
weimen and chyldren.And he sent awaye the people/and toke
shyppe and cam in to the parties of magdala:

The xvi. Chapter.

Mar.
viij.
Luc.ix.

THen cam to him the pharises
with the saduces also /and dyd tēpte him /desyr
inge that he wolde shewe thē some sygne frō he
ven. He answered and saide vnto them: At even
ye saye/we shall have fayre wedder.and that be cause the skye
ys reed:ɤi the mornige:ye saye/todaye shalbe foule wedder/ɤ
Luc.rij. that because the skye is trōbelous and reed. O ye ypocrij rṣ/ye

G ij

describes the case as follows: "So Packington came
to William Tyndale, and said, 'William, I know thou
art a poor man, and I have gotten thee a merchant.'
'Who?' said Tyndale. 'The Bishop of London.'
'He will burn them,' said Tyndale. 'Yea, marry,'
quoth Packington. And so forward went the bar-
gain. The Bishop had the books, Packington the
thanks, and Tyndale the money" (Hoare, Evolution
of Eng. Bible, p. 148).

192. With persistent energy the enemies of Tyndale's translation tried to obliterate it. All the
machinations of the court seem to have been employed
to stamp out so dangerous a heresy. Even King
Henry, who had paid no heed to Tyndale's appeals,
described the works as "imagened and onely fayned
to enfecte the peopull." The success of their cam-
paign of destruction may be partially inferred from
the scant remnants now extant of Tyndale's translation. Of the quarto edition begun at Cologne and
completed at Worms, there is known to be in existence just one little fragment, now in the Grenville
Library in the British Museum. It consists of thirty-
one leaves and contains a prologue, a list of New
Testament books, a wood-cut of an angel holding up
an inkstand into which Matthew is dipping his pen,
and Matthew 1: 1 to 22: 12. Eight of these sheets
were printed by Quentel in Cologne in 1525, and carried by Tyndale to Worms. Of the octavo edition
one copy, perfect except for a missing title-page, is
now preserved in the Baptist College at Bristol, Eng-

land; another copy, very imperfect, in the library of
St. Paul's, London. The fierceness and destructive-
ness of the opponents of Tyndale's translation systematically followed up and destroyed the thousands
of copies that had been widely sold throughout England and Scotland. Of the estimated 18,000 copies
printed between 1525 and 1528, the two copies just
mentioned are the only known fragments.

193. Tyndale's English New Testament is unique.
It is not a translation of a translation, as is Wycliffe's,
but is rendered out of the original Greek text of the
New Testament, probably as published by Erasmus
in 1516, and revised in 1522. He made use of such
helps as the Vulgate, Erasmus' Latin translation of
his own Greek text, and Luther's German translation.
Many of the errors charged against Tyndale's English New Testament are due to the differences between Erasmus' Greek text and the Latin Vulgate.
The violent opposition of the church authorities was
due to causes other than the mere putting of the Bible
into the hands of the common people. Tyndale had
followed the custom common in the issuance of the
Vulgate, and had incorporated marginal notes in his
earlier editions. These were largely controversial,
and only served to fire the wrath of his adversaries.
In later editions, however, they were omitted. Again,
he was not careful to retain in his translation the long-
cherished words of the Vulgate and of the church,
but freely translated the Greek into words that
seemed to him best to convey the thought of the orig-

inal. Such freedom brushed away many age-long cherished ecclesiastical terms, and launched upon the public words that sounded strange in so dearly beloved a book as the Bible. Then the determination and persistency of Tyndale's friends in their clandestine methods of importing his New Testaments into England, and their success in giving it a wide distribution, only inflamed the church authorities to more desperate methods of suppression. But its real value, despite all opposition, was so great as to make it a really dangerous weapon against many of the hollow claims of the church. Its close-fitting faithfulness to the Greek established its importance as the best and truest translation of the Bible for all classes.

194. As soon as Tyndale's New Testament had been well launched upon the English reading public, he took up the work of translating the Old Testament out of the Hebrew text. In 1530 he published a translation of the Pentateuch, accompanied with marginal notes that are severely controversial. Their form would indicate that they were printed separately, for Genesis and Numbers appear in blackface type, as over against the other three, which are plain Roman. In 1531 the book of Jonah appeared in translation,—the Pentateuch and Jonah being the only portions of the Old Testament published during Tyndale's lifetime. He spent the next three years busily engaged in a revision of his earlier work. In 1534 he published a revision of his Pentateuch, 1530 edition, and of the New Testament of the

1525 edition. The motives that led him to revise his translation of the New Testament rather than to complete that of the Old Testament, were (1) to meet the sharp criticism that had been hurled at his first edition, and (2) to checkmate a revision, wholly unauthorized, by his old amanuensis, George Joye, which appeared the same year. Joye had corrected some of the earlier printers' errors, made changes that more closely harmonized with the Vulgate, and his own theological opinions. Tyndale made several important improvements upon his earlier editions. He supplied brief introductions to each of the New Testament books, except Acts and Revelation, took the sting out of many of his marginal notes, and at the end of the volume added the " Sarum " epistles, extracts from the Old Testament to be used in the church services "upon certain days of the year." In this collection Tyndale also included several passages from the Apocrypha. This was the end of Tyndale's printed work.

195. The persistent and continued efforts of Tyndale and his friends had made a distinct gain in the distribution of the New Testament. Though the opposition to his work had somewhat lost strength he dared not return to England. In fact, his work had already so impressed Cromwell and Cranmer that they began to agitate a translation of the Bible into English under royal patronage. Tyndale, however, took up his residence at the " English House," an English merchants' club, in Antwerp. Here he

worked, apparently safe, amid a lot of his merchant friends. But the bitterness of the opposition now showed itself by sending or employing an Englishman, Henry Philips, a Romanist, to do the treacherous deed. After pretending to great friendship for Tyndale, he stealthily and murderously betrayed him, in May, 1535, into the hands of officers of Emperor Charles V. They seized him and carried him off and thrust him into a dungeon in Vilvorde Castle, near Brussels. While confined in this place he was permitted, it is thought, in response to an appeal to the governor of the castle, to use his Hebrew Bible, grammar, and dictionary, and possibly his Greek New Testament. For during his imprisonment he is credited with having once more revised his New Testament, adding headings to the chapters of the Gospels and the Acts. While here he is also thought to have translated Joshua to 2 Chronicles, though its publication was left in the hands of his friend, John Rogers. There is no evidence that Henry VIII or Cromwell had anything to do with his arrest or imprisonment, nor, on the other hand, is there any scrap of evidence to show that either of them lifted a finger to release him from the grasp of his enemies. On October 6, 1536, Tyndale was brought to trial, and being proved a heretic, was condemned to death. He was tied to a stake, praying in these, his last words: " Lord, open the King of England's eyes," and then was strangled and burned.

196. But Tyndale won his battle. In the face of

fierce opposition on the part of the church authorities, he determined to give the Bible to the common
people in their native tongue, the English language.
With slight regard for self, his whole purpose con-
centrated on the one task, he made himself an exile,
fled from place to place to accomplish his task, and
finally succeeded, by the help of close friends, in
printing and having distributed in England, in large
numbers, his New Testament in the English language.
Though the books were bought up and burnt in quantities, their very appearance and use created an appetite for the Bible in English that could not be satisfied.
The flames might burn, and annihilate the books, but
the appetite created thereby was inextinguishable.
Popular requirements soon reached the throne, and,
in spite of earlier adverse action towards Tyndale's
work, made an impression that could not be erased.
The court and the government wisely recognized the
necessity of providing some edition of the English
Bible for popular use. Even in 1534, before Tyndale's
death, a convocation under the presidency of Cranmer petitioned the King that he would " vouchsafe
to decree that a translation of the Scriptures into
English should be made by certain honest and learned
men whom the King should nominate; and that the
Scriptures so translated should be delivered to the
people according to their learning." This was one
of the fruits of the life and labors of the indefatigable
and immortal Tyndale.

197. Tyndale's victory had far-reaching results.

He was a master of a simple and forceful literary style. This, combined with exactness and breadth

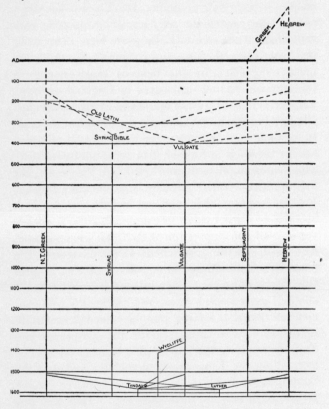

DIAGRAM SHOWING THE BEGINNINGS OF MODERN VERSIONS, EARLY IN THE SIXTEENTH CENTURY.

of scholarship, led him so to translate the Greek New Testament into English as largely to determine the character, form, and style of the Authorized Version. There have been some painstaking calculations to determine just how large a part Tyndale may have had in the production of the version of 1611. A comparison of Tyndale's version of 1 John and that of the Authorized Version shows that nine-tenths of the latter is retained from the martyred translator's work. Paul's Epistle to the Ephesians retains five-sixths of Tyndale's translation. These proportions are maintained throughout the entire New Testament. Such an influence as that upon the English Bible cannot be attributed to any other man in all the past (Demaus, William Tindale, p. 162).

More than that, Tyndale set a standard for the English language that moulded in part the character and style of that tongue during the great Elizabethan era and all subsequent time. He gave the language fixity, volubleness, grace, beauty, simplicity, and directness. His influence as a man of letters was permanent on the style and literary taste of the English people, and of all who admire the superiority and epochal character of the literature of the sixteenth century.

CHAPTER XXII

VERSIONS CLOSE TO TYNDALE'S

198. Tyndale's last words and prayer, "Lord, open the king of England's eyes," as he was being strangled by the executioner, to be burnt at the stake were even at that moment being fulfilled. The one man upon whom was laid the burden of carrying out the spirit of the petition of the convocation of 1534 was Myles Coverdale. Now, this man Coverdale attempted through the liberal members of the old party to work "out a reformation from within through them." He was early an intimate friend of Cromwell and More, and it may be that under their encouragement he began to prepare for his translation of the Bible. If Foxe is to be believed, Coverdale met Tyndale in Hamburg, and helped him on his translation of the Pentateuch. However this may be, one thing seems certain, viz., that he was busily engaged in preparing a translation of the Bible into English, though it is positively asserted that he was neither a Hebrew nor a Greek scholar. King Henry's antipathy to Tyndale and his work, on the one hand, and the growing popular demand for the Bible in English, on the other, may have led the monarch to approve of the plan of his friend Coverdale, thus encouraging him to complete his transla-

tion. Besides, Cromwell, Secretary of State, gave him his active support in getting his work before the public.

199. The moral and financial support of high officials immediately brought Coverdale's work into publicity. While Tyndale was incarcerated in Vilvorde Castle, in Belgium (in 1535), an English Bible suddenly appeared in England. It had evidently crept in from the continent. It was printed in black letter, small folio size, and dated, "fynished the fourth daye of October." Either Coverdale's relation to the authorities or his desire to court their approval is seen in an effusive dedication to Henry VIII, signed by his " humble subjecte and dayle oratour, Myles Coverdale." It gave neither printer's name nor place of printing. The title-page of the original edition stated that this Bible had been "translated out of Douche [German] and Latyn in to Englishe." The first imprint of this edition left out " Douche and Latyn." It has been ascertained that the printed sheets reached London in the winter of 1535-36, and that they were bound and supplied with a new title-page by Nycolson, which carried on it "faythfully translated in Englysh and newly oversene and corrected." The cutting out of " Douche and Latyn " from the title-page, as in the second issue mentioned above, probably avoided the current antagonism in the church to Lutheranism, and also may have led the reader to suppose that the book was translated out of the original Greek and Hebrew. At any rate, the book

MYLES COVERDALE

seems not to have been arrested in its circulation, though there does not seem to have been either any royal prohibition or sanction for the earlier editions.

200. Myles Coverdale must be credited with having published the first complete Bible in the English language. In contrast with the incomplete work of Tyndale, it was not translated from the original Hebrew and Greek texts, but was based on (1) the Zürich Bible of Zwingli and Leo Juda, completed in 1529; (2) Luther's German; (3) The Vulgate; (4) the Latin text of Pagninus (1528); and (5) probably on Tyndale's work in the Pentateuch. In the New Testament Coverdale's main sources of help were Tyndale's latest (1534-5) revision and Luther's German (1522). In that part of the Old Testament of which Tyndale had published no translation, viz., the historical books, Joshua to 2 Chronicles, the poetical and prophetical books, Coverdale made the most familiar use of Zwingli's Zürich Bible. It is apparent then that Coverdale was essentially an editor, who gathered together the best materials within reach, and so selected and so modified them as to construct a Bible that would meet both the demands of the public and those of the ecclesiastical authorities. His great good sense, as shown in the use of language to secure beauty, harmony, and melody, made him a wise editor. His essentially peaceful nature led him to restore many beloved ecclesiastical terms that Tyndale had thrown out for new and more exact translations of the original Greek and Hebrew texts.

Indeed, so happy are some of the translations of Coverdale that they were perpetuated in the Authorized Version.

201. Coverdale's Bible so met the requirements of all parties that it immediately achieved popularity. In 1537—one year after the martyrdom of Tyndale—two revised editions appeared, carrying this statement, "set forth with the king's most gracious license." In 1538, he published a revised New Testament with the Latin in parallel columns. Thus within twelve years from the issuance of Tyndale's New Testament, which had to be printed abroad and clandestinely carried into England, we find the entire Bible, translated, printed, and distributed with royal approval—and this within one year after the treacherous destruction of Tyndale.

The character and position of the men who fostered the enterprise doubtless aided in the reception accorded Coverdale's work. Tyndale was a genius, was self-poised, original, and creative. He was every whit a scholar, and stood absolutely on his convictions, regardless of consequences. Coverdale was an imitator, a follower in the tracks of others, harmonistic, sympathetic, and gentle. He was modest, dependent, and regarded, always and everywhere, the interests of others in his decisions. Tyndale had the conviction that he had a great mission in this world and bent everything to accomplish that end. Coverdale apparently came into his own without any burning zeal that could not be quenched. Tyndale's tre-

The XI. Chapter.

A Ende thy vytayles ouer thē waters, and so shalt thou fynde thē after māny yeares. Geue it awaye amonge seuen or eight, for thou knowest not what miserye shal come vpō earth. Whē the cloudes are full, they poure out rayne vpon the earth. And whē ȳ tre falleth, (whether it be toward the south or north)in what place so euer it fall, there it lyeth. He that regardeth ȳ wynde, shal not sowe: and he that hath respecte vnto the cloudes, shal not reape. Now like as thou knowest not the waye of the wynde, ner how ȳ bones are fylled in a mothers wombe: Euen so thou knowest not the workes of God, which is the workemaster of all.

B Cease not thou therfore with thy handes to sowe thy sede, whether it be in ȳ mornynge or in the euenynge: for thou knowest not whether this or that shall prospere, ȝ yf they both take, it is the better. The light is swete, ȝ a pleasaunt thinge is it for the eyes to loke vpon the Sonne. Yf a man lyue many yeares, and be glad in them all, let him remembre the dayes of darcknesse, which shal be many: ȝ when they come, all thinges shal be but vanite. Be glad then (O thou yonge man)in thy youth, and lat thine hert be mery in thy yonge dayes: folowe the wayes of thine owne hert, and the lust of thine eyes: but be thou sure, that God shal bringe the in to iudgment for all these thinges.

mendous energy and love of the right led him to translate into English the best biblical texts that he could find. Coverdale's marvelous capacity for harmony, in spite of his lack of scholarship, led him to compile and to publish the first complete Bible in the English language. Each man was a kind of complement to the other, and together they were able to set forth the English Bible in such form and character as to command the English Bible-reading public.

202. Bible translation and revision were now in the air. Popular demands and royal favor joined hands to aid such work. John Rogers, an Oxford graduate of 1525, went to Antwerp some years afterwards as chaplain to the "English House," in which Tyndale was making his home. Here he soon became a close friend of the translator, and, as some think, of Coverdale. When Tyndale was spending his last days in Vilvorde Castle, he turned over to John Rogers his unpublished work, his translation of Joshua to 2 Chronicles inclusive. Rogers doubtless was acquainted with the version that Coverdale published in 1535. But now, being in possession of all that Tyndale had translated, both published and unpublished, he seems to have desired to give it to the public in a complete edition. Accordingly he prepared a Bible with Tyndale's work from Genesis to 2 Chronicles inclusive, Coverdale's version for the rest of the Old Testament and the Apocrypha, and Tyndale's New Testament of his last revision in 1535. This mass of material was revised with few

changes, furnished with introductions, summaries of chapters, illustrations, and some controversial marginal notes.

That the name "William Tyndale" should not appear on the title-page seemed essential to the public sale of the work, therefore it bears the name, "Thomas Matthew," supposed to be either a pseudonym for John Rogers, or the name of some merchant who backed up the enterprise in a financial way. At any rate, the book began to be printed, it seems, in Antwerp, where Rogers had for several years held the somewhat leisurely office of chaplain. When the printing reached Isaiah there was a stoppage for lack of funds. Two London merchants came to the rescue and carried the work through to completion in 1537.

203. This Matthew Bible was 12 by 8 inches in size and printed in black letter. Its boldest stroke is its dedication to "The moost noble and gracyous Prynce Kyng Henry the Eyght and Queen Jane," and signed "Thomas Matthew." The "Prayer of Manasses," omitted from Coverdale, was taken from the French Bible of Olivetan. The dedication may have been advised by such men as Cranmer and Cromwell, who seem to have welcomed its appearance. Cranmer in a letter to Cromwell says, "You shall receive by the bringer thereof a bible in English, both of a new translation and of a new print . . . so far as I have read thereof, I like it better than any other translation heretofore made. . . .

I pray you, my Lord, that you will exhibit the book unto the King's highness, and to obtain of his grace, if you can, a license that the same may be sold and read of every person, without danger of any act, proclamation, or ordinance, heretofore granted to the contrary, until such time that we bishops shall set forth a better translation, which I think will not be till a day after doomsday." Within a week Cromwell replies that he had "obtained of his grace that the same shall be allowed by his authority to be bought and read within this realm" (Park. Soc. Letter, 194).

Thus Henry VIII, who had proscribed Tyndale's New Testament in 1525, who apparently made no effort to save the life of its translator in 1536, within one year after his martyrdom authorized the sale and use of Tyndale's work, though under another name. Thus, by the influence of Cranmer, the co-operation of Cromwell, and the authorization of Henry VIII the Matthew Bible was given free course on English soil. Being a compilation, as it were, of Tyndale and Coverdale, it was the best English Bible in print.

204. There were now two English Bibles, Coverdale's and Matthew's, which were sold on authorization of the king. But the decree had gone no further. Cromwell was a shrewd politician and a far-sighted churchman. He doubtless saw the deficiencies of the two English revisions that were so freely circulated by royal decree. Coverdale's Bible had been compiled from various sources, and not trans-

lated from the original Hebrew and Greek. Matthew's Bible was a compilation of translations of varying values, whose marginal notes carried here and there a sting of a controversial character. Besides, royal discovery of the Tyndale translations under the mask of "Matthew," might precipitate a storm in the court. Consequently Cromwell secured the services of Coverdale to prepare a revised Bible that should be free from the objections of the two already authorized. Coverdale was to make the translation, as far as possible, more faithfully to represent the Hebrew and Latin texts of the Complutensian Polyglot. Coverdale's deficiency in Hebrew and Greek learning seems to have been supplemented by his employment of scholars efficient in these languages. His editorial sagacity, his popular grasp of the needs of the times, his power to use others, and his favor at court, seem to have combined in him just those elements of character that could produce a Bible that would be acceptable to all parties.

205. The editorial work having been done, Coverdale could find no facilities in London for executing the work on the scale that he had marked out for it. With Richard Grafton, the London publisher, he went to Paris in the spring of 1538. With Regnault, the French printer, and under royal license, the printing began. But the inquisition uttered its voice, and ordered the work to be confiscated. By shrewd management and trickery equal to that of the inquisitors, Coverdale safely transferred printed sheets, printers,

¶ The.xx.Chapter.

¶ Hezekia is sycke,& receaueth the sygne of his health. He receaueth rewardes of Benodach,& is reprehended of Isay because he shewed hym the treasure. He dyeth and Manasseh his sonne raygneth in his steade.

Boute that tyme was Heze=kia sycke vnto the deeth. And the prophete Isay the sonne of Amoz came to him, and sayde vnto hi: Thus sayth ẙ Lozde: put thyne houstholde in an ozdze, foz thou shalt die, and not lyue. And Hezekia turned his face to ẙ wall, & pzayed vnto the Lozde, sayeng : I beseche the now, O Lozd, remembze how I haue walked be=foze the in trueth and with a perfecte herte,& haue done that which is good in thy syght, and Hezekia wepte soze.

And it foztuned that afoze Isay was gone out into ẙ myddle of ẙ courte, ẙ wozde of ẙ Lozd came to hi, sayeng:turne agayne, and tell Hezekia the captayne of my people : Thus sayth the Lozd God of Dauid thy fa-ther: I haue herd thy pzayer , & sene thy tea=res. And beholde, I will heale the, so that on the third daye ẙ shalt go vp into the house of ẙ Lozd. And I will adde vnto thy dayes yet fyftene yeare, and will delyuer the & this cytie out of the hand of the kynge of Assy=ria,& wyll defende this citie foz myne awne sake,& foz Dauid my seruauntes sake. And

The Great Bible.   A.D. 1539
2 Kings 20 : 1-7

presses, type and other outfit to London. In April, 1539, Coverdale's new revision was completed. Because of its splendid proportions and magnificent form it was called "The Great Bible." It was in large folio, black letter, and carried neither notes nor dedication. Its unique title-page reads: "The Byble in Englyshe, that is to saye the content of all the holy Scripture, both of ye Olde and Newe Testament, truly translated after the veryte of the Hebrue and Greke Textes, by ye dylygent studye of dyverse excellent learned men, expert in the forsayde tonges. Printed by Rychard Grafton and Edward Whitchurch. Cum privilegio ad imprimendum solum, 1539. . . . Fynisshed in Apryll, Anno MCCCCCXXXIX. A Dño factū est istud."

One of the remarkable features of this book is its artistic frontispiece. It consists of a design of Hans Holbein, nine by fourteen inches, in which the king's authority is set forth with startling definiteness. The galaxy of worthies here delineated—the king handing the Bible to Cromwell and Cranmer—was apparently one of the methods of Coverdale for securing royal patronage and favor in the distribution and use of this new work.

206. What now were the biblical contents of this Great Bible? The title-page specifies that Coverdale had made use of Hebrew and Greek experts in its preparation. But the short space of time between the appearance of his own revision and the Great Bible would scarcely permit much expert work

to be done. The Old Testament is Matthew's (Rogers-Tyndale-Coverdale) edition, revised on the basis of Sebastian Münster's Latin translation of 1535. In the New Testament, Tyndale's translation was the basis, revised by making comparison with the Latin translation of Erasmus, and also of the Vulgate. So that the result of Coverdale's careful editorial supervision, " The Great Bible " was only a revised edition of John Rogers' " Matthew " Bible, which was the most complete presentation of the translation work of William Tyndale, whose martyrdom had occurred only three years earlier (in October, 1536).

207. The hand of Cromwell had been supporting Coverdale in his great work, so that without fear of interference he could prosecute his plans on a large scale. In fact, " the King's most honourable Council " had taken enough active interest in the enterprise to cut out all marginal notes. The publication of the so-called extra volume of annotations was postponed indefinitely. Furthermore Cromwell, as the king's right-hand officer, showed his interest in the work by promulgating in 1536, but not issuing until September, 1538, an order to the clergy throughout the kingdom to provide before a specified day " one boke of the whole Bible, in the largest volume, in Englyshe, sett up in summe convenyent place within the churche that ye have cure of, whereat your parishioners may most commodiously resort to the same and rede yt." What a revolution! In 1525-6,

Tyndale's New Testament was publicly burned at St. Paul's. In 1538 the same book, under another cover and name, was ordered by sanction of royal authority, if not decree, to be placed in public places, where all could read it. Tyndale had been martyred, but his battle had been won. The Bible in English was commanded to be put in every parish church in the land. The church historian Collier says that a paper dating from 1539 declares: " Englishmen have now in hand, in every church and place, the Holy Bible in their mother tongue, instead of the old fabulous and fantastical books of the "Table Round," "Lancelot du Lake," "Bevis of Hampton," "Guy of Warwick," etc., and such other, whose impure filth and vain fabulosity the light of God has abolished utterly " (After Hoare, p. 194).

208. Although Archbishop Cranmer was not actively engaged in the production of the Great Bible, he soon championed its cause. King Henry VIII gave to Cromwell the absolute right of licensing the publication of the Bible for five years. For the second edition Archbishop Cranmer prepared a Preface, and this edition appeared in April, 1540. In July and November two other editions (third and fourth) followed. In 1541 three editions (May, November, and December) were issued from the London presses. Six of them carry Cranmer's Preface ; and the third and fifth have on their title-pages the names of Tunstall and Heath, who had " overseen and perused " the book " at the commandment of the

King's Highness." So Bishop Tunstall, who had so
vigorously condemned, bought up, and burned Tyndale's New Testament, now formally, on the title-
pages indorses its publication and use.   Suspicion
had been attached to Cromwell's acts and name, for
he was sent to the executioner's block in July, 1540.
But the Bible had free course for a time.   The seven
editions of the Great Bible within two years testified
to its immense popularity and the public demand for
it.   Indeed, so firm a hold did it take upon the
church authorities that it formed the basis of the
English Prayer-Book, and was secure in its authority
as the Bible of the English people for thirty years.

Its presence in the churches where every one could
approach and read it, became an actual menace to the
preacher and the public services.   For readers would
crowd about it, read and discuss it, while the preacher
was trying to deliver his sermon.   These events became so aggravating to the clergy that Henry VIII
issued a warning or injunction that every preacher
charge his congregation to use this Bible "most hum-
bly and reverently," not "having thereof any open
reasoning in your open taverns or alehouses," using
it "quietly and charitably every one of you to the
edifying of himself, his wife and family" (Strype's
Cranmer, Vol. II, p. 735-6).

Whatever else may be said of the open Bible, it is
perfectly plain that the authorization of Cromwell,
in putting it within the reach of every one,
aroused the English nation to a new conception of

the meaning of Bible truth, and of their own personal relation to a forgiving and redeeming Saviour. It also widened the breach between the stern ecclesiastical sustainers and those who looked askance at the wornout tenets of the church, clinging rather to the more liberal personal type of religion.

209. During the same year that Coverdale was completing the printing of his Great Bible, an Oxford scholar, a layman and lawyer, R. Taverner, was printing another revision. Taverner was a good Greek scholar, but apparently was unacquainted with Hebrew. He dedicated it to King Henry in dignified, courteous, and straightforward language. The Old Testament followed the Matthew revision with only slight changes, occasioned by comparison with the Vulgate. The New Testament revision bears some marks of his Greek scholarship.

Taverner's Bible appeared in 1539, in two editions, a folio and a quarto; his New Testament appeared the same year, separately in two editions, a quarto and an octavo. The whole Bible was but once reprinted; his Old Testament was adopted in a Bible of 1551. Otherwise his revision was entirely superseded by the Great Bible, now circulated and used by royal authority.

CHAPTER XXIII

THE GENEVAN, BISHOPS', AND DOUAI VERSIONS

210. Cromwell's political and religious policy had caused his downfall and execution. His wholesale confiscation and destruction of shrines, images, and other religious symbols; his forcible plundering of abbots, monks, and monasteries; his wrecking of even the buildings connected with worship, stirred up a revolution among the Roman Catholic subjects throughout the kingdom. Cromwell's head was only one of their demands. The exalted place that he had given the English Bible and the reformation movement could not long be maintained. A most determined reaction set in against everything that looked like Lutheranism or the reformation that had made such astounding progress on the continent, particularly in Germany. King Henry VIII was in danger. He was forced not simply to modify, but almost to reverse the policy inaugurated by Cromwell. In 1543 "Parliament proscribed all translations bearing the name of Tyndale." It also required that the notes in all other versions should be expunged. Furthermore, it was enacted that no laboring men or women "should read to themselves or to others, publicly or privately, any part of the Bible, under pain of imprisonment." In 1546 King Henry proscribed every

Bible and every separate New Testament, except the Great Bible. The reading and use of this was restricted to the upper classes—to the people of leisure, as it were. At this time Bibles and Testaments were burned by the hundreds to satisfy the anti-reform movement, which had taken off the head of Cromwell. Tunstall and Heath, who had caused their names to be printed on the title-pages of the Great Bible in approval thereof, now said " they never meddled therewith " (Strype, Eccles. Memorials, Vol. I, p. 633). At the climax of this reaction against the reformation King Henry died (January 28, 1547). It looked as if Bible translation work had received its death blow.

211. With the accession of Edward VI, the sun rose on the reformation. This young king, even at his coronation, affirmed his devotion to the Bible, commanding that it be carried before him. His religious and political policy was that of the reform party. During his reign of six and one-half years (1547-53) the English Bible was reprinted many times and in many editions. Thirty-five editions of the New Testament and thirteen of the Old were issued from the press. The king's attitude and policy were set forth in certain injunctions issued at his coronation. Among these we find that every beneficed person shall provide " one book of the whole Bible of the largest volume in English, . . . the Paraphrasis of Erasmus also in English upon the Gospels," and shall set up the same " in some con-

venient place within the . . . church, . . .
where their parishioners may most commodiously
resort unto the same and read the same." What a
reversal of the last policy of King Henry! Reformers, too, who had fled to the continent to escape the
wrath of King Henry, now came back to meet the
welcome of the new ruler, and of Archbishop Cranmer. These warm friends of the new king formed
a choice group for promoting the reform. Calvinism and Lutheranism were flourishing under the
new protectorate, as over against the policy of the
last years of Henry's reign.

212. At the close of Edward's all too short reign,
Mary Tudor came to the throne (1553). England
again fell back into the hands and power of Roman
Catholicism. Mary quickly turned the tables upon
Protestantism. She inaugurated a reign of terror, by
lighting the fires of Smithfield. Archbishop Cranmer
and John Rogers, with hundreds of others, were
burnt at the stake. Myles Coverdale, now Bishop of
Exeter, escaped with difficulty to the continent.
Scores of reformers took the same road to safety.
But the fierceness of Mary's persecution defeated its
own purpose. The burning of such men as Archbishop Cranmer caused a revolt in the hearts even
of his opponents. The use of the English Bible in
public was prohibited, and the copies placed in
churches by the order of Edward VI were removed
and burnt. But there was no searching nor spying
out hidden copies in order to destroy them. The hor-

rors of Smithfield and the suppression of the English Bible had driven into voluntary exile some of the best biblical scholars of England. These men drifted to Germany and Switzerland, and naturally took up the cause they loved so dearly. After five years (1553-58) of bloody persecution and terror, in which some of the best men of England had suffered martyrdom, Mary died.

213. One of the direct results of the persecution of Mary was the flight of some of the reformers to Geneva, Switzerland, the home of Beza, the most noted biblical scholar of the time, and of Calvin, the theologian. The city of Geneva was the home of free thought, hampered by no political or religious restrictions. It was a home of biblical scholars of more than one nationality. Beza's critical and exegetical work had done much to clear up some of the difficulties of translation and interpretation. The company of English scholars now improved their long desired opportunity to revise the Great Bible and bring it up to the new standards of scholarship. Whittingham, a brother-in-law of Calvin, seems to carry the credit for the preparation and printing of the Genevan New Testament in 1557, with an introduction by Calvin. The reviser's preface contains some instructive information. He says, "I have divided the text into verses [first marked on the margins of Stephanus' Greek Testament of 1551] and sections according to the best editions in other languages." He provided marginal notes wherever he

could thereby explain obscure Hebrew or Greek phrases. He also introduced in italics words required to complete the sense, but lacking in the original tongues.

This was the most complete and accurate English New Testament that had yet appeared. Its merits soon won for it a hearty welcome, even in England. Its notable reception led its promoter to engage in a larger work for the cause of the reformation and of biblical learning.

214. Whittingham, with the aid of a group of scholars, whose names we know only in part, and Coverdale was probably one of them, assiduously worked on a revision of the Great Bible. This work continued " for the space of two years and more day and night." It is reported that " Whittingham, with one or two more, did tarry at Geneva an year and a half after Q. Elizabeth came to the Crown [Nov., 1558], being resolved to go through with the work" (Woods, Athenæ Oxon.). Thus it is evident that not all the group of scholars worked during the entire time of revision. The work was completed and the new Bible published in 1560, dedicated to Queen Elizabeth in simple, dignified language. The printing was done at the cost of the congregation at Geneva, among whose members we find John Bodley, the father of the founder of the Bodleian Library, at Oxford. He secured from Queen Elizabeth the exclusive right to print the Bible in England for seven years. In 1561 he printed a folio edition in Geneva.

1 **P**Aul ꞏan Apostle (not ꞏof men, nether by ᵇ mã, but by IESVS CHRIST, and God the Father ẃ hathe raifed him from the dead)

2 And all the brethren ẃ are with me, vnto ỹ Churches of Galatia:

3 Grace *be* with you and peace from God the Father, & *from* our Lord Iefus Chrift,

4 Which gaue him felf for our finnes, that he might deliuer vs ꞏ from this ꞏ prefent euil worlde according to the wil of God euen our Father,

5 To whome ꞏbe glorie for euer and euer, Amen.

6 I marueile that ye are fo fone remoued a-way vnto another "Gofpel, from him that had called you in the ᵈ grace of Chrift,

7 Which is not another *Gofpel,* faue ỹ there be fome which trouble you, and intende to ꞏ peruert the Gofpel of Chrift.

8 But thogh that we, or an ᶠ Angel from heauen preache vnto you other wife, thẽ that which we haue preached vnto you, let him be accurfed.

9 As we faid before, fo fay I now againe, If anie man preache vnto you otherwife, thẽ ỹ ye haue receiued, let him be accurfed.

The size of the Genevan version was a quarto,—small in comparison with the folios of Coverdale, Matthew, and the Great Bible. Another innovation was the abandonment of black letter for the plain, simple Roman type. As in the New Testament of 1557, the chapters were divided into verses. The margins carried terse, sensible, explanatory notes, that smacked somewhat of Calvinism, though without controversial bitterness.

215. The Geneva Bible immediately sprang into full-grown popularity. Its superiority to every other preceding version, and the silent assent of Queen Elizabeth to its distribution and use, gave it a tremendous impetus as an instrument of popular religious reform. In the Old Testament the learned revisers took as their basis the Great Bible, and thoroughly revised the translation on the evidence of the best texts. The most sweeping changes were made in the prophetical and hagiographical books—books unrevised by Tyndale. The New Testament work, based on Tyndale's last revision, was largely affected by Beza's Latin translation and commentary.

The Geneva Bible, however, did not displace the Great Bible, which had been once more required in the churches for ecclesiastical use, though its presence everywhere soon instituted comparisons that were detrimental to this long-established Bible of the parish church. Thus the two books were used side by side from the beginning of Queen Elizabeth's reign, until the appearance of the Bishops' Bible in

1568. Thenceforth the Geneva Bible was required in increasing ratio, so that by 1611, one hundred and twenty editions had appeared. Between 1568 and 1611 sixteen editions were issued in octavo, fifty-two in quarto, and eighteen in folio.

216. Archbishop Parker, who was a devoted and learned biblical scholar, took steps in 1563-4 for a revision of the Great Bible. His plan involved the dividing of the whole Bible into parts, and the assigning of one part to each of a large number of scholars. He assigned to himself the offices of general editor and of overseer of the printing of the text. At least nine of the revisers were bishops, hence the resultant Bible was to be called " The Bishops' Bible." The directions given the revisers included specifications that they were to follow the Great Bible, except where " it varieth manifestly " from the Hebrew and Greek. They were to regard especially the Latin versions of Münster and Pagninus. " Bitter notes " and controversial matter were to be omitted. " Genealogies " and other non-edifying passages were to be so indicated as to be passed over by the reader. Language that gave offense to good taste was to be " expressed with more convenient terms and phrases." Several of the bishops engaged on the work carried on a frank correspondence with Archbishop Parker. The work was evidently done without conference or consultation among the revisers, so that we may be prepared for a considerable degree of unevenness in the outcome. On the completion of the revision, the edi-

3 *A voyce crieth in wildernesse: Prepare the way of the Lorde, make strayght the path of our God in the desert.

4 All valleys shalbe exalted, and euery mountayne and hyll layde lowe: what so is croked shalbe made strayght, and the rough shalbe made playne.

5 *For the glorie of the Lorde shall appeare, for all fleshe shall at once see that the mouth of the Lorde hath spoken it.

6 The same voyce spake: Nowe crye. And the prophete aunswered, what shall I crye: *That all fleshe is grasse, and that all the goodlinesse therof is as the floure of the fielde.

7 The grasse is withered, the floure falleth away, for the breath of the Lord bloweth vpon them: of a trueth the people are grasse.

23

8 The grasse withereth, and the floure fadeth away: *yet the worde of our God endureth for euer.

9 Go vp vnto the hye hyll O Sion thou that bryngest good tidinges, lyft vp thy voyce with power O thou preacher Hierusalem, lyft vp without feare, & say vnto the cities of Iuda: Beholde your God,

The Bishops' Bible. A.D. 1568
Isaiah 40 : 3-9

torial work, and the printing (in 1568), Parker made
an effort to secure for the new Bible the recognition
of the Queen. But so far as evidence goes, it was
not granted. Convocation, however, decided (1571)
that "every archbishop and bishop should have at his
house a copy of the Holy Bible of the largest volume
as lately printed at London . . . and that it
should be placed in the hall or the large dining room,
that it might be useful to their servants or to strang-
ers." Every cathedral was to have a copy, and so
were all other churches, "as far as it could be conveniently done."

217. The title-page of the Bishops' Bible bore the
title, "The Holie Bible, containing the Old Testament
and the New," and a portrait of Queen Elizabeth.
As a frontispiece of the book of Joshua there was
a portrait of Lord Leicester, and of the Psalms, one
of Cecil, Lord Burleigh. The division into verses followed that of the Geneva Bible. Then the book was
provided with almanacs, calendars, tables, pictures,
and maps. Besides the Preface of Archbishop Parker,
the Bible contained that of the martyr Cranmer, which
was found in the Great Bible.

The internal character of the work is about what
would be expected. The contents were of unequal
merit. In the Old Testament the readings of the
Great Bible are quite faithfully followed, while the
Apocrypha is almost identical with it, though the
Great Bible was based largely on a Latin text. The
New Testament, on the other hand, exhibited marks

of real scholarship in its revision. In the second edition in 1572, the New Testament was notably revised and improved, while the Old remained as it had been.

But the authorization of the bishops was enough to displace the Great Bible at once from public use. For its last edition appears to have been printed in 1569, only one year after the publication of the Bishops' Bible. This new Bible was far from satisfactory to the increasingly large number of able scholars. Its ponderousness and its ecclesiastical sanction were not enough to popularize it. Its illustrations were such as to make it an object of reproach—the second edition being called the "Leda" Bible, from its objectionable picture of "Leda and the Swan." It was held in high ecclesiastical regard for about forty years, and passed through twenty editions, six in quarto, one in octavo, and thirteen in folio—the last bearing the date of 1606.

218. Protestant refugees from the persecutions of Queen Mary revised and produced the Geneva Bible. On the other hand, upon the accession of Queen Elizabeth some of the Romanist party, now forced to the background, migrated to the continent. The popular demand for the English Bible, and the answer to this demand by the Protestant revisions now freely circulated, led the Romanists to see the necessity of providing a version for their own adherents. In 1568, the year of the issuance of the Bishops' Bible, some of the Romanist refugees to the continent established an English college at Douai, in Flanders. This

city was the seat of a university founded by Philip II
of Spain in 1562, and was an important continental
center of English Roman Catholicism. The founder of
this English college, William Allen, was an Oxford
man and a canon under Queen Mary. He projected
the plan of producing an English Bible for English
Roman Catholics. The translation of the work, however, was prosecuted under the oversight of Gregory
Martin, another Oxford graduate. During the progress of the work political upheavals compelled the
removal of the college from Douai to Rheims in 1578.
By 1582 the entire work of translation had been completed, and the New Testament section published.
The next year after its appearance Fulke printed in
parallel columns the Rheims New Testament and the
second edition (1572) of the Bishops' Bible, and
added to each chapter a keen reply to the controversial
marginal notes of the Rheims version. Fulke's work
had the merit at least of popularizing this particular
version. In 1593 the college, being compelled to
leave Rheims, returned to Douai. Here the translation of the Old Testament, hitherto unprinted for
lack of funds, was published in 1609-10. Hence this
is called the Douai Version. The New Testament
was reprinted three times between its first appearance in 1582 and 1750, and the Old Testament but
once—bespeaking the slight demand for this version.

219. The Douai version (1609-10) carries this on
its title-page: "The Holie Bible, Faithfully Translated
into English out of the authenticall Latin." A com-

paratively long preface apologizes to the reader for the production and publication of such a version, assigning as a reason the prevalence and wide-spread use of various heretical and false versions. To counteract these menaces to the church of Rome, and to vindicate the good name of Roman Catholic scholarship, this particular version, well fortified with controversial notes, was issued.

As stated on the title-page, the Douai version is a translation " from the authenticall Latin," the Vulgate, because " it is the same which St. Augustine so commendeth . . . " and was declared by " the Holy Council of Trent to be authentical . . . ;" because " the adversaries themselves, namely, Beza, prefer it before all the rest." These, among ten reasons, are assigned by the New Testament translators for the use of the Vulgate as the original, or basis, of their work. No acknowledgment whatever is made to the various English versions that had appeared, though the resemblance to the Genevan is often striking. Some use is said to have been made of the Hebrew and Greek originals, but it was slight and the result of small value.

The translation itself is extremely literal, and even carries over into English sentences that are obscure in the Latin. The translators say: " we presume not to mollify the speeches or phrases, but religiously keep them word for word, and point for point, for fear of missing or restraining the sense of the Holy Ghost to our fancy." The adoption of such a policy

1  ND there vvere in the Church vvhich vvas at Antioche, Prophets and Doctors, among vvhom vvas Barnabas, & Simon that vvas called Niger, and Lucius of Cyréne, and Manahen vvho vvas the foster-brother of Herod the Tetrarch, and Saul.

2 † And ᶜ as they vvere "ministring to our Lord, and fasting, the holy Ghost said: "Separate me Saul and Barnabas vnto the vvorke, vvhereto I haue taken them.

3 † Then they "fasting and praying, and "imposing hands vpõ them, dimissed them.

4 † And they being "sent of the holy Ghost, vvent to Seleucia, and thence sailed to Cypres. † And vvhen they vvere

5 come to Salamina, they preached the vvord of God in the synagogs of the levves. And they had Iohn also in their mi-

6 nisterie. † And vvhen they had vvalked through out the

ᶜ Λ Λ θ ο υ-
ρ ο υ ϩ ω ν
α υ τ ω ν

carried over into English words and phrases that are stiff, formal, wooden and often meaningless. The Psalter is the most defective part of their Bible, for its translation was made not from Jerome's Latin translation, but from his second revision of the Old Latin, that is found incorporated in the Latin Bible adopted by the Council of Trent.

The Rhemish New Testament, however, through its popularity attained through Fulke's publication, exercised some influence in the preparation of the Authorized Version of 1611.

CHAPTER XXIV

THE AUTHORIZED VERSION OF 1611

220. The reign of Queen Elizabeth (1558-1603) was replete with great events. In the religious sphere we have (1) the appearance (1560) of the Geneva Bible that soon attained large popularity and use; (2) the publication (1568) of the Bishops' Bible that immediately displaced the Great Bible as the ecclesiastical version in use in the churches; (3) the Rhemish New Testament (1582) as the product of the English Catholic college at Rheims, Flanders, and its completion, the Douai Old Testament (1609-10) at Douai; (4) the tolerance enjoyed by the reform party in England, securing for them practically unrestricted growth. The two events in the political sphere that contributed to the success and liberties already achieved were the execution of Mary Stuart (1587) and the overwhelming defeat of the Spanish Armada in 1588. In the literary world there arose a galaxy of scholars and writers which has made the period unique in England's history, and given the language a purity, style, and beauty that has never been surpassed by any subsequent age. Among these worthies may be mentioned Shakespeare, Spenser, Bacon, Hooker, Jonson, and Richard Hakluyt. The religious and intellectual forces set to work greatly

272

stirred up and molded the desires, aspirations, and endeavors of the Englishmen of the close of the sixteenth century. Scholarship had achieved a high standard of excellence and was not satisfied with anything small or less than the best.

221. James I came to the throne in 1603. His early life and training had made him a student of the Bible. He had even tried his hand at authorship, having written a paraphrase of the book of Revelation, and translated some of the Psalms. The beginnings of the movement that ended in the translation of the so-called "Authorized Version" were apparently unpremeditated. King James had summoned a Conference to meet at Hampton Court in January, 1604, to consider complaints by the Puritans. The item of importance for our consideration is found in the Preface of the Authorized Version:

"The very historical truth is that upon the importunate petitions of the Puritans, at his Majesty's coming to this crown, the conference at Hampton Court having been appointed for hearing their complaints: when by force of reason they were put from all other grounds, they had recourse at the last to this shift, that they could not with good conscience subscribe to the Communion [Prayer-] book, since it maintained the Bible as it was there translated [in the Great Bible], which was, as they said, a most corrupted translation. And although this was judged to be but a very poor and empty shift, yet even hereupon did his Majesty begin to bethink himself of the good that might ensue by a new translation, and presently after gave order for this translation which is now presented unto thee."

The one man who presented this question to the Conference was Dr. Reynolds, president of Corpus Christi College, Oxford. His examples of " a most corrupted translation " were cited from the Great Bible and the Bishops' Bible, for from the translation of the former of these the Prayer-Book had been constructed.

So far as is known the Conference adjourned without taking any definite steps towards meeting the issue. of the Puritans. But the strong words of the Oxford president had been sown in fruitful soil.

222. The charge of the Puritans that mistranslations of the Scriptures were found in the Prayer-Book was the first definite step towards a revision. James I was thoroughly in accord with the idea of a new revision of the Bible, for he himself is cited concerning the best translation of that day, the Genevan, by Bancroft, in these words, " but the worst of all [the translations] his Majesty thought the Geneva to be." James entered heartily into the preparation and execution of a plan to provide a uniform translation " by the best learned in both the Universities; after them to be reviewed by the bishops and the chief learned of the church; " to be ratified by the Privy Council, and by royal authority.

James seemed to regard this as the opportunity of his life to do a popular and permanent piece of work on the Bible. He entered into the plan with energy, enthusiasm, and a determination to carry it through to a successful issue. His own Bible-trained spirit

and his theological turn of mind made the whole enterprise congenial to him. The extemporized suggestion of Dr. Reynolds soon sprang forth into full
fruition. It is not known with whom James made
all the plans and arranged all the details. But about
six months later, not only the general plan of procedure, but the list of scholars who were to do the
work, had been fully prepared. By July 22, 1604,
James wrote to Bancroft that he had "appointed certain learned men to the number of four and fifty for
the translating of the Bible." The only prerequisite
for the position of translator seems to have been
proved efficiency as biblical scholars. The list included Anglican churchmen, Puritans, and laymen.
Though James' letter mentions fifty-four, the list that
has been preserved contains only forty-seven. The
discrepancy between the original number and the
actual workers is supposed to be accounted for by
resignations and deaths between the time of appoint-
ment and the time when the real work began.

223. The revisers were organized into six groups,—
two at Westminster, two at Oxford, and two at Cambridge. Each of the six groups worked on a specified portion of Scripture, separately at first. The
Westminster group revised Genesis to 2 Kings inclusive, and Romans to Jude inclusive; the Oxford
group took Isaiah to Malachi inclusive, and the Gospels, the Acts, and the Apocalypse; the Cambridge
group revised 1 Chronicles to Ecclesiastes inclusive,
and the Apocrypha.

The competency of the revisers was undoubted. Nevertheless, such an array of scholarship could not do the work harmoniously without stringent rules. To guide them fifteen specific rules were provided by

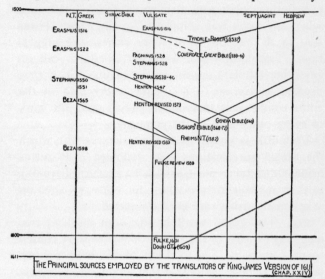

THE PRINCIPAL SOURCES EMPLOYED BY THE TRANSLATORS OF KING JAMES VERSION OF 1611 (CHAP. XXIV)

the scheme for work. Some of the most important things required were that (1) the Bishops' Bible should "be followed, and as little altered as the truth of the original will permit;" (2) the old ecclesiastical words should be retained; (3) there were to be no marginal notes at all, except such as should be needed for the explanation of the Hebrew or Greek words; (4) whenever Tyndale's, Matthew's, Coverdale's, Whitchurch's [The Great Bible, here named after one of its printers] or the Geneva translation, agreed better with the original text than the Bishops' Bible, it was to be used. It was provided, too, that a comparison of translations of each individual translator with every other one in each company should be made, and when any book was completed by any group it was sent to all the other groups for review and suggestion. Translators, too, were authorized to call on any other scholars outside of the regular list, if they deemed it wise so to do. Thus every man of the entire company of forty-seven passed upon the work of every other man in the company.

Very little is known as to the strictness with which the fifteen specifications were followed. It seems evident that there must have been practical harmony in their methods of procedure, for the work sped on at a commendable rate until completed.

224. The group work having been finished, two members of each of the three companies were chosen to pass upon the final revision of the work for the press in London. It is said that a copy of the whole Bible was sent to London by each of the three companies. The six final revisers thus chosen put the finishing touches, the harmonistic elements, upon the work submitted by the three companies, and made the final preparations for the press.

The entire time for carrying out the great enterprise is sometimes divided into two periods, (1) the first three years (1604-07) were occupied in perfecting the preliminary arrangements, and, on the part of some of the translators, in carefully working over in private study the material soon to be handled by the entire body of revisers; (2) the next two to three years were consumed in the individual and co-operative labor of the six groups of revisers, during which the revision work was finished. Then the following nine months were occupied upon the final revision in London. At the conclusion of this work the revised version appeared from the press of R. Barker in 1611. It was a folio volume in black-letter type, without notes.

225. The revision carried on its title-page, "newly translated out of the original tongues; and with former translations diligently compared and revised by his Majesty's special command." This "translation," as has been already mentioned, was really a revision based on the Bishops' Bible, with a free use by the revisers of the Genevan, the Rheims New Testament, and the material of Tremellius (1579), Beza (1556, 1565 and 1598), and other Latin versions. When we consider that the Bishops' Bible was based on the Great Bible, and the Great Bible was a slightly revised edition of Tyndale's work, we begin to appreciate the part that Tyndale's work occupies in this new version of 1611. There was no standard or "received" Hebrew text of the Old Testament, hence the revisers were obliged to use the four current Hebrew Bibles and the Complutensian and Antwerp Polyglots; in the Greek New Testament they had Beza's improvements on Erasmus and on Stephanus. The Old Testament far surpassed any English translation in its faithful

ND I sawe when the Lambe opened one of the seales, and I heard as it were the noise of thunder, one of the foure beastes, saying, Come and see.

2 And I saw, and behold, a white horse, and hee that sate on him had a bowe, and a crowne was giuen vnto him, and hee went foorth conquering, and to conquere.

3 And when hee had opened the second seale, I heard the second beast say, Come and see.

4 And there went out another horse that was red: and power was giuen to him that sate thereon to take peace from the earth, and that they should kill one another: and there was giuen vnto him a great sword.

5 And when hee had opened the third seale, I heard the third beast say, Come and see. And I beheld, and loe, a blacke horse: and hee that sate on him had a paire of balances in his hand.

King James', or the Authorized Version. A.D. 1611
Revelation 6 : 1-5

representation of the Hebrew text, and did it in a simplicity of language admirably representative of the Elizabethan age. The New Testament is so chaste and expressive in language and form that it is even said to surpass the original Greek as a piece of literature.

226. Another significant statement appeared on the title-page of the version attributed to the activity of King James, hence often called "King James' Version," or the "King's Bible." This is, "appointed to be read in the churches." Although the promotion and preparation of this Bible was under a direct order of the King and his chief advisers, there is no record of any order, act, or decree, authorizing or sanctioning its use as implied in the above statement. Neither parliament, convocation, privy council, nor king, is known to have laid down any law that would entitle this version to be named what, for long centuries, it has been called, "the Authorized Version."

Notwithstanding its royal and scholarly paternity, its birth occurred without any blast of trumpets, any royal edict or public proclamation. It seems that the mere fact of its almost national character was regarded as a sufficient guarantee of its rapid adoption and use in the churches and in private reading. At any rate, the King's name, and the eminence of the many great scholars who brought about its production, gave it an immediate hearing. It met opposition, of course, as does any new revision, even in these days. It soon outran in popularity the Bishops' Bible, that had not been reprinted since 1606. With the Genevan Version it waged a running fight for a full half-century. But character and merit won the contest, and the "Authorized Version" completely took the field.

227. The first edition of the "Authorized Version" appeared in 1611. In 1614 another edition was printed which contained more than 400 variations from the first. But the sharp criticisms that were hurled at the new version, largely by Hugh Broughton, whose irascible disposition had deprived him of a place, as his scholarship deserved, on the translation committee, forced a revision in 1629. The so-called final revision of the Authorized Version was printed in 1638. Within less than fifty years after the appearance of King James' Version, agitation was begun for a new revision of the Bible. In 1653 the Long Parliament submitted a bill calling for such revision. The reasons that lay back of the bill were in part errors, mainly printers', and some in translation, and also the so-called prelatical language of the version. The matter went so far as to be put into the hands of a committee appointed especially to take charge of the scheme. Some preliminary work was begun, but the dissolution of Parliament put an end to the proposed concerted action. Some of the most noted men of the century were on the committee which was dissolved. Among these may be named Walton, bishop of Chester, who, with the active support of Oliver Cromwell, edited the colossal Polyglot Bible, and also

through his arduous textual studies, pointed out the variations existent between manuscripts, particularly of the New Testament. Cudworth, the eminent theologian and philosopher, was another whose work has given him a permanent place in history.

228. The King James Version was winning the day. Its rivals had fallen out one by one, and the popular agitation for revision had dwindled into insignificant proportions. Private attempts either at betterment or radical revision were not infrequent, but they remained almost private, and rarely exercised any large influence. Explanatory notes were called for, and editions like that of 1649 began to appear, with more or less of this additional matter. Bishop Lloyd's Bible in 1701 was the first to incorporate in it the biblical chronology that had been worked out by Archbishop Ussher (who died 1656). This system, which fixed the creation at 4004 B. C., has been generally followed by biblical scholars until recent times, when extensive discoveries of chronological material in the Orient have shown conclusively that it is greatly in error in all of its earlier calculations, and in most of its later dates before the fall of Samaria (722 B. C.). In 1762 the Cambridge Bible, by Dr. Paris, introduced 383 marginal notes and other changes; and in 1769 Dr. Blayney introduced into the Oxford Bible 76 changes, including many on weights, measures and coins. These were practically private changes made to elucidate the text as it had been preserved from its final revision. As late as

1873 the Cambridge Paragraph Bible gave a list of variations from the text of the King James Version as it first appeared in 1611, that covered sixteen closely printed pages. The Oxford Parallel Bible of 1885 made a selection from these variants and put them in the margin.

229. For almost three centuries the Authorized, or King James, Version has been the Bible of the English-speaking world. Its simple, majestic Anglo-Saxon tongue, its clear, sparkling style, its directness and force of utterance, have made it the model in language, style, and dignity of some of the choicest writers of the last two centuries. Added to the above characteristics, its reverential and spiritual tone and attitude have made it the idol of the Christian church, for its own words have been regarded as authoritative and binding. It has endeared itself to the hearts and lives of millions of Christians and has molded the characters of the leaders in every walk of life in the greatest nation of the world. During all these centuries King James' Version has become a vital part of the English-speaking world, socially, morally, religiously, and politically. Launched with the endorsement of the regal and scholarly authority of the seventeenth century, its conquest and rule have been supreme. No version of private origin, even in the face of advances in scholarship, could compete with it. Only when such another organization as produced it came to the field was it obliged to yield the day—to the Revised Version.

CHAPTER XXV

THE REVISED VERSION

230. The Authorized Version held undisputed sway in the English-speaking world for more than two centuries. There were only occasional efforts now and then to improve that version, and they were purely personal and unauthorized. In fact, after the abortive effort of the Long Parliament to secure a new translation, the main ecclesiastical and national interests pursued other lines of action. The early half of the eighteenth century was submerged religiously in controversies that dealt with theological questions more from a dogmatic and philosophical point of view than from that of the Scriptures. The second half of that century was largely occupied by the English in political and economic questions. The ecclesiastical life of the nation in this century was at a low ebb, awaiting some thunderbolt of discovery or invention to arouse it to new energy and action. The beginnings of the nineteenth century saw new movements in every line of activity. Discovery, invention, scholarship, politics, religion—all aroused to new life as the century advanced, promising not only larger action, but a wider horizon for the future.

231. Biblical scholarship, though confined to comparatively a few men, had made some decided prog-

ress, particularly on the textual and philological side
during the preceding century. The most prominent
workers in this line were Kennicott, de Rossi, and
Davidson, who carefully collated critical material of
great value. New international relations, new incen-
tives to travel and investigate, also took possession of
biblical students. In 1844 Tischendorf's discovery of
the Sinaitic manuscript (Codex Sinaiticus), Tregelles' publication of a critical text of Revelation based
on many manuscripts in the principal libraries of Europe; and in 1857 and thereafter, his Greek New Testament opened the eyes of scholars to the immense
possibilities of improvements in translations of the
Bible. The number of biblical scholars was increasing, and the textual material which could be used in
Bible study, particularly of the New Testament, was
multiplying as rapidly as old manuscripts were dug
out of the old libraries of Europe and the monasteries
of the East. These " finds " revealed some of the
most glaring defects of the Authorized Version and
initiated efforts to produce new revisions or translations of parts or of the whole Bible. In 1857 five
English clergymen published translations of the
Gospel of John and of Paul's Epistles. Of these
translators, Dean Alford and Bishop Ellicott were
afterwards chosen to be members of the Committee
of Revisers. Four English scholars, Drs. Gotch,
Davies, Jacob and S. G. Green, prepared a Revised
English Bible. G. R. Noyes, of Harvard University,
published a translation in 1869, with some notes by

Ezra Abbot in 1870. The American Bible Union, too, gathered together a choice biblical exegetical library at large expense, and prosecuted a new translation of the Bible. The New Testament was translated and published in full. Parts of the Old Testament were published with comments by T. J. Conant, a leader in American biblical scholarship. All these efforts on both sides of the sea were indicators of the drift of scholarly opinion and movement in the last half of the nineteenth century. The large amount of new textual material, particularly of the New Testament, brought to light by the investigations of scholars, pushed the sentiment for a new revision of the Bible to the front.

232. The first public move towards a new revision was made February 10, 1870, in the Upper House of the Convocation of Canterbury. Bishop Wilberforce (of Winchester) presented a resolution that a committee of both Houses be appointed to report on the desirableness, on the basis of certain principles named in the document, of a revision of the Authorized Version of the New Testament. By an amendment the Old Testament was included. This important resolution was seconded by Bishop Ellicott (of Gloucester and Bristol), and it was adopted by the body. Two such names at the head of such a proposal were sure to give it a strong impetus. The committee provided for in the resolution was appointed to report in the following May. After due consideration this committee almost unanimously recommended, and both

Houses of Convocation adopted, a resolution that a revision should be undertaken. It also provided that a body of its own members should be nominated to undertake the work of revision, who should "be at liberty to invite the co-operation of any, eminent for scholarship, to whatever nation or religious body they may belong." The Church of England took the lead in the management of the movement, and a committee of sixteen men was appointed to carry out the letter and spirit of the resolution. This committee decided to invite about forty biblical scholars to become members of the Revision Committee. With Episcopalians in the lead, the committee was made up of members of nearly all evangelical bodies, including Baptists, Congregationalists, Methodists, Presbyterians and Unitarians; but no Roman Catholics accepted. The full number of this committee was fifty-four, the same as that originally named on King James' Revision Committee.

233. According to the Preface of the Revised Version, some of the general principles which were agreed to on May 25, 1870, by the Revision Committee of Convocation for their guidance were: "(1) To introduce as few alterations as possible into the Text of the Authorized Version consistently with faithfulness; (2) to limit as far as possible, the expression of such alterations to the language of the Authorized and earlier English Versions . . . .; (4) that the Text to be adopted be that for which the evidence is decidedly preponderating; and that when the text so adopted

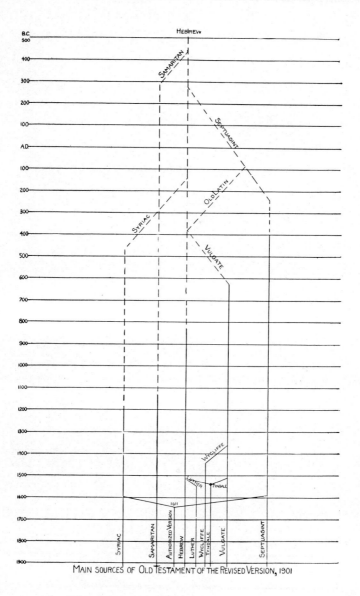

MAIN SOURCES OF OLD TESTAMENT OF THE REVISED VERSION, 1901

differs from that from which the Authorized Version was made, the alteration be indicated in the margin; (7) to revise the headings of chapters and pages, paragraphs, italics, and punctuation." A discussion of the method of carrying out these instructions follows likewise in the same Preface.

The general committee was organized into two Companies, the Old Testament and the New Testament, of twenty-seven members each. The New Testament Company was formally organized and began work in the famous Jerusalem Chamber of Westminster Deanery, London, June 22, 1870, and on the 30th the Old Testament Company began its long and arduous toil. Each Company was required to work through its portion of the Bible twice. These Companies met together in sessions at stated intervals, and these sessions were for the most part of ten days each—and they generally sat six hours a day. On the first revision the readings to be retained were settled by a majority vote, but on the second revise it required a two-thirds vote of those present to fix the new text.

234. In 1870 Dr. Angus visited America, and, at the request of Bishop Ellicott, held a conference with some American scholars on the possibility of co-operation with the British Revision Committee. A plan of such co-operation was framed, and a list of American biblical scholars representative of the leading religious bodies and denominations of the country was drawn up. The British Revision Committee approved

the plan and list of names. Accordingly a body of thirty men was organized December 7, 1871, which first began active service October 4, 1872, as Old and New Testament Companies, after the pattern of the British organizations. These two American Companies after beginning their service, met for committee work one session every month, except July and August, in the Bible House in New York. Of the New Testament Company, ex-President Woolsey of New Haven was chairman, and Professor William Henry Green, of Princeton, occupied the same position for the Old Testament Company. The details of the plan of co-operation with the British Revision Committee were not easily arranged or adjusted. It was not until 1875 that a mutually agreeable and workable scheme was concluded. Dr. Schaff's statement of the substance of the agreement is sufficiently clear (Companion to Greek Testament and Revised Version, pp. 400-1) : "The English Revisers promise to send confidentially their Revision in its various stages to the American Revisers, to take all the American suggestions into special consideration before the conclusion of their labors, to furnish them before publication with copies of the Revision in its final form, and to allow them to present, in an Appendix to the Revised Scriptures, all the remaining differences of reading and rendering of importance, which the English Committee should decline to adopt; while, on the other hand, the American Revisers pledge themselves to give their moral support to the authorized editions of the University Presses, with a view to their freest circulation within the United States, and not to issue an edition of their own, for a term of fourteen years."

235. The New Testament Companies were naturally the first to complete their task. The whole time devoted to the work by the British Company was ten and one-half years. The first revision was completed at the end of six years. The second by the end of two and one-half more. The remainder of the time was occupied in the consideration of the suggestions from America on the second revision, and of many details, and of special questions that had arisen. As a rule the British Company held a session of four days every month, except August and September, in each year from June, 1870. The average attendance of members of the Revision Committee for the whole time was sixteen each day, out of the original of twenty-seven; but the actual number of the Company was twenty-four—the changes occurring either from death or resignations having lowered the average.

Thus after about 400 days of sittings on their work the British New Testament Company affixed their names to the Preface to their version, November 11, 1880. On May 17, 1881, Bishop Ellicott, one of the two original movers of the resolution in 1870, to undertake the work of revision, laid the first copy of the Revised New Testament before the Convocation of Canterbury, and then gave in a brief address an account of the production of the volume. On that Tuesday, May 17, the Revised New Testament was published and put on sale in England, and on Friday, May 20, in the United States.

236. The reception accorded this work has been unprecedented in the history of the Bible. One million copies were ordered in advance from the Oxford University Press, and nearly as many from that of Cambridge. Dr. Schaff reports that a telegram from London, May 21, 1881, reported the sale of two million copies of the Revised New Testament in that one city. The pressure for copies in New York and Philadelphia began before daybreak of May 20. The agent of the Clarendon Press in New York alone sold 365,-000 before the end of the year, largely, however, during the first few days. Other agents in Philadelphia sold about 110,000 copies. Within a few days after its appearance more than a score of reprints of different kinds were thrown on the market. Two firms sold during the summer of 1881 about 165,000. It is estimated that almost three million copies of the Revised New Testament were sold in England and America in all editions within less than one year after its publication. In addition to these recorded sales there were various periodicals and papers that did large service, either by the publication of a part or the whole of the new volume. The Chicago Tribune and the Chicago Times published the book entire in their issues of May 22, 1881. The Gospels, Acts, and Romans, containing about 118,000 words, were telegraphed from New York, and the remainder of the

book was set up from copies received in Chicago on the evening of May 21.

Thus the Revised New Testament sprang at once into a full-fledged popularity, and was widely and, for a time, eagerly read by the religious and literary elements of the English-speaking world.

237. The work of revising the Old Testament was greater and more extensive in time. It was not concluded until 1884, fourteen years after the beginning of the task. This space of time wrought many changes in the personnel of the British Old Testament Company. Only fifteen of the original twenty-seven lived to see the completion of their work; ten had died and two had resigned; their places being filled by others until 1875, after which no one was added to the Company. The Revision was completed in eighty-five sessions, ending June 20, 1884; and it occupied 792 days, or more than two and one-half years of working days. The greater part of the sessions were for ten days each, and each day the Company generally sat six hours.

The British Company had gone twice through the Pentateuch before co-operation with the American Company had been arranged. The first revision of the British Company was submitted to the American, and in every case except that of the Pentateuch, the British had the benefit of their criticisms and suggestions before they took up their second revision. The second revision was also submitted to the Americans and their latest thoughts were in the hands of the

British Company at their final review.   As in the case
of the New Testament, the Revised Old Testament
carries an Appendix that contains many of the American preferences which were not adopted by the British Company. The Preface of the completed Old
Testament was signed by the British Old Testament
Company in Jerusalem Chamber, July 10, 1884; and
the entire Revised Version appeared bound in one
volume, May 19, 1885. Its reception was general,
cordial, and thoughtful.   There was no such phe-
nomenal and popular demand for the entire Revised
Bible as there had been just four years before for the
Revised New Testament.   But there was a healthy
and encouraging call for the product of such long
years of toil on the part of such an eminent body of
biblical scholars.

238. The real bases of the Revised Version were
the original texts used by the revisers. (1) The Old
Testament text was the Massoretic Hebrew, substantially the same as that used by the Company that produced the Authorized Version. The additional material at the command of the Revisers was due to the
collation of the variant readings of Hebrew manuscripts and of such early versions as the Septuagint
and the Vulgate.   It should be no surprise, then, that
there are so few striking changes between the Old
Testament of the Authorized and that of the Revised
Versions. (2) The Greek text of the New Testament used by the Revisers presents the greatest improvements over that used by the revisers of King

James. Since 1611 all the great New Testament manuscripts (Chapter XIV) had been discovered. As members of the British New Testament Company were Drs. Scrivener and Hort, two of the most able textual critics of the New Testament. The text used by the revisers was the result of a critical examination and estimate of all the known Greek New Testament manuscripts. The differences of the Greek text used by the revisers from that used by those who prepared King James' Version, according to Dr. Scrivener's notes (as cited by Dr. Schaff, Companion, p. 419, note) are seen in the case of 5,788 readings. Only about one in four of these makes any material difference in the substance of the text. Another estimate placed the number of changes in the English text at 36,191, or an average of four and one-half changes in each of the 7,960 verses. In other words, the Revised Version of the New Testament differs in more than 36,000 places from the Authorized Version—at first thought almost a revolutionary change.

239. There is a remarkable contrast apparent when the translations of the Authorized and Revised Versions of the Old and New Testaments are compared. In 1611 the Hebrew language was quite imperfectly understood, while the Greek had been well mastered. Consequently the Hebrew Old Testament was often inaccurately rendered into English, and beautiful English it was; while the New Testament was a fairly good and accurate translation of the Greek text. But the Old Testament of the Revised Version, although

based on practically the same Hebrew text as that used for the 1611 version, is a much clearer translation of the Hebrew, making sense of many passages that were obscure in King James. This improvement is very marked in the prophetical and poetical books, where obscurities, as we all know, were frequent and many.

The New Testament of the Revised Version shows its greatest gains over its predecessor in the purity of the Greek text used as already mentioned (§238) and in the rendering of such passages as require a more discriminative recognition of the principles of the grammar and of the syntax of New Testament Greek. This one fact has introduced large improvements in the translation of some of the most difficult passages in the cogent arguments of Paul in his epistles. Readers cannot but note the excellent improvements of the Revised Version over the Authorized in these very particulars.

240. Two hundred and seventy years wrought a noticeable change in the English language. The Authorized Version has been in use nearly three hundred years, and, of course, contains scores and hundreds of words and expressions whose meanings have become greatly modified, or entirely changed. One of the urgent tasks of the revisers was to weed out these obsolete words, archaisms, and expressions that do not now mean what they did originally, nor what the original text now means. The archaic character, and bald expressions of the Authorized Version have

been some of the targets at which scoffers have aimed their shafts—evidently forgetting, or winking at, the entirely different modern sense of the Hebrew and Greek originals. Again, many of the apparently plain and even immodest expressions of the Authorized Version, though entirely common and proper three centuries ago, are quite barred from good literature to-day.

The revisers were required to translate the originals into modern, modest, and yet forcible language that would properly represent the original texts, and at the same time give no needless offense to any thoughtful reader. This modernization of the language of Scripture, and, as far as possible, the translation of the same original by the same English word, were two of the hard tasks of the revisers. Such changes in words were made as "Holy Spirit" for "Holy Ghost," "Sheol" or "Hades" for "hell," "strange" for "outlandish," "smooth" for "peeled," "inwards" for "purtenance," "condemnation" for "damnation," "falsehood" for "leasing." The second task had been disregarded by the 1611 revisers; in fact, they often rather tried to use synonyms for the same Greek word, and thus give variety and beauty to the English language, and in this they were marvelously successful.

241. The Revised Version also possesses other qualifications for its claim to pre-eminence. The old arbitrary chapter and verse divisions—almost always misleading—have been relegated to the margin, so

that the text reads continuously like any other regular
book. The narrative is broken up into paragraphs
corresponding to the divisions and sub-divisions of
thought. The chapter headings, chronological material, and antiquated marginal references, that have
come to occupy so prominent a place in the Authorized Version and have been the direct cause of so
much misunderstanding and misinterpretation, have
been omitted. In short, the Revised Version was
intended to reproduce as faithfully as possible in English the best original texts of the Old and New Testaments, abandoning the man-made and fallible chapter
and verse breaks, the chapter headings, the chronological material, and the marginal references. In addition, some of the poetical sections in the Old Testament are put into verse-formation, the better to
show forth the character of the original thought. This
fact is observed particularly in the so-called poetical
books, and but rarely in the prophets, though there
are in these latter books many beautiful poetic sections
and passages where such formation would better represent the original.

242. The Revised Version was produced by the
hearty co-operation and skill of about seventy-five of
the leading biblical scholars of Great Britain and
America, who represented the most prominent religious bodies of the two great English-speaking countries. The age of the Authorized Version, its antiquated
language, and its recognized defects of several kinds,
were some of the reasons for the production of a

modern version of the Bible. Thus the sentiment and scholarship of the age demanded a revision, and the best critical and exegetical scholarship of the times produced it. What more could we expect than that the churches of the day would gladly welcome such a revision as would remove the defects of the Authorized Version, and at the same time represent the best scholarship of the times?

These existing conditions brought about for the Revised Version a hearty welcome by most of the better trained and more intelligent Bible students of the day. They early recognized its merits as more truly representing the original texts, and its clearness of statement in language that accords more nearly with such language as we use in the simple, dignified tongue of to-day. But these linguistic and literary improvements did not everywhere meet instant approval. There were critics with sharp pens, who found many defects in the version. Then the tender and sacred associations with King James' Version held any variation therefrom as almost sacrilegious, and refused to let go of so precious a volume for a new and modern version. All these considerations, however, as in the history of earlier versions were not sufficient to outweigh in the minds of the more intelligent readers the recognized superiority of the Revised Version. From its first appearance it has won favor and has increased in use and in influence throughout the English-speaking world. Not many years hence the Authorized Version will be put on the shelf as the most venerable and influential among all the past versions of the Bible.

243. The production and merits of the American Standard Revised Version of 1901 deserve some especial notice. It will be remembered (§234) that an American Revision Committee was not organized until 1871, and that its work did not begin until October 4, 1872, more than two years after that of the British Committee. Its task was to pass in review the two revisions of the British Committee and to make any suggestions or emendations that seemed to be required from the viewpoint of American scholarship, or from the needs of the American churches. But the actual terms on which the two committees finally jointly prosecuted their work were not concluded until 1875. This agreement provided that the suggestions of the American Committee should be duly considered by the British Committee before the final conclusion of their labors, and that they (the British Committee) should allow the American Committee to present in an Appendix to the Revised Scriptures, all the remaining differences of reading and rendering of importance which the British Committee should decline to adopt. This Appendix was to be published in every copy of the Revised Bible during a term of fourteen years. " The American Committee on their part pledged themselves to give, for the same limited period, no sanction to the publication of any other editions of the Revised Version than those issued by the University Presses of England."

THE

HOLY BIBLE

CONTAINING THE

OLD AND NEW TESTAMENTS

TRANSLATED OUT OF THE ORIGINAL TONGUES

BEING THE VERSION SET FORTH A D 1611

COMPARED WITH THE MOST ANCIENT AUTHORITIES AND REVISED

A.D. 1881–1885

Newly Edited by the American Revision Committee

A.D 1901

STANDARD EDITION

NEW YORK

Thomas Nelson & Sons

37 EAST 18TH STREET

Title-Page of the American Standard Revised Version

244. The pledge of the American Committee tied its hands, for a period of fourteen years from 1885. Even the possibility that the British Committee might in some subsequent edition make use of the Appendix suggestions of the American Committee disappeared at the disbanding of the former Committee very soon after the publication of the Revised Version in 1885. The American Revision Committee, however, continued its organization, for it saw the possibility that an "American recension" of the Revised Version might be called for. This Committee suspected, too, that some person or persons would probably, in the near future, transfer the American preferences in the Appendix to the main body of the text and thus issue a so-called American edition of the Revised Version. Such an edition in the thought of the public would be the product of the American Committee, or at least be attributed to it as its originator. Such a conclusion manifestly would be unjust, for the Appendix which contained the American preferences "had been prepared under circumstances which rendered fullness and accuracy almost impossible." Such a list of differences, even reduced to its smallest compass, as appeared in the Appendix to the regular Revised Version evidently could not be compiled until the Revision proper had been concluded. And its compilation required long and careful consideration of many points involved in previous discussions. But the British public had become impatient at the long delay in the issuance of the revision of the Old Testament, and de-

manded of the University Presses a speedy delivery.
The Presses, on their part, insisted on a prompt transmission by the American Committee of the Appendix.
" Prepared under such pressure, and in such haste, it
was obviously inevitable that it should be marked by
grave imperfections " (Preface to Am. Rev. Ver.).
Evidently then the mere incorporation of this Appendix in the text could not in any true sense produce
an " American recension " of the Revised Version.

245. Another pressing need of an American Revised Version is seen in the use in the 1885 edition
of a large number of words and phrases whose meaning and whose strange spellings are wholly antiquated.
Some of these are, " bewray," " grisled," " holpen,"
" hough," " marish," " pourtray," " sith," " strowed."
Then there are many words that are English but not
American in meaning. " Corn " means grain of all
kinds in England, but only maize or Indian corn in
America. " Chargers " are not " platters," but
" horses " here. " Traders " are not " chapmen " with
us, nor are " merchants " " occupiers." " Fat " is not
" vat " here, nor is " the capital " of a column called
a " chapiter." Our soldiers are not arrayed in " har-
ness," nor do we take our shoes " to be clouted."
What is " go to "? To retain such words in our Bible
would necessarily require a glossary to explain them.

Some other characteristics of the 1885 version required Americanizing. The use of " a " and " an "
before strong aspirates and vowels is in utter confusion. " My " and " mine," " thy " and " thine " suffer

likewise at the hands of the revisers. " Which,"
meaning " who," is an archaism that should be thrown
out; " the which " belongs to the same class. " God
forbid " and " would God " are not a translation of the
Hebrew. They are simply " far be it " and " would
that." These and scores of other Anglicisms are
found in the 1885 edition—many of them puzzling and
confusing to American readers.

246. The Revised Version of 1885 swept away
all the excrescences of the Authorized Version, such
as chapter headings, chronology, marginal references,
etc., and began anew. Its sole marginal references
were such as cited the readings of the ancient versions. The American Committee voted against the
British selections for the margin, because, as Dr.
Osgood of the Old Testament Company states,
out of the two hundred and forty references, one hundred and fifty-one are not supported by the versions,
and in thirty-three places not a version supports the
reference. The American Committee therefore took .
in hand the matter of reducing and largely reduced
the number of references to versions.

Early in the work of revision the British Committee
considered the matter of furnishing the Revised Version with a complete set of marginal references. After
considerable progress had been made in that direction,
especially by Dr. Scrivener, it was decided to issue
the Revision without any such helps. But " in
1895 the University Presses undertook to meet the
increasing demand, both at home and in America, for

an edition of the complete Revised Version with marginal references." A committee was appointed to superintend the work. The general editorship was put into the hands of Dr. Stokoe, of Oxford. The Revised Version " with revised marginal references " appeared from the University Presses in 1898. In the preface to this edition this statement occurs : " The marginal references given in the original edition of the Authorized Version of 1611 have been retained as far as possible, and the contributors have availed themselves largely of the references in Dr. Scrivener's Paragraph Bible, which they were instructed to make the basis of their work."

247. The surviving members of the American Revision Committee were keenly conscious of the defects of the Version of 1885, and early after its appearance began to plan the preparation of an edition that would fully represent the results of their own research and the requirements of the American Bible-reading public. Their task was not simply to incorporate in the body of the Bible their preferences as expressed in the appendices to the Revised Version, but thoroughly to revise those preferences in accordance with their own opinions. Their published list of preferences was so condensed as not fully to represent them. Being now untrammeled by any relations with the British Committee they went well beyond that published list, and introduced into the text emendations, corrections, and changes (originally adopted by a two-thirds majority of their own committee), neither

approved by the British Committee nor inserted in the Appendix. Again, this American Committee freely revised the translation, language, phrases, and thought where it seemed to them best for the better expression for American readers of the original languages.

With their practical ideas of simplicity, clearness, and value, the Committee made ample preparations to issue a complete edition. Accordingly they prepared, with the aid of scholars not members of the Committee, a full set of new marginal references; they revised and greatly reduced the references to ancient versions or texts; they printed at the top of each page in a brief, succinct form the contents of that page; they re-paragraphed the whole Bible; and sought to remove inconsistencies of punctuation.

An outline of the enormous task undertaken and completed by the surviving members of the American Committee is given in the " Preface to the American Edition."

248. About two years before the expiration of the period of fourteen years, already noted (§243) the American Revision Committee entered into an agreement with Thomas Nelson & Sons, of New York City, by which that firm was authorized to publish, in or after the summer of 1899, the American Standard Edition of the Revised Bible. The members of the Committee, who had been at work for some years, agreed on their part to prepare the text for the press. Their work on this edition, as on that that appeared

1881-1885, was purely a gratuitous service, rendered the cause of religion in general and Christianity in particular.

Just before the expiration of the fourteen years, the University Presses of Oxford and Cambridge, issued the " American Revised Version," an edition in which the American Appendix had been taken and incorporated into the text, and accompanied by the marginal references prepared by the special British Committee already described. In other words, the University Presses took the precaution to supply the American market with an " American Revised Version," while the American Committee were still restrained by their pledge to those Presses from issuing or sanctioning the issuance of any other than the Revised Version, of 1885. Naturally a storm arose, which gradually calmed down upon the advance to the front of the work of the American Revision Committee.

249. The Standard American Edition of the Revised Version, authorized by the American Committee of Revision, was published August 26, 1901, by Thomas Nelson & Sons, of New York City. It embodies the ripest scholarship of Great Britain and America (1881-1885), fully revised and corrected (1901) to suit it to the demands and requirements of American Bible students and readers. As it now stands it is the most perfect English Bible in existence, and will be the standard version for English readers for decades to

come. It is the crystallization of the best elements of ripe scholarship and sound learning, and is a fitting climax to the tremendous advances made in biblical learning during the last half of the nineteenth century. The hearty reception given it, and the readiness with which it has been adopted by scholars and the churches are a glowing tribute to its excellence and its adaptability to the requirements of the religious life of America.

250. This American Revised Version has achieved an ever-increasing popularity since its appearance five years ago (1901). The fact that it has been indorsed almost universally by religious teachers and leaders of all shades of belief, has given it a secure foothold. Its value is now being recognized by every one who has taken the trouble to compare its readings with those of the Authorized Version. Its adoption, too, by the American Bible Society, has given its translation a new value among Bible students in general, and promises for it general acceptance among the American Bible-reading public in far less years than the most sanguine had dared to hope. So constant has been the demand for this unrivaled Bible that the enterprising publishers who own the copyright have issued it in more than 100 different styles. The American public is quick to appreciate its real worth, and within a few short years will surely see its general adoption in every line of biblical and religious service.

BIBLIOGRAPHY

INTRODUCTION

CHAPTER I

Kenyon, F. G., Our Bible and the Ancient Manuscripts, 1895, Chap I; Variorum Teachers' Bible, in Foot-Notes.

CHAPTER II

Kenyon, F. G., Our Bible and the Ancient Manuscripts, Chap. II; Variorum Teachers' Bible.

Part I. The Old Testament

CHAPTER III

Weir, T. H., A Short History of the Hebrew Text of the Old Testament, 1899; Ginsburg, C. D., Introduction to the Hebrew Bible, 1897; Merrill, G. E., Parchments of the Faith, 1894, Chaps. III, IV; Briggs, Study of Holy Scripture, Chaps. III and VII.

CHAPTER IV

Mills, Three Months' Residence at Nablus, 1864; Price, Ira M., The Monuments and the Old Testament, 1905, Chap. XXIV; Eckstein, A., Geschichte und Bedeutung der Stadt Sichem, 1886; Green, W. H., Introduction to the Old Testament: The Text, pp. 129-141; Barton, W. E. "The Samaritan Pentateuch," in Bibliotheca Sacra, October, 1903; Watson, W Scott, "A Critical Copy of the Samaritan Pentateuch, written in A. D. 1232," in Hebraica, Vol. IX (1892-93), pp. 216-225; Vol. X (1893-94), pp. 122-156; Margoliouth, G. Descriptive List of the Hebrew and Sa-

maritan Manuscripts in the British Museum, 1893; König,
Ed. "The Samaritan Pentateuch," Hastings, Dictionary of
the Bible, Extra Volume.

CHAPTER V

Swete, H. B., An Introduction to the Old Testament in
Greek, 1900; Hastings, Dictionary of the Bible, Article
"Septuagint" by Nestle; Cheyne, Encyclopædia Biblica,
Art. "Texts and Versions," §§ 46-55; Merrill, G. E., Parch-
ments of the Faith, Chap. V; Briggs, Study of Holy Scrip-
ture, Chap. VIII.

CHAPTER VI

Swete, Introduction to Old Testament in Greek; Burkitt, F. C., Fragments of the Books of Kings according to
the Translations of Aquila, 1897; Field, Origenis Hex-
aplorum quae Supersunt, 1875; Art. "Hexapla" in Dictionary of Christian Biography; in same see "Symmachus,"
"Theodotion."

CHAPTER VII

Article by H. J. White on "Vulgate" in Hastings, Dic-
tionary of the Bible; Berger, S., Histoire de la Vulgate
pendant les premiers siècles du moyen âge, Paris, 1893;
Art. "Hieronymus" (Jerome) in Dictionary of Christian
Biography; Life of Jerome in Select Library of Nicene
and Post-Nicene Fathers, Vol. VI, pp. XVI-XXV, 1903;
Copinger, W. A., Incunabula Biblica, or the First Half-
Century of the Latin Bible, London, 1892; White, H. J.,
"The Latin Versions" in Scrivener-Miller, Introduction to
the Criticism of the New Testament, 4th ed., 1894, Vol. II,
pp. 56-90; Kenyon, F. G., Handbook to the Textual Criti-
cism of the New Testament, 1891, pp. 184-203; Smith, H.
P., "The Value of the Vulgate Old Testament for Textual
Criticism" in Presbyterian and Reformed Review, April,
1891.

CHAPTER VIII

Article by Eb. Nestle on "Syriac Versions" in Hastings, Dictionary of the Bible, for list of monographs on the books of the Old Testament; Barnes, W. E., "On the Influence of the Septuagint on the Peshitta," Journal of Theological Studies, II, 186, 187; Wright, W., A Short History of Syriac Literature, London, 1895; Barnes, W. E., "The printed editions of the Peshitta of the Old Testament," in Expository Times, Sept., 1898, pp. 560-562.

CHAPTER IX

Article by T. Walker on "Targum" in Hastings, Dictionary of the Bible, for literature in general, and on the three divisions of Old Testament; by Schiller-Szinessy in Encyclopædia Britannica; Green, W. H., Introduction to Old Testament: The Text, pp. 102-110; Merrill, Parchments of the Faith, Chap. VI.

CHAPTER X

Articles on "Egyptian Versions," "Ethiopic Version," "Armenian Version," "Arabic Versions," under these heads; and "Georgian Version," "Gothic Version," and "Slavonic Version" under "Versions (Georgian, Gothic, Slavonic)" in Hastings, Dictionary of the Bible; Kenyon, F. G., Our Bible and the Ancient Manuscripts, pp. 73-77.

CHAPTER XI

Article on "Texts and Versions" in Encyclopædia Biblica; Kenyon, F. G., Our Bible and the Ancient Manuscripts, Chap. V, § 5.

CHAPTER XII

Articles on "Apocrypha," by M. R. James, in Encyclopædia Biblica; by F. C. Porter in Hastings, Dictionary of the Bible; by G. F. Moore in Jewish Encyclopedia; Churton, Uncanonical and Apocryphal Scriptures, 1884;

Bissell, The Apocrypha of the Old Testament, 1890 (Commentary in the Lange series); Ball, C. J., Variorum Apocrypha, 1892; The Revised Version of the Apocrypha, 1895.

Part II. The New Testament

CHAPTER XIII

Westcott and Hort, Introduction to the Text of the Greek Testament, Vol. II, §§ 98-106; Scrivener-Miller, A Plain Introduction to the Criticism of the New Testament; Mitchell, E. C., Critical Handbook of the Greek New Testament, new ed., 1896, pp. 87-113; Sitterly, Praxis in Manuscripts of the Greek Testament, 1898; Lake, K., Text of the New Testament, 1900; Merrill, G. E., The Parchments of the Faith, Chaps. VIII-X; Schaff, Introduction to the American Edition of Westcott and Hort's The New Testament in the Original Greek, pp. xiii-xxxv.

CHAPTER XIV

In addition to the citations under Chapter XIII, Merrill, Parchments of the Faith, Chaps. XI-XV; Abbot, Ezra, "Comparative Antiquity of the Sinaitic and Vatican Manuscripts" in Journal of the American Oriental Society, Vol. X, pp. 189-200; Kenyon, F. G., Facsimiles of Biblical Manuscripts in the British Museum, 1901, Chap. III; Harris, J. R., The Annotators of the Codex Bezae, 1901.

CHAPTER XV

Schaff, P., Companion to the Greek Testament of the English Version, pp. 208-224; Murray, J. O. F., "Textual Criticism (of New Testament)," Hastings, Dictionary of the Bible, Extra Vol. §§ 24-68; Westcott and Hort, Introduction to New Testament in Greek, 1882; Warfield, B. B., Textual Criticism of the New Testament, 1890.

CHAPTER XVI

Article, "Vulgate" by H. J. White, Hastings, Dictionary of the Bible; Burkitt, F. C., The Old Latin and the Itala (Cambridge Texts and Studies, iv. 3, 1896); Article "Latin Versions—The Old," by H. A. A. Kennedy, Hastings, Dictionary of the Bible; Berger, S., Histoire de la Vulgate, 1893; Kaulen, Handbuch zur Vulgate, 1870; Kenyon, F. G., Our Bible and the Ancient Manuscripts, Chaps. VIII and IX; and other articles cited under Bibliography, Chap. VII.

CHAPTER XVII

The literature on Chaps. VIII and X, and additional thereto; Bewer, J. A., The History of the New Testament Canon in the Syrian Church, 1900; English translation from the Arabic of Tatian's Diatessaron by H. W. Hogg, in Ante-Nicene Christian Library, additional Vol. (1897), pp. 35-138; Zahn-Hjelt, Die altsyrische Evangelienübersetzung und Tatians Diatessaron, 1903; Murdock, James, The Syriac New Testament translated into English from the Peshitto Versions, Boston, 1893. Burkitt, F. C., on "Coptic and other Versions," in Encyclopædia Biblica, Vol. IV, cols. 5006-5012.

CHAPTER XVIII

The literature on Chapter XV, and additional thereto: Scrivener-Miller, Introduction to the Criticism of the New Testament, 4th ed., 1894; Gregory, C. R., Textkritik des Neuen Testamentes, 1900; Nestle, Eb., Introduction to the Greek New Testament, 1901; Vincent, M. R., History of the Textual Criticism of the New Testament, 1900; Kenyon, F. G., Handbook to the Textual Criticism of the New Testament, 1901; Lake, K., The Text of the New Testament (elementary), 1900.

Part III. English Versions of the Bible

CHAPTER XIX

Article by J. H. Lupton on "Versions (English)," in Hastings, Dictionary of the Bible, Extra Vol., pp. 236-238; Kenyon, F. G., Our Bible and the Ancient Manuscripts, pp. 189-199; Watson, R. S., Cædmon, the First English Poet, 1875; Turk, M. H., The Legal Code of Ælfred the Great, 1893, pp. 33-37; Skeat, W. W., The Holy Gospels in Anglo-Saxon, Northumbrian, and Old Mercian Versions, 1871-77; White, R. M., The Ormulum, 2d ed., 1878; Wright, T., The Religious Poems of William de Shoreham, 1849; Bramley, H. R., The Psalter or Psalms of David and Certain Canticles . . . by Richard Rolle, of Hampole, 1884. Eadie, J., The English Bible, 1876, Vol. I, pp. 3-36; Pattison, T. H., Hist. of the English Bible, 1894, Chap. I.

CHAPTER XX

Article by Lupton, "Versions (English)," in Hastings, Dictionary of the Bible, Extra Vol., pp. 238-241; Kenyon, F. G., Our Bible and the Ancient Manuscripts, pp. 199-208; Forshall-Madden, The Holy Bible of the Wycliffite Versions, 4 vols., 1850; Lechler, John Wycliffe, 1878; Bender, W., Der Reformator J. Wiclif als Bibelübersetzer, 1884; Matthew, F. D., J. Wyclif's English Works, 1880; Skeat, W. W., Preface to the New Testament in English (Purvey's revision), 1879, and "Dialect of Wyclif's Bible" in Transactions of Philological Society, Part I, for 1895-96; Westcott, History of the English Bible, Chap. I and App. I; Eadie, J., The English Bible, Vol. I, Chaps. I-V; Pattison, Hist. of Eng. Bible, Chap. II.

CHAPTER XXI

Demaus, R., William Tindale, ed. 1904; Article by Lupton, "Versions (English)," in Hastings, Dictionary of the

Bible, Extra Vol., pp. 241-244; Westcott, History of the
English Bible, Chap. II, § 1, and III, § 1; Hoare, H. W.,
Evolution of the English Bible, 1901, Chap. V; Kenyon, F.
G., Our Bible and the Ancient Manuscripts, pp. 211-218;
Anderson, C., Annals of the English Bible, 1845, Vol. I,
pp. 1-551; Fry, Fr., A Bibliographical Description of the
Edition of the New Testament, Tyndale's Version in Eng-
lish, 1878; Eadie, J., The English Bible, Vol. I, Chaps. VI-
XVI; Tyndale's Works, by Parker Society; Pattison, Hist.
of Eng. Bible, Chap. III.

CHAPTER XXII

Fry, Fr., The Bible by Coverdale, 1867; Westcott, His-
tory of the English Bible, Chap. II, §§ 2-5, and App. IV;
Chap. III, §§ 2-5; Anderson, C., Annals of the English
Bible, Vol. I, pp. 551-592, Vol. II, pp. 1-252; Hoare,
Evolution of the English Bible, Chap. VI; Coverdale's
Works, by Parker Society; Eadie, J., The English Bible,
Vol. I, Chaps. XVII-XXXI.

CHAPTER XXIII

Hoare, H. W., Evolution of the English Bible, Chap.
VII; Kenyon, F. G., Our Bible and the Ancient Manu-
scripts, pp. 224-229; Anderson, C., Annals of the English
Bible, Vol. II, pp. 253-532; Eadie, J., The English Bible,
Vol. II, Chaps. XXXII-XLII; Westcott, History of the
English Bible, Chap. II, §§ 7 and 8, and Chap. III, §§ 6-8;
Article by Lupton, "Versions (English)" in Hastings, Dic-
tionary of the Bible, Extra Vol., pp. 249-253; Carleton, J.
G., The Part of Rheims in the Making of the English
Bible, 1902.

CHAPTER XXIV

Scrivener, F. H. A., The Authorized Edition of the
English Bible (1611), 1884; Article by Lupton, "Versions
(English)," in Hastings, Dictionary of the Bible, Extra

Volume, pp. 253-257; Westcott, History of the English Bible, 1868, Chap. II, § 9, III, § 9; Anderson, Annals of the English Bible; Eadie, J., The English Bible, Vol. II, Chaps. XLIII-XLIX; Kenyon, F. G., Our Bible and the Ancient Manuscripts, pp. 234-245; Hoare, H. W., Evolution of the English Bible, Chaps. VIII and IX; Pattison, Hist. of Eng. Bible, Chap. VI.

CHAPTER XXV

Article by J. H. Lupton, "Versions (English)," in Hastings, Dictionary of the Bible, Extra Vol., pp. 258-271; Hoare, H. W., Evolution of the English Bible, Chap. IX; Kenyon, F. G., Our Bible and the Ancient Manuscripts, pp. 235-245; Kennedy, Ely Lectures on the Revised Version of the New Testament, 1882; Westcott, Some Lessons of the Revised Version of the New Testament, 1897; Documentary History of the American Committee on Revision, 1885; Burgon, J. W., The Revision Revised, 1883 (a sharp arraignment of the Revisers); Whitney, S. W., The Revisers' Greek Text; Schaff, P., Companion to the Greek Testament and English Version, 1883; Chambers, T. W., A Companion to the Revised Old Testament, 1885.

CHRONOLOGICAL TABLE

Carrying the most important dates mentioned in the text
of the book.

B. C.

About   432.—Expulsion of Manasseh from the priesthood
at Jerusalem, and probable establishment of
Jehovah worship at Samaria, with the Pentateuch as the Scriptures of the Samaritans.

284-132.—Probable date of the translation of the
Septuagint.

A. D.

128.—Aquila's Greek translation of the Old Testament.

About   150.—The Syriac Old Testament.

180-192.—Theodotion's Greek translation of the Old
Testament.

193-211.—Symmachus' Greek translation of the Old
Testament.

In 200.—The Old Latin Version of the Bible extant.

186-254.—Origen: Hexapla of the Old Testament.

260-340.—Eusebius of Cæsarea: Revision 'th help of
Pamphilus of Origen's Greek text, with
other readings.

Before   311.—Lucian's revision of the Septuagint.

Before   311.—Hesychius' revision of the Septuagint.

310-383.—The Gothic Version of Ulfilas.

383-404.—Jerome's revisions and translations.

About   400.—The Ethiopic Version.

About   400.—The Armenian Version.

After   400.—The Targums in written form.

400-500.—The Georgian Version.

About 590.—The Sahidic Version.

597.—Augustine, the monk, lands at Kent, England.

About 670.—Cædmon's paraphrases of the Bible.

About 700.—The Bohairic Version.

674-735.—Venerable Bede—the Gospel of John.

Before 709.—Aldhelm of Malmesbury—first Anglo-Saxon translation of the Psalms.

Before 709.—Egbert—a translation of the Gospels.

848-901.—King Alfred—embodied Pentateuchal laws in his national code.

About 950.—Aldred—interlinear Anglo-Saxon paraphrase of the Gospels (Lindisfarne Gospels).

970-1000.—Abbot Ælfric produced "the Durham Gospels," also an Anglo-Saxon version of the Pentateuch, Joshua, Judges, etc.

(1066.—The Norman Invasion—Battle of Hastings.)

About 1215.—The Ormulum—metrical version of parts of the Gospels and the Acts.

About 1320.—Psalter in English prose, credited to William of Shoreham.

About 1320.—Birth of John Wycliffe.

1338.—Wycliffe entered Oxford.

About 1340.—Rolle of Hampole translated the Psalter into English, with Commentary.

1361.—Wycliffe made master of Balliol College, Oxford.

1374.—Wycliffe appointed to a living at Lutterworth.

1380.—Wycliffe's translation of the New Testament completed.

1382.—Wycliffe's Bible with help of Nicholas of Hereford completed.

1384.—Death of Wycliffe.

1388.—Purvey's harmonization of Wycliffe and Hereford's work.

1408.—Action forbidding use of unauthorized Bibles.

(1453.—Constantinople captured by the Turks.)

1454.—Printing from movable types invented.

1455.—First complete Bible—the Vulgate—printed.

(1458.—Greek language first taught in the University of Paris.)

(1470.—Printing press introduced into England by Caxton.)

(1476.—First Greek grammar published.)

(1480.—First Greek lexicon published.)

1484.—Birth of William Tyndale.

(1488.—First Hebrew Bible printed.)

(1492.—Grocyn became first teacher of Greek at Oxford.)

(Columbus discovered America.)

(1497.—Vasco da Gama rounded the Cape of Good Hope.)

(1503.—First Hebrew grammar published.)

(1506.—First Hebrew lexicon published.)

1516.—First Greek New Testament—Erasmus'—appeared.

(1520.—Magellan sailed around the world.)

1522.—Luther's New Testament in German.

1523.—Tyndale goes to London to translate the Bible.

1524.—Tyndale withdraws from London to Hamburg and Wittenberg.

1525.—Tyndale's New Testament printed at Cologne and Worms.

1526-9.—Tyndale's New Testaments burned at St. Paul's in London.

1528.—Latin Bible of Pagninus.

1529.—Zürich Bible completed.

1530.—Tyndale printed his translation of the Pentateuch.

1534-5.—Sebastian Münster's Latin Version of the Old Testament.

Tyndale's revision of his Pentateuch and New Testament.

1535.—Olivetan's French Bible.

Tyndale treacherously arrested and imprisoned.

Coverdale's Bible reaches England.

1536.—Tyndale strangled and burned at Vilvorde Castle, October 6.

1537—Coverdale's Bible licensed by royal authority.

John Rogers' "Matthew" Bible distributed by authority of Henry VIII.

1539.—"The Great Bible," edited by Coverdale, authorized by Cromwell.

Taverner's Bible.

1540.—The Great Bible issued with Cranmer's Preface.

1543.—Royal restrictions on public and private reading of the Bible.

1545-6.—Council of Trent, establishing Roman Catholic canon of the Bible.

1546.—Wholesale destruction of Bibles.

1547.—Death of Henry VIII, and accession of Edward VI.

1551.—Castalio's Latin Bible.

Stephanus' Greek New Testament.

1553.—Death of Edward VI, and accession of Mary Tudor.

1553-8.—Persecution and martyrdom of Cranmer, Ridley, Latimer, John Rogers, and hundreds of others.

1557.—Geneva New Testament, by Whittingham.

1558.—Death of Mary Tudor, and accession of Elizabeth.

1560.—Genevan Version of the Bible.

1568.—The Bishops' Bible.

1579.—The Latin Old Testament by Tremellius.

1582.—The Rheims New Testament.

(1588.—The Spanish Armada defeated.)

1603.—Death of Elizabeth, and the accession of James I.

1604.—Hampton Court Conference.

1609-10.—The Douai Old Testament.

1611.—The Authorized Version.

1614.—Slightly altered edition of Authorized Version.

1629.—A revision of the Authorized Version.

1701.—Bishop Lloyd's Bible with Ussher's chronology.

1762.—Cambridge Bible by Blayney.

1844.—Tischendorf's discovery at Mt. Sinai.

1857.—Tregelles' critical Greek text of Revelation.

1870.—First definite step toward revision.

1881.—Revised Version—New Testament.

1885.—Revised Version of Bible complete.

1895.—Revised Apocrypha.

1901.—American Standard Revised Version.

TOPICAL INDEX

Figures refer to pages, and those in heavy type give the main description. Stars indicate illustrations.

ABBOT, Ezra, 157, 285

Abishua, reputed writer of Sam. roll, **45**

Abraham, Apocalypse of, Pseudepig. book, 125

Abraham, Isaac and Jacob, Testament of, Pseudepig. book, 125

Achiacharus, Story of, Pseudepig. book, 127

Act., abbreviation for Acts and Epistles of cursive Manuscripts, 142

Acta Pauli, 180

Adam, Testament of, Pseudepig. book, 125

Adler, see Assemani

Adrian, brought original of Cotton Manuscript to England, **213**

Ælfric, translates Gospels into the Anglo-Saxon, **213**; archbishop of Canterbury translated parts of Old Testament, **214**

*Alcuin, revised Vulgate for Charlemagne, *168

Aldhelm, abbot of Malmesbury, minstrel preacher, 209; first known translator of Psalter into Anglo-Saxon, 210

Aldred, a priest, wrote interlinear Anglo-Saxon paraphrase in Cotton Manuscript, 213

Alexander II, Czar, patron of Tischendorf, 144; published Codex Sinaiticus, 146

Alexander the Great, 49

Alexandria, home of Jews, 50

Alexandrian type of New Testament Manuscript, 194

Alford, dean, co-translator of John and Epistles, 284

Alfred, king of England, to whom a Psalter was attributed, **211–12**

Allix, Peter, discovered Codex Ephræm in Paris, 153

Ambrose, on Old Latin, 160

*American Standard Revised Version, **298–305**; specimen page, *4; title page, *298

Ammonius of Alexandria, sections of the Gospels, 138

American Revision Committee, organization, **288;** co-operation with British Com., 288–91; preparation of American Revision, 298–305; expunging archaisms, 300; new marg. refs., 301; issuance of American Standard Revised Version, 304

Angus, Dr., enlists American scholars in BIBLE REVISION, **287**

Aphraates, Syrian church father, quotes New Testament, 87

Apoc., abbreviation for Apocalypse in New Testament cursive Manuscript, 142

Apocalypse, absent from Peshitta, 180

Apocrypha of Old Testament, Chapter XII

Apocryphal books of Old Testament, **121–2;** classified and described, **122–3;** why not in Canon? **129–130**

Apocryphal books in Septuagint, **55**

Apocryphal books in the Vulgate, **77**

"Apocryphal Correspondence of St. Paul and the Corinthians," in Syriac, 180

Apost., abbreviation for the Lectionary of Acts and Epistles in cursive Manuscripts, 142

*Aquila, translator of Greek Version, *64

Arabic Versions, **108, 187–8**

Aramaic, Old Testament text, 92 ff.; geographical divisions, 182

Aristeas, letter of, 51

Aristion, presbyter, to whom Mark 16:9–20 is assigned, **186**

Armenian Version, **106–7**

Aseneth, Life of, Pseudepig. book, 125

*Ashburnham Pentateuch, *84

Assemani and Adler, describe Syriac Lectionary in Vatican, 188

Athanasius, St., Epistle of, 57; the humble, 148

Athos, Mt., Iberian Monastery on, 103

Augustine, St., and Old Latin Bible, 160; on Vulgate, 166, lands at Kent, England, 207

*Authorized Version, Chap. XXIV; specimen page, *278

BALL, C. J., edited Variorum Apocrypha, 128
Barnabas, Epistle of, 145
Bartolocci, G., librarian Vatican, 150
Barton, W. E., owner of Sam. Manuscripts, 46
Baruch, Apocryphal book, 124
Baruch, Apocalypses of, Pseudepig. book, 126
Baruch, Rest of the Words of, Pseudepig. book, 126
Bede, tells of Cædmon, 208; story of his death, **210–11**
Beer and Brockelmann, editing new Syriac Bible, 91
Bel and the Dragon, part of Apocryphal Additions to Daniel, 123
Ben Asher, 33
Bensly, with Harris and Burkitt transcribed Old Syriac text, 177
Bentley, R., 150, 175, 201
Berger, S., on Old Latin and Vulgate Manuscripts, 83, 175
Beza, T., owner of Codex D, biblical scholar at Geneva, 155, 190, 263
Biblical Aramaic in Old Testament, **20**
Birch, A., New Testament scholar of Copenhagen, 150
*Bishops' Bible, appearance and character, *266–8
Blayney, Dr., of Oxford, 46, **281**
Bodley, John, member of Geneva group of scholars, 264
Bohairic Version,‘**101**
Bomberg ed. of Hebrew Bible, 37
Brescia Hebrew Bible, 36
British and Foreign Bible Society, issue Ethiopic New Testament, 186
Burkitt, F. C., with Bensly and Harris transcribed Old Syriac text, 177; views on the Diatessaron and Old Syriac, 178; on origin of Bohairic dialect, 184.

CÆDMON, Celtic-Saxon poet singer, **208–9**
Cairo, Egypt, former center of Samaritan colony, 45; Tischendorf copied Codex Sinaiticus, **145**
Canon of the Jews, **30**
Cassiodorus, textual work of, 83, **166–7**
*Catharine, St., monastery of, at Mt. Sinai, 57, *143–5, 177
Chajim, Jacob ben, 37

Challoner and Troy, revised Douai Bible, 175
Charlemagne, 83; employed Alcuin to revise Vulgate, **168,** 174
Charles I, and Codex Alexandrinus, 148
Chrysostom, St., of Constantinople, 192
Classification of New Testament Manuscripts, Chap. XVII
Clement, St., Epistles of, to Corinthians in Syriac, 182, 192, 194
Clement VIII, pope, edited official Vulgate, **173–4**
Cochlæus, enemy of Tyndale at Cologne, **236–7**
*Complutensian Polyglot, 36, 60, *116, 189
Conant, T. J., translator for American Bible Union, 285
Conybeare, F. C., opinion of Armenian Version, 106
Cook, S. A., 20
Coptic Versions, **100, 183–5**
Corssen, P., Vulgate scholar in Germany, 175
*Coverdale, Myles, ed. first complete English Bible, *248–9; specimen page, *250; two revisions, **250;** *Great Bible, *254–8
Cranmer, archbishop, aid to Coverdale's Bible work, **252–8;** burnt at stake, 262
Cromwell, T., friend of Coverdale, **252–8**
Cureton, W., edited Old Syriac text, 177
Cuthbert, St., story of Bede's death, **210–11;** gospels of, **213**
Cyprian, and Old Latin Version, 160, 163, 192
Cyril, with Methodius, translated Slavonic Bible, 104
Cyril, of Alexandria, 194–5

DAMASCUS, former center of Samaritans, 45
Damasus, pope, friend of Jerome, 78
Daniel, Additions to, Apocryphal book, 123
David the philosopher, cited in Armenian Version, 107
Demaus, author of life of Tyndale, 238, 246
*Diagrams:
    Origen's Hexapla, *67
    Relations of rival Greek Bibles and revisions to Sept., *72
    Sources of Minor Eastern Versions, *105

General relations of ancient versions to the Hebrew, *111
Beginnings of modern versions in 16th century, *245
Sources of revisers of Authorized Version, *276
Sources of Old Testament Revised Version, opp. *287
Diatessaron, of Tatian, 176-7
Didymus, 195
Dillmann, A., edited Ethiopic text of Gen.-Kings, 102
Dionysius, 194
Discoveries in the fifteenth and sixteenth centuries, 233
Douai Version, 269-71
Durham, Book of, 213

EADFRITH, bishop of Lindisfarne, copied Cotton Manuscript of Gospels, 212-13
*Ecclesiasticus (Wisdom of Jesus, son of Sirach), Apocryphal book, *124
Egbert, bishop of Holy Island, translated Gospels, 210
Elijah, Apocalypse of, Pseudepig. book, 126
Elizabeth, queen of England, 263-71
Ellicott, bishop, co-translator of John and Epistles, 284; seconded move for Revision, 285; presented copy of Revision, 289
Enoch, Book of, Pseudepig. book, 126
Enoch, Secrets of, Pseudepig. book, 126
Ephraem Syrus, commentary of, 86, 177; sermons of, 153
Epiphanius of Cyprus, 68
Erasmus, edited first Greek New Testament, 189, 190, 224
Erizzo, count, edited Syriac Lectionary, 182
Errors of transcription, classes of, 27-30
Esdras, Apocalypse of, Pseudepig. book, 126
1 Esdras (3 Esdras in Vulg.), Apocryphal book, 123
4 Esdras (2 Esdras in A. V.), Apocryphal book, 124
Esther, Additions to, Apocryphal book, 123
Estienne, see Stephanus
*Ethiopic (or Ge'ez) Version, 101, *102, 186
Eusebius, of Caesarea, 68, 70; with Pamphilus revises Origen, 70, 87; adopts Ammonite sections of New Testament, 139

Euthalius of Alexandria, stichoi of, 139
Evan., abbreviation for Gospels in cursive Manuscripts, 141
Evst., abbreviation for Lectionaries of Gospels in cursive Manuscripts, 142
Exemplar Parisiense, a text of the Vulgate in Paris, 170

FAYYUMIC version, 185
Fenton, Bible in Modern English, 2
Field, F., Hexapla, 70
Forshall and Madden, edited Wycliffe's Bible, 226
Fulke, reply to notes in Rheims New Testament, 269

GALL, St., monastery of, 169
Gasquet, challenges authenticity of Wycliffe's Bible, 226
Gaster, M., discovers Hebrew text of Song of Three Children, 123
Gaza, former center of Samaritans, 45
Geneva, Switzerland, center of biblical scholars, 263
*Geneva Bible, completed, *264-5
Georgian version, 103, 188
Gerizim, Mt., site of Samaritan temple, 42, 43
Gibson, Mrs., with Mrs. Lewis discovered Syriac Manuscripts at Mt. Sinai, 177; edited fragments of the Gospels, 182-3
Ginsburg, C., author of Massoretic version, 20
Gospels, written reports, 133
Gotch, Dr., co-reviser of English Bible, 284
*Gothic version, 102, *187
*Great Bible, *254-9
Green, S. G., co-reviser of English Bible, 284
Green, W. H., chairman American Old Testament Revision Com., 288
Gregory, C. R., author Prolegomena to Greek New Testament, 157
Gregory, pope, put Old Latin and Vulgate on a par, 165
Griesbach, J. J., New Testament textual critic, 206
Gutenburg and Fust, printed first Latin Bible at Mayence, 171
Gwilliam, G. H., with Pusey edited latest ed. of Peshitta, 178
Gwynn, J., discovered and edited Apocalypse of Syriac Bible, 181

HAMPTON COURT CONFERENCE, 273-4

Harding, Stephen, abbot of Citeaux, 169

Harris, J. R., on Codex Bezæ, 156; with Bensly and Burkitt transcribed Old Syriac text, 177

Hartmut, abbot of St. Gall, 169

Hebrew Language, alphabet, rolls, 26; pointed, 32-34; Manuscripts, 34-5; printed texts, 36-7

*Hebrew Bible, first printed in America, *38

*Hebrew Papyrus, *Frontispiece

Henry VIII, and the Bible, 237-9, 253, 261-2

Hentenius, J., edited Vulgate, 172

Hereford, Wycliffe's aid in translation, 222-3

Hesychius, of Egypt, version of, 71, 200

Hetzenauer, edited Vulgate, 174

Hexapla of Origen, diagram of, 67

Hilary of Poitiers, and Old Latin Bible, 160

Hoare, H. W., Evolution of English Bible, 239, 257

Holmes and Parsons, 59

Horner, G., edited Bohairic Gospels, 184

*Hort, F. J. A., with Westcott on Greek New Testament Manuscripts, Chap. XVII, and often; portrait, *194

Hug, L., examined Codex B in Paris (1809), 150

*JACOB BEN AARON, high-priest of Samaritans to-day, *46

Jacob, of Edessa, 87

Jacob, Dr., co-reviser of English Bible, 284

Jacobite branch of Syrian Church, 181

James I, King of England, Chap. XXIV

James, M. R., classification of Apocryphal and Pseudepigraphical books, 122-7

Jason, of Cyrene, author of sources of 2 Macc., 122

Jerahmeel, Chronicle of, Pseudepig. book, 123

Jeremiah, Epistle of, Apocryphal book, 124

Jeremiah, Prophecy of, Pseudepig. book, 126

Jerome, St., education, 78; revision work, 79-81; personality, 81; criticism of, 82

Jesus, son of Sirach, Wisdom of, Apocryphal book, 124

Jews in Egypt, 50 ff.

Job, Testament of, Pseudepig. book, 125

Joye, Geo., Tyndale's amanuensis, 242

Jubilees, Book of, Pseudepig. book, 125

Judith, Apocryphal book, 123-4

KENNICOTT, collector of variants of Old Testament text, 38

Kenyon, F. G., author of Criticism of New Testament, 311

Kipling, T., edited codex Bezæ, 155

LACHMANN, K., New Testament textual critic, 190-1

Lagarde, P. de, 72; edited Syriac Lectionary, 182

Lanfranc, archbishop of Canterbury, 37, 169

Langton, S., archbishop of Canterbury, divided Bible into chapters, 170

Lascaris, J., brought codex Ephræm to Europe, 153

*Latin Bible of Jerome (Vulgate), *78

Latin versions, Chaps. VII and XV; printed Bibles, 171-5

Laud, archbishop, once owned codex Laudianus (e), 162

"Leda Bible," 268

Lee, edited Syriac Bible, 91

Lewis, Mrs., see Mrs. Gibson

Lindisfarne Gospels, 213

Lloyd, bishop, issued Bible in 1701 with Ussher's chronology, 281

Lollards, established by Wycliffe, 223

Lord's Prayer in language of King Alfred, Wycliffe, and Am. Rev. Version, 228

Lucar, Cyril, of Constantinople, 147-8

Lucian, of Samosata, revision of Origen, 70, 200

Lucifer, of Cagliari, and Old Latin, 160

Lysimachus, translator of book of Esther, 52

1 MACCABEES, Apocryphal book, 122

2 Maccabees, Apocryphal book, 122

3 Maccabees, Apocryphal book, 123

4 Maccabees, Apocryphal book, 123

Madden, see Forshall.

Mai, cardinal, edited codex B, 151
Malkite (Greek) church uses degenerate Syriac Bible, 182
Manasseh, supposed founder of Samaritan Pentateuch as Bible of Samaritans, 42
Manasses, Prayer of, Apocryphal book, 124
Maniacoria, cardinal, revised Vulgate, 170
Manuscripts, biblical, list of—
*Codex Alexandrinus (A), 57, **147**, *148, 149
—— Ambrosianus, (F), **59**, 88-9
*—— Amiatinus (A), **84**, *166-7
—— Basiliano-Vaticanus (N), **59**
*—— Bezæ (D), **155-6**, *190
—— Bezæ (d), 161
—— Bezæ (Evan. d), **164**
—— Bobiensis (k), 162
—— Bodleianus (E), **59**
—— Brixianus (f), **161**
*—— Claromontanus (d), **163**, *164
—— Claromontanus (Paul. d), 164
—— Coislinianus (M), 70
—— Colbertinus (c), 70
—— Complutensis, **84**
—— Corbeiensis (ff), **163**
*—— Cottonianus (D), 58, *212-3
—— Dublinensis (O), **71**
*—— Ephræmi (C), 58, *153-5
—— Firkowitch, Hebrew, **35**
—— Friderico-Augustanus, **144**
—— Gennadius (Slavonic), **104**-106
—— Gigas Holmiensis (g), **162**
—— Laudianus (e), **162**
*—— Marchalianus (Q), **71**, *72
—— Orient. 4445, **34**
—— Palatinus (e), 162
—— Perpignan Manuscript, **165-6**
—— Rich, 89; (Evan. e), 164
—— Samaritan, **46**
—— Sarravianus (G), **70**
*—— Sinaiticus (S), **57**, *16, **143-7**
—— Usserianus (r), 166
—— Vallicellianus (V), 168
*—— Vaticanus (B), **57**, *136, **150-3**, 194
*—— Vercellensis (a), **161**, *162
—— Vercellensis (Evan. a), 164
—— Veronensis (b), **161**
—— Veronensis (Evan. b), 614
—— Vindobonensis (Vienna Genesis) (L), **59**
—— 1700 (Syriac), **182**
Manuscripts, number of New Testament, 134-40
Marcion, biblical scholar, 134
Martin, abbé, translator on Douai Bible, 269
Mary Deipara, St., Monastery of, 88, 177
Mary Tudor, queen of England, **262-3**
Massoretes, 33
Mazarin Bible, printed 1455, 171
Medici, Catharine de, once owner of Codex C, 153
Melito of Sardis, 87
Memphitic version, 184
Mercati, G., discovered palimpsest of Hexapla, 68, 69
Mesrop, St., reputed translator of Georgian version, **103**
Methodius with Cyril, translated Slavonic version, 104
Mico, abbé, collated Cod. B for Bentley, 150
Mill, J., edition of New Testament, 154; on variants, **200**
Mitchell, E. C., Critical Handbook to New Testament, 157
Montanus, Arias, 37
Moses, Apocalypse of, (same as Book of Jubilees) Pseudepig. book, 125
Moses, Magical Books of, Pseudepig. book, 126
Moses, Revelation of, Pseudepig. book, 126-7
Moulton, R. G., Modern Reader's Bible, 2
Münster, S., Latin text, 256
Muralt, de, examined Cod. B in Rome (1844), 150

Nablus, modern home of Samaritans, 43
Napoleon took Cod. B to Paris, 150
Nestle, Eb., catalogue and number of New Testament Manuscripts, 139, 140
Nestorians, 88; New Testament of, **180**
Neutral type of New Testament Manuscripts, **194**
New Testament, writing, Manuscripts, versions, criticism, Part II, 131 ff.

Nicholas V, pope, secured Cod. B, 150
Nitrian desert, Egypt, source of Syriac Manuscripts, 88, 177
Noah, Book of, Pseudepig. book, 125
Noyes, G. R., translator of Bible, 284

Old Latin version, 75; classification of texts, 76–77; Chap. XV; 160
Old Syriac version, 176–8
Old Testament, Hebrew, writing, Manuscripts, versions, printed editions, Chap. III
Onkelos, author of Targum, 64, 94
Origen, Hexapla ed. of Sept.,65–70, 192, 194–5, 199
Ormulum, metrical version of parts of Gospels and Acts by Orm, 215
Oxford Parallel Bible, 282
*Oxyrhynchus papyrus of Sept., 56, *58

Packington, merchant friend of Tyndale, 238–9
Pagninus, Latin text of, 249
Palimpsest Manuscript, meaning of word, 58; Cod. Bezæ, 153
Pamphilus, co-reviser with Eusebius of Origen's Sept., 70, 87
Paris, Dr., edited Cambridge Bible, 281
Paris Polyglot, 37
Paul, bishop of Tella, translated Origen's fifth col. into Syriac, 69, 178, 181
Paul., abbreviation for Pauline Epistles of cursive Manuscripts, 142
Pelagius and Old Latin text, 160
Pentateuch adopted by Samaritans, 43
Peshitta Syriac version, 17, 178, 192
Petermann, author of Samaritan gram., 46
Philostorgius, authority on Ulfilas, 102
Philoxenus, bishop of Mabbogh, revised Peshitta, 181
Platt, T. P., edited Ethiopic New Testament, 186
Polycarp, translated Syriac Bible, 87; revised with Philoxenus of Mabbogh, 181
Polyglot Bibles:
　　Complutensian (1514–17), 36, 60, 189
　　Paris (1629–45), 37
　　London (Walton) (1654–7), 37

Primasius, commentary on Apocalypse, 163
Psalter, Additions to, Pseudepig. book, 126
*Psalter fragment of papyrus, *58
Pseudepigrapha, defined, 121–2; books of, 125–7
Purvey, John, harmonized Wycliffe's and Hereford's work, 224–5

Renaissance of Bible languages, 232–3
Revised Version, Chap. XXV
Revisers of 1611 version, organized, 275; rules for work, 276–7; revision completed, 277–8
Revision Committee of 1870; representation, 286; rules for work, 286–7; completed New Testament, 289; completed Old Testament, 291–2; texts used, 292–3; improvements, 293–5; improvements in form, 295–6
Reynolds, Dr., a Puritan, incited James I to Bible revision, 274
*Rheims New Testament, 268–9, *270
Roe, Sir T., presented Cod. A to Charles I, 148
Rogers, John, edited "Matthew" Bible, 250–3; burnt at stake, 262
Rolle, Richard, translated Psalter, 216
Rossi, G. B. de, compiled variants in Hebrew Manuscripts, 38
Roye, Tyndale's amanuensis, 237
Rushworth Gospels, 213

Sa'adya the Gaôn, translated Arabic Pentateuch, 108
Sahidic version, Old Testament, 100; New Testament, 183–4
*St. Petersburg Hebrew Manuscript, 916 A.D., 15, 20, *34
Sale of Revised Version, 290
Samaritan Pentateuch, Chap. IV, Manuscripts, text variants
Samaritans, 39–44
Sancto Caro, Hugo de, 37
Sarcey, M. de, French diplomat, 45
Scaliger, J., linguist, 43
Schaff, P., on New Testament text criticism, 199 ff, 288, 290
Scrivener, F. H. A., classif. of texts, 154; edited Codex Bezæ, 155; edited Textus Receptus, 190–1; on variants in New Testament, 200
*Septuagint, Chap. V; translation, 52; purpose, 53; order of Jer.

52, 53; canon, **54, 55;** *papyrus of third century, *56; first printed, first great edition, Holmes and Parsons, printed editions, 60

Sepulveda, made known Cod. B, 150

Shepherd of Hermas, 145

Shoreham, William of, made translation of Psalter, **216**

Sibylline Oracles, 126

Sixtus V, pope, published Sixtine ed. of Vulgate, **172**

Soden, H. von, surveys New Testament criticisms, 157

Slavonic version, **104, 188**

Solomon, Psalms of, Pseudepig. book, 126

Solomon, Testament of, Pseudepig. book, 125

Solomon, Wisdom of, Apocryphal book, 124

Spalatinus, tribute to Tyndale, 237

Stephanus, R., edited Vulgate, **171;** edited Greek New Testament, **190**

Strozzi, P., once owner of Cod. C, 153

Swete, H. B., text of Sept., 60

Symmachus' Greek version, **65**

*Syriac Palimpsest at Mt. Sinai, *182

Syriac versions, Chaps. VIII. and XVI

*Syriac Vulgate, Westcott and Hort's designation of Peshitta, *90, 178

Syrian type of New Testament Manuscripts, **192–3**

Syro-Hexaplar version of Paul of Tella, **69,** 72, 87

*TARGUM of Onkelos, 94; Jerusalem II, of Jonathan, Jonathan bar Uzziel, 95; of prophets, 96; rolls, 97; value, 98; in alternate verses, *94

Tatian, Diatessaron of, 138; **176–7**

Taverner, made translation of Bible, **259**

Tertullian, gives Old Latin quotations, 160, 192

Textual criticism, Old Testament, Chaps. III–X; New Testament, Chaps. XIII–XVIII, rules for, **201–5**

Textus Receptus, origin and character, **190,** 195, 196

Thecla, supposed writer of Cod. A, 148

Theodore of Mopsuestia, 89, 192

Theodotion, Greek version of Old Testament, **64**

Theodulf, revised Vulgate, **168**

Thomas of Heraklea, revised Syriac Bible, **181**

Thompson, Sir E. M., edited Cod. A, 149

Three Children, Song of the, part of Apocryphal Additions to Daniel, 123

Tischendorf, L. C. F., discovery at Mt. Sinai, 57, **143–5;** edited S, and C, 154, 190–1

Tobit, Apocryphal book, 123

Tregelles, bibl. critic, 150, 190–1, 284

Tremellius, Latin text of, used by revisers 1611 version, 278

Trent, Council of, 119, **171**

Troy, archbishop of Dublin, revised Douai Bible, 175

Tunstall, bishop of London, Tyndale's enemy, Coverdale's friend, 234–58

Twelve Patriarchs, Testament of, Pseudepig. book, 125

*Tyndale, W., Chap. XXI; *230; birth and education, 233–4; in London, 235; in Hamburg and Wittenberg, Cologne and Worms 236; books destroyed, 238–40; kidnaped and destroyed, **242–3;**

ULFILAS, translator of Gothic version, **102**

Uncial texts, meaning of, **136–40**

*University of Chicago New Testament Manuscript, *140

Urmia Syriac text, 91

Ussher, archbishop, author of biblical chronology, 281

VALLE, P. DE LA, Italian traveler, 45

Variants in Old Testament, Chap. I

Variorum Apocrypha, edited by Ball, 138

Variorum Teachers' Bible, 11

Vercellone, C., edited Cod. B, 151

Versions, value of, 110–8

Vulgate version, Chaps. VII and XV

WALTON, B., Polyglot Bible, 37

Watson, W. S., owner of Samaritan Manuscript, 46

Wearmouth and Jarrow, schools at, 169

*Westcott, bishop B. F., with Hort, New Testament textual critics, edited text, Chap. XVIII; portrait, *192

Western type of New Testament Manuscripts, **193–4**

White, H. J., studies of Vulgate, 175

Whittingham, prepared Geneva New Testament, **263–4**
Widmanstad, A., edited Peshitta, **178**
Wilberforce, bishop, resolution on new revision, 285
Woide, C. G., and Cowper, edited New Testament of Codex A, 149 ; also known fragments of Sahidic New Testament, 183
Woolsey, Ex-Pres., chairman American New Testament Revision Company, 288
Wordsworth, bishop, student of Old Latin and Vulgate texts, 175

*Wycliffe, J., version of, Chap. XX; sketch of life, *218; clash with Rome, 220; translated Bible into English, **221–2;** specimen page, *222; Hereford's help, 222–3; Lollards, 223; death, 224

XIMENES, cardinal, editor Complutensian Polyglot, 36, 60, 189

ZEPHANIAH, Apocalypse of, Pseudepig. book, 126
Zohrab, edited Armenian Bible, 108, 186
Zwingli, edited Zürich Bible, 249

SCRIPTURE INDEX

Numbers refer to pages. Stars refer to illustrations on which text is found.

GENESIS

1 : 1-12 . . . . . *116
1 : 20 7
3 : 20 7
4 : 8 . . . . . 47, 53
5 47
6 : 3 . . . . . . 3, 9
7 : 3 47
11 :10 f 47
12 : 9 7
14 : 17 56
19 : 20 35
23 21
24 : 10 7
24 : 38-43 . . . . *56
40 : 15 7
43 : 9 7
44 : 31 47
49 : 7 48
49 : 10 . . . . 4, 9, 47

EXODUS

4 : 18 47
8 : 10, 11 35
12 : 46 . . . 47, 54
15 31
17 : 14 21
18 : 1 47
20 : 2-17 . *Frontispiece
20 : 17 48
21-23 22
24 : 7 22
29 : 9-21 . . . . . *102

LEVITICUS

8 : 7 30
11 86
20 : 10 28

NUMBERS

1 : 22b-38a *84

DEUTERONOMY

5 : 21 48
14 86
19 : 2-5 . . . . . *90
27 : 4 . . . . 44, 48
27 : 5-28 : 18 . . . *38
32 57

JOSHUA

1 : 1-2 : 5 . . . . *94
13 : 26 30

JUDGES

4 30
5 31
5 : 14 22
6 : 32 29
10 : 8 30

1 SAMUEL

2 : 1-10 57
3 : 13 27
9 : 20 4
10 : 25 22
12 : 11 29
13 : 1 29
14 : 18 9
27 : 8 29

2 SAMUEL

3 : 17 29
5 : 8 4
6 : 5 53
11 : 14 22
21 29
22 32

1 KINGS

1 : 1-3 : 4 23
12 : 18 29

2 KINGS

8 : 10 8
17 : 24 40
17 : 24-41 41
20 : 1-7 . . . . . *254
20 : 12 29
20 : 20 23
23 : 15-19 . . . . *64

1 CHRONICLES

2 35
8 : 29-38 28
9 : 35-44 28
29 : 29 22

2 CHRONICLES

1 : 13 10

(no heading)

3 : 4 28
10 : 18 29
32 : 30 23
33 124

EZRA

4 : 2 41
4 : 8-6 : 18 20
4 : 9, 10 41
7 : 12-26 20

NEHEMIAH

8 : 1-8 92
8 : 8 32
13 : 23-27 42
13 : 28 42

ESTHER

1 : 15-2 : 14 . . . . *16

JOB

1 : 1-8a *78
7 : 20 27
40 : 15 7
41 : 1 7

PSALMS

11 : 7-15 : 4 . . . 56, *58
18 32
22 69
22 : 1 93
22 : 16 10
35 : 7 28
50 : 18 34
59 : 10 34
73 : 4 27
100 : 3 29

ECCLESIASTES

11 : 1-9 . . . . . *250

ISAIAH

1 : 1 . . . . . . *222
1 : 1-4a *168
8 : 20 5
14 : 31-16 : 3 . . . *34
23 : 13 5
39 : 1 29
40 : 3-9 . . . . . *266
40 : 9 5
52 : 2 8

53 : 1 5
61 : 1f 31

JEREMIAH
6 : 7 30
10 : 11 20
15 : 19 53
25 : 13 52
27 : 1 29
32 : 9-15 22
43 and 44 50
46-51 52
51 : 1 7

EZEKIEL
5 : 12-17 . . . . *72
23 : 42 53
32 : 31 53
34 : 16 53

DANIEL
2 : 4-7 : 28 . . . 20

AMOS
6 : 12 27

MATTHEW
1 : 1-4a *140
1 : 1-17a *182
1 : 16 205
2 : 2 5
5 : 46 7
6 : 11 7
6 : 13 8
15 : 27-16 : 3 . .*238
20 : 16-23 . . .*154
25 : 41 5
27 : 46 93

MARK
3 : 14 203
7 : 3-7 . . . . .*187
9 : 49 203
11 : 25 203
16 : 1-20 . . . 147
16 : 9ff 8
16 : 9-20 . . . 185

LUKE
1 : 4 5
1 : 35 5
4 : 17f 31
4 : 32b-5 : 6 . .*166
6 : 1-9 . . . . .*190
12 : 31 204

JOHN
1 : 1-4 136
1 : 9 5
1 : 18 147
3 : 31b, 32a . . 8
8 : 1-11 186
9 : 11 227
16 : 23-30 . . .*162
17 : 2 7

ACTS
13 : 1-6 . . . .*270
15 : 21 31
20 : 28 147

ROMANS
7 : 4-7 . . . .*164
8 : 28b 204

1 CORINTHIANS
2 : 13 6
5 : 8 133

2 CORINTHIANS
2 : 17 6
3 : 1-4 : 6 . . .*136
10 : 10 133
11 : 28 133

GALATIANS
1 : 1-9 . . . . .*264

COLOSSIANS
1 : 2 6
4 : 16 132

PHILIPPIANS
3 : 18 133

2 THESSALONIANS
3 : 17 133

1 JOHN
5 : 9-2 John 13 .*148

REVELATION
6 : 1-5 . . . . .*278

APOCRYPHA

ECCLESIASTICUS
48 : 17 23
51 : 6c-12+ . . .*124

BARUCH
3 : 20 222

1 MACC.
1 : 56, 57 25

By the same author

A Syllabus of Old Testament History
Seventh edition, 1908

The Monuments and the Old Testament
Fifth edition, 1907